DATE DUE

DEMCO 38-296

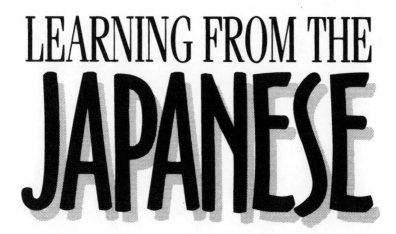

LEARNING FROM THE JAPANESE

The economic growth of Japan over the last 125 years has been faster than that of any other country in the world. With the collapse of the Soviet economy in the early 1990s, Japan has become the major non-Western model for late developing countries. This book looks at Japan's early economic modernization to see if today's low-income countries can learn any lessons. The author focuses on education, technology policy, capital formation, the transfer of savings from agriculture to industry, state aid to the private sector, improvement engineering in the informal sector, low wages, industrial dualism, export expansion, and resistance to Western imperialism (a strategy which included acquiring its own empire) under Japan's "guided capitalism." He criticizes modernization scholars for underemphasizing the damage of imperialism and the importance of economic autonomy and technological learning, the dependency school for prescribing trade reduction and neglecting market exchange-rate policies, and world-system theorists for rejecting the possibility of global economic growth.

Dr. Nafziger notes that today's developing countries must be selective in choosing components of the Japanese model and concludes that the development model favored by Western countries, the IMF, and the World Bank resembles that of early capitalist Japan—economic liberalization with state action but with little attention to achieving political democracy.

LEARNING FROM THE
JAPANESE

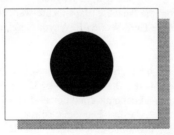

Japan's Pre-War Development and the Third World

E. Wayne Nafziger

An East Gate Book

M.E. Sharpe
Armonk, New York
London, England

An East Gate Book

Copyright © 1995 by M. E. Sharpe, Inc.

Library of Congress Cataloging-in-Publication Data

Nafziger, E. Wayne.
Learning from the Japanese : Japan's pre-war development
and the Third World / E. Wayne Nafziger.
p. cm.
"An East gate book."
Includes bibliographical references and index.
ISBN 1–56324–485–3. — ISBN 1–56324–486–1 (pbk.)
1. Japan—Economic conditions—1918–1945.
2. Japan—Economic policy.
3. Economic development. I. Title.
HC462.8.N22 1995
338.952′009′041—dc20
94–27010
CIP

Printed in the United States of America

The paper used in this publication meets the minimum requirements of
American National Standard for Information Sciences—
Permanence of Paper for Printed Library Materials,
ANSI Z 39.48-1984.

∞

BM (c) 10   9   8   7   6   5   4   3   2   1
BM (p) 10   9   8   7   6   5   4   3   2   1

To my colleagues at
the Graduate School of International Relations,
International University of Japan,
Yamato-machi, Niigata,
from whom I learned about the Japanese economy

Contents

Preface

"Are we watching the 'death of the Japanese model'?" the *Toronto Globe and Mail* recently asked. Economic growth in Japan, as in the other industrialized countries, decelerated steadily during the past three decades. Why, then, write a book about Japan's development? Japan grew faster than any Western country, not only from 1970 to 1994, but also from 1870 to 1994. Japan deserves attention as a developing country from the Meiji Restoration (1868) to World War II. During those seven decades, Japan grew more rapidly than any other country in the world. Japan stressed education, savings, technological borrowing and modification, learning by doing, and market exchange rates; modernization also engendered pathologies, however, such as income concentration, labor repression, authoritarianism, militarism, and imperialism. This book concentrates on what Third World economies can learn from Japan's early modernization.

I began this book in 1983, when I was visiting professor at the International University of Japan. Kansas State University supported me for two leaves of absence, which James Ragan, Peter Nicholls, Jarvin Emerson, and William Stamey helped me obtain. Herbert Bix, Roger Buckley, Patrick Gormely, Sadasumi Hara, Yujiro Hayami, Chihiro Hosoya, Ichirou Inukai, Shigeru Ishikawa, Takafumi Kaneko, Hiroshi Kitamura, Hirohisa Kohama, Fumie Kumagai, Ryoshin Minami, Tsuneo Nakauchi, Seiji Naya, Konosuke Odaka, Kazushi Ohkawa, Yoshi Okada, Saburo Okita, Katsuo Otsuka, John Power, Mark Selden, Toshio Shishido, Howard Stein, Rodney Wilson, Hiroyuki Yoshioka, and many others facilitated my research. Elfrieda, Brian, and Kevin Nafziger tolerated inconveniences in Japan and the United States, leaving me more time for research. I am grateful for all these, but I am solely responsible for errors.

I also thank the following for permission to reproduce copyrighted materials: the World Future Society for my "The Japanese Development Model," in Howard F. Didsbury, Jr., ed., *The Global Economy: Today, Tomorrow, and the Tran-*

sition (Washington, D.C., 1985); the World Bank for a graph and tabular material from *Global Economic Prospects and the Developing Countries* (Washington, D.C., 1993), *World Development Report 1988* (New York: Oxford University Press, 1989), and *World Development Report 1993* (New York: Oxford University Press, 1993); the International Monetary Fund for tabular material from *World Economic Outlook* (Washington, D.C., 1990); the Population Reference Bureau for a graph and tabular material from Madgda McHale and John McHale, "World of Children," *Population Bulletin*, vol. 33, no. 6 (January 1979), and *1993 World Population Data Sheet* (Washington, D.C., 1993); St. Martin's Press for a table from Jogindar S. Uppal, *Economic Development in South Asia* (New York: St. Martin's Press, 1977); and Macmillan Press for tables from Ryoshin Minami, *The Economic Development of Japan: A Quantitative Study*, trans. Ralph Thompson and Ryoshin Minami (Houndmills, England: Macmillan, 1986), © 1986 by Macmillan Ltd.

List of Tables and Figures

Tables

Figures

Abbreviations

AL(s) Adjustment loan(s): Sectoral adjustment loans (SECALs) of the World Bank or structural adjustment loans (SALs) of the Bank or IMF

DCs Developed countries

EU European Union (formerly European Community)

FAO Food and Agriculture Organization of the United Nations

F.o.b. Free on board

IMF International Monetary Fund: International organization established at Bretton Woods, New Hampshire, in 1944 for the initial purpose of providing credit to ease short-term international payments imbalances

JDM Japanese development model

LDCs Less developed countries

MFA Multifiber Arrangement

MNCs Multinational corporations

NICs Newly industrializing countries (South Korea, Taiwan, Hong Kong, and Singapore)

OECD   Organisation for Economic Cooperation and Development: A major bilateral donor group that includes the United States, Canada, Western Europe, Japan, Australia, and New Zealand

SA   Structural adjustment: the process of undergoing a SAP

SALs   Structural adjustment loans: World Bank/IMF loans to affect the supply side, which support sectoral, relative price, and institutional reform to improve efficiency and long-term growth

SAPs   Structural adjustment programs: World Bank/IMF programs involving policy-based SALs

SECALs   Sectoral adjustment loans: World Bank loans emphasizing trade, agricultural, industrial, public enterprise, financial, energy, educational, or other sectoral reforms

SOEs   State-owned enterprises

UNCTAD   United Nations Conference on Trade and Development, comprising 127 African, Asian, and Latin American members

Modern Japanese History
by Reign Period: A Chronology

Meiji: 1868–1912, initiated by the restoration of the emperor
Taisho: 1912–26
Showa: 1926–89
Heisei: 1989 to present

LEARNING FROM THE
JAPANESE

The Japanese
Development Model

This book focuses on two poles of the world's economic development performance. One pole includes the slowest-growing countries since the mid- to late nineteenth century, fifty-four countries of Africa and Asia. Japan occupies the other pole, the fastest-growing economy since the 1870s. The purpose of this study is to examine lessons from the growth of Japan from the restoration of the Meiji emperor in 1868 through the beginning of World War II in 1939, and the application of these lessons to less-developed countries (LDCs) today.

Meiji Japan imitated, borrowed from, and modified many techniques and approaches from the advanced Western economies. A question today is: Can Asian and African LDCs be as successful emulating, borrowing, and adapting innovations and procedures from Japan?

My approach is that of a development economist, focusing on the economic growth and structural change of Third World countries, rather than that of an economic historian.[1] Social scientists studying developing countries have examined the experience of today's rich countries for lessons to apply to contemporary LDCs.

The Decline of the American Model

In the past, one of the major developed-country (DC) models was that of the United States (or sometimes the West generally). The premise of Walter W. Rostow, *Stages of Economic Growth* (1961), was that economic modernization implies a change from an underdeveloped economy to one similar to the United States and other Western economies. His theory was the vogue among many U.S. government officials in the 1960s, especially in the international agencies, since it promised hope for sustained growth in LDCs after substantial initial infusions of foreign aid. Rostow compared LDCs at independence to the formation of nation-states in the West. He assumed that the development of underdeveloped countries will parallel earlier stages of today's advanced countries. For Rostow, today's modernized societies, the archetype of which is the United States, provide an image of the future of traditional societies.

Rostow's work met with mixed reviews. Rostow was accused of overambition. Ian Drummond complained that "probably no theory has been so widely circulated from so slight a base of organized fact and careful analysis" (1961: 112–13).

Another economic historian, Alex K. Cairncross, argued that one can believe in Rostow's takeoff into sustained growth only if one's knowledge of history is flimsy and out of date. Cairncross contended that many of Rostow's conditions were defined so vaguely that they stretch to cover any case and he seemed only too willing to admit exceptions when takeoff occurred at a time other than his theory suggests (1961: 454).

Rostow's premise that economic modernization implies a change from an underdeveloped economy to one similar to those in North America, Western Europe, and Japan today poses a problem. He assumes that the development of underdeveloped countries will parallel earlier stages of today's advanced countries, but he neglects the relationships of contemporary underdeveloped countries with rich countries within the world capitalist system.

It is not my purpose here to critique in detail Rostow's United States-and Western-based model of economic growth, which is widely discussed in the development literature.[2] Indeed, since Rostow's writing, the United States' growth of real (inflation-adjusted) GNP per person has been slow—only a little more than 1 percent annually (World Bank 1991b: 205). Moreover, since the mid-1970s, the average material levels of living of the bottom 75 percent of the U.S. population have fallen. As a result, few serious scholars use the United States as a model for Third World development.

The Decline of the Soviet Model

The 1917 Communist revolution in Russia provided an alternative road to economic modernization. The main features of Soviet socialism, beginning with the first five-year plan in 1928, were replacing consumer preferences with planners' preferences, the Communist party dictating these preferences to planners, state control of capital and land, collectivization of agriculture, the virtual elimination of private trade, plan fulfillment monitored by the state banks, state monopoly trading with the outside world, and a low ratio of foreign trade to GNP. The Soviets diverted savings from agriculture to industry (especially metallurgy, engineering, and other heavy industry) through collectivizing farming (1928–38), enabling the state to capture a large share of the difference between state monopsony procurement at below-market prices (sometimes below cost) and a sales price closer to market price. In a few decades the Soviet Union was transformed into a major industrial power. Moreover, a 60 percent illiteracy rate, an average life expectancy of about forty years, and widespread poverty before the revolution gave way to universal literacy, a life expectancy of seventy years, and economic security in the 1970s (Gregory and Stuart 1986: 141–52).

After World War II, from the granting of independence to India in 1947 through the 1970s, many LDCs were attracted by the Soviet model. Indeed, in the mid-1950s, Jawaharlal Nehru, India's first prime minister, wanted to combine democratic socialism with G.A. Fel'dman's model of rapid increase in investment in machines to make machines, used by Joseph Stalin in the 1930s. Nehru, however, abandoned the Fel'dman-Stalin approach in the mid-1960s as a result of slow growth in agriculture and capital goods, as well as balance-of-payments crises from rapidly growing food and capital imports. In India's mixed economy, the demand for capital goods was not sufficient, the squeeze on current consumption from the unbalanced investment promised to be at least a generation, and planners' control was too limited to implement the strategy (India, Planning Commission 1969; Nafziger 1990a: 274–76; Taylor 1979: 119–27).

While few LDC leaders questioned the success of the first fifty years of socialism in the USSR, its leadership's acknowledgment in the 1980s that centralized socialism was responsible for economic weaknesses of low consumption levels and low productivity (especially in agriculture) increased the doubts of Third World leaders about the Soviet model. In 1985–91, Mikhail Gorbachev's perestroika, or economic restructuring, recognized that the Soviets could no longer rely on major sources of past growth—substantial increases in labor participation rates (ratio of the labor force to population), rates of investment, and educational enrollment rates. For Gorbachev, continued growth required increased productivity per worker through agricultural decollectivization, more decentralized decision making, a reduced bureaucracy, greater management and worker rewards for increased enterprise profitability, more incentives for technological innovations, and more price reform.

Most developing countries became disillusioned with the Soviet model in the early to mid-1980s, after a decade of slow Soviet growth. Yet growth even decelerated during Gorbachev's leadership through 1989, and output fell after that until the breakup of the Soviet Union, when Boris Yeltsin replaced Gorbachev in Moscow in 1991. The coup de grace for the application of the Soviet model came with the fall of Central European Communist governments in 1989–90 and the disintegration of the Soviet Union in 1991. Most interpret these events as an admission of the failure of the Soviet approach.

The Japanese Model as an Alternative

While economists became interested in Japan as a model for economic development in the 1960s and 1970s, the recent declines in the consideration of the

American and Soviet models further increased the appeal of the Japanese approach.

Japan's 1868 level of economic development was only slightly higher than other countries of Asia and Africa. Since 1868, Japan has widened its income gap vis-à-vis the rest of Asia and Africa (except during World War II). Raymond W. Goldsmith (1983: 15–16) states that Japan's level of real income per head in 1868 was about equal to that reached by India in the 1950s, and was higher, if you adjust for the consumption of basic commodities of food, clothing, housing, and services (Lockwood 1954: 4; Nakamura 1983: 2).

Japan had the world's fastest growth in real GNP per capita from 1870 to 1986—3.5 percent annually (a thirty-one-fold increase per century), compared to more than 2 percent yearly for Sweden, Germany, and Russia, the next fastest growers.[3] (A 2 percent increase multiplies income seven times per century.) If computed through the early 1950s, Japan's growth is second to Sweden's (table 1.1).

Modernization versus Dependency–World System Paradigms

Developing Asian countries like Thailand, Malaysia, and Indonesia are "looking East" to learn development lessons from the experience of the major non-Western industrialized country, Japan. Modernization and dependency–world system scholars have two competing explanations for Japan's successful economic development. Capitalist Japan has become a substitute for the capitalist West as a favorite of modernization theorists who contend that, among non-Western societies, Japan's traditional institutions, values, and social system were uniquely positioned to promote rather than block modern economic development. Ironically, dependency and world system theorists point to Japan's emergence as the most successful non-Western economy as evidence for an alternative explanation: among African and Asian countries, only Japan was autonomous enough economically and militarily to resist late nineteenth-century and twentieth-century Western imperialism, to chart its own development planning, and to appropriate the gains from technological learning by doing (Moulder 1977: 1–23, 199–203; Nafziger 1976: 18–34; Norman 1975: 3–108).[4]

Benjamin Higgins, expressing a modernizing perspective, singles out Japan as "the only country in recent decades to have 'graduated' from the ranks of . . . an underdeveloped country" to an advanced country. He attributes this dramatic progress to "reactive nationalism," to land reform, to other institutional reform, to government assistance to private enterprise, to drastic monetary and fiscal measures, to the "efforts of government to transfer and develop a technology suitable to Japanese conditions," and to an open economy (Higgins 1968: 617–19).[5]

Modernization scholars stress that if Japan industrialized, it must be because Japan is the only Third World nation with a culture and social structure favorable to economic development. According to Edwin O. Reischauer and John K. Fairbank,

Table 1.1

Annual Rate of Growth of Real GNP per Capita (percent)

Annual growth rates

Country	(1) 1860 or 1870 to 1910	(2) 1910 to 1950	(3) 1950 to 1975	(4) 1975 to 1986	(5) (long period) 1860 or 1870 to 1986	Multiplica- tion of 1860 GNP per capita in 1986
Japan	2.9	1.8	7.6	3.4	3.5	76
Sweden	2.4	2.6	2.6	2.4	2.5	23
Germany[a]	2.0	0.7	4.5	2.4	2.1	14
Canada	2.2	1.3	2.4	2.2	2.0	11
Denmark	1.8	1.3	2.9	2.5	1.9	11
France[b]	1.5	0.9	3.8	2.3	1.9	11[c]
United States	2.5	1.1	2.0	2.0	1.9	11
Russia–USSR[d]	1.0	2.0	2.7	1.9	1.8	9[c]
Ireland	1.7	1.4	2.6	1.9	1.8	9
Italy	0.8	1.3	4.3	2.2	1.8	9
United Kingdom	1.2	1.2	2.2	1.8	1.4	6

Sources: Kuznets 1956: 13; Morawetz 1977: 80; Organisation for Economic Cooperation and Development 1988: 44; Ofer 1987: 1778; U.S. Congress 1988. The 1975 to 1986 rates (except for the USSR) are estimates based on World Bank 1987a: 6–9.

Note: As Nafziger (1990a: 8–68) explains, long-period growth rates and per-capita income multiples, subject to serious price-index number and subsistence valuation problems, are rough approximations.

[a]Since World War II, West Germany.
[b]Figures for period (1) and the long period begin in 1840.
[c]Multiplication for period 1860–1986 at same annual growth rate as that in column 5.
[d]The periods are: (1) 1870–1913 and (2) 1913–50.

> The great differences . . . in the speed and nature of their responses to the West in the past century . . . must be attributed mainly to the differences in the traditional societies of the countries of East Asia. Only such differences can explain why a basically similar impact could have brought such varied initial results . . . why relatively small Japan, for example, soon became a world power, while China sunk to the status of an international problem. [1958: 670]

Marion Levy, Jr., comparing "traditional" China and Japan, contends that "it was not differences in the new forces introduced to China and Japan that accounted for their different experiences in industrialization. It was rather differences in the social structure into which the new forces were introduced" (1955: 496).

Frances V. Moulder, a dependency scholar, challenges the contention of modernizing scholars that Japan's traditional society was more conducive to economic modernization than was China's. Instead, China's incorporation into the world economy led to the "dismantling of [an] already weak imperial state." In contrast, "Japan's greater autonomy . . . permitted transformation of [a] weak feudal state into a bureaucratic or national state." Dependency scholars contend that Japan was virtually the only Asian, African, or Latin American country to modernize rapidly because it was the only nation largely to escape the pressures to become an economic satellite to Western nations within the world system. Modernizing scholars, however, deny that, in comparison with other Third World countries, Japan's more autonomous position relative to Western nations in the international capitalist system in the late nineteenth and early twentieth centuries had any relationship to faster economic modernization in Japan than in the third world generally (Moulder 1977: vii–viii, 1–23, 199–203).

According to dependency theorist Celso Furtado (1968, 1970, 1973: 118–23), since the eighteenth century global changes in demand resulted in a new international division of labor in which the peripheral countries of Asia, Africa, and Latin America specialized in primary products in an enclave controlled by foreigners while importing consumer goods that were the fruits of technical products in the metropolitan countries of the West. The increased productivity and new consumption patterns in peripheral countries benefited a small ruling class and its allies (less than a tenth of the population), who cooperated with the DCs (capitalist developed countries) to achieve modernization (economic development among a modernizing minority). The result is "peripheral capitalism, a capitalism unable to generate innovations and dependent for transformation upon decisions from the outside" (Furtado 1973: 120).

Andre Gunder Frank, a major proponent of the dependency thesis, criticized the view of modernization scholars that contemporary underdeveloped countries resemble the earlier stages of now-developed countries. Many of these scholars viewed modernization in LDCs as simply the adoption of economic and political systems developed in Western Europe and North America.

For Frank, the presently developed countries were never *under*developed, though they may have been *un*developed. His basic thesis is that underdevelopment does *not* mean traditional (that is, nonmodern) economic, political, and social institutions but LDC subjection to the colonial rule and imperial domination of foreign powers. In essence, Frank sees underdevelopment as the effect of the penetration of modern capitalism into the archaic economic structures of the Third World. He sees the deindustrialization of India under British colonialism, the disruption of African society by the slave trade and subsequent colonialism, and the total destruction of Incan and Aztec civilizations by the Spanish conquistadors as examples of the *creation* of underdevelopment.[6]

More plainly stated, the economic development of the rich countries contributes to the underdevelopment of the poor. Development in an LDC is not self-generating or autonomous, but ancillary. The LDCs are economic satellites of the highly developed regions of North America and Western Europe in the international capitalist system. The Asian, African, and Latin American countries that are most *weakly* integrated into this system tend to be the most highly developed. Japanese economic development after 1868 is the classic case illustrating Frank's theory. Japanese industrial growth remains unmatched: Japan was never a capitalist satellite. Modernizing economists fail to consider that Japan's adaptation and development would probably not have occurred had the Japanese not resisted Western economic domination. Conceivably, African and other Asian countries might have used strategies similar to those of Japan to develop rapidly if they had been free to borrow, adapt, innovate, and plan in light of indigenous goals and strengths.

Brazil illustrates the connection between the satellite relationship and underdevelopment. Since the nineteenth century, the growth of the major cities, São Paulo and Rio de Janeiro, has been satellite development—largely dependent on outside capitalist powers, especially Britain and the United States. As a result, regions in interior Brazil have become satellites of these two cities and, through them, of these Western capitalist countries.

Frank suggests that satellite countries experience their *greatest* economic development when they are *least* dependent on the world capitalist system. Thus, Argentina, Brazil, Mexico, and Chile grew most rapidly during World War I, the Great Depression, and World War II, when trade and financial ties with major capitalist countries were weakest. Significantly, the most underdeveloped regions today are those that have had the closest ties to Western capitalism in the past. They were the greatest exporters of primary products to, and the biggest sources of capital for, developed countries, and were abandoned by them when for one reason or another business fell off. Frank points to India's Bengal, the one-time sugar-exporting West Indies and Northeastern Brazil, the defunct mining districts of Minas Gerais in Brazil, highland Peru, and Bolivia, and the former silver regions of Mexico as examples. He contends that even the *latifundium*, the large plantation or hacienda that has contributed so much to underdevelopment in Latin America, originated as a commercial, capitalist enterprise, not as a feudal institution, which contradicts the generally held thesis that a region is underdeveloped because it is isolated and precapitalist.

It is an error, Frank feels, to argue that the development of the underdeveloped countries will be stimulated by indiscriminately transferring capital, institutions, and values from developed countries. He suggests that, in fact, the following economic activities have contributed to underdevelopment, not development:

1. Replacing indigenous enterprises with technologically more advanced, global, subsidiary companies;
2. Forming an unskilled labor force to work in factories and mines and on plantations;

3. Recruiting highly educated youths for junior posts in the colonial administrative service;
4. Workers migrating from villages to foreign-dominated urban complexes;
5. Opening the economy to trade with, and investment from, developed
   countries.

According to Frank, a Third World country can develop only by withdrawing from
the world capitalist system. Perforce such a withdrawal means a large reduction in
trade, aid, investment, and technology from the developed capitalist countries.

Economic, political, and military power enables the DCs to transform con-
flicts of economic interests between DCs and LDCs into harmonies of interests
between elites of both countries. In most contemporary low- and lower-middle-
income countries, large portions of the political elite and local bourgeoisie rely
on and profit from economic and military assistance and political support from
Western countries for position, success, and even survival. Economic and political interests of local elites depending on activities of foreign governments and
businesspeople and international agencies are constraints on foreign and domestic economic policies. Foreigners and international agencies transfer technology,
contribute development planning assistance, provide foreign economic and military aid, make loans, write down debt, establish branches of multinational corporations, set conditions for relieving chronic current-account deficits, and can
determine import restrictions, as discussed in chapters 2, 3, and 8. Domestic
elites, because of their dependence, protect foreign interests, often at the expense
of local economic interests. During crises, indigenous elites often act in harmony
with outside economic interests, even when military force and aggressive diplo-
macy are absent (Galtung 1971: 83–84; Nafziger 1983: 18–19). In the next
chapter, I discuss Jürgen Osterhammel's concept of imperialism, which I use in
this book. These relationships between DCs and LDC elites are an integral part
of Osterhammel's concept.

World system theorists such as Immanuel Wallerstein contend that a limited
number of states that experience the discontent of rural workers and the urban
poor are able to channel this social movement into a national movement that
calls for a basic transformation of the world capitalist system of inequality.
Under the banner of nationalism, some weak states have accumulated the capital,
acquired the technology, built the military strength, and developed a core economy relative to a regional peripheral zone so as to transform themselves into
strong states. These states shift from peripheral to semiperipheral, from an assim-
ilated to an autonomous zone, from a colony or satellite to an independent entity
(and perhaps a regional imperial power). Since world economic growth is limited, only a few can escape this peripheral role in the global capitalist system
(Wallerstein 1974, 1980a: 167–223, 1980b, 1983: 17–21, 1989, among others).

The last section of this chapter provides a brief introduction to this book's
position on dependency and world system views.

Tokugawa Feudalism, 1603–1868

As background, I discuss feudalism before examining the post-Meiji Restoration (1868) period. Shogun Iemitsu's 1637 policy of "closing the country" (*sakoku*), so any Japanese leaving Japan and returning was to be put to death, lasted until the last tottering Tokugawa years. Isolation from Europe's empire building allowed more autonomous political development but increased relative economic backwardness, at least during Europe's industrial revolution of the early nineteenth century.

In the first half of the nineteenth century, Japan's economy was no more advanced than that of Western Europe in the eighteenth century and of most Asian and African LDCs in the mid-twentieth century. The overwhelming majority of Japan's 28–30 million people were unfree, poverty-stricken peasants, living mostly in self-sufficient rural villages. The chief source of wealth was the cultivation of rice, carried on by primitive methods that had changed little over the centuries.

Yet, in keeping with centralized government, Japan's premodern road system was well developed. Moreover, while in 1850 the means were available to meet basic needs within the traditional society, because of high income inequality the average Japanese was not well fed, well housed, or well dressed (Lockwood 1954: 3; Ohkawa and Rosovsky 1973: 5–8), with the average material well-being among the bottom half of the population probably no higher than the average sub-Saharan African today.

E. Herbert Norman indicates Japan's feudalism represented "one of the most conscious attempts in history to freeze society in a rigid hierarchical mold" (1975: 119). Every social class and subdivision had regulations on clothing, ceremony, and behavior. The Tokugawa rulers distinguished between samurai (feudal warrior class) and commoner, and emphasized class hierarchy in every conceivable way. Some *chonin* (merchants), who held lower status, however, were invited by the *shogun* (overlords) to occupy government positions. Farmers—85 percent of the working population in the early nineteenth century—could not engage in other occupations or migrate to the towns. Yet class and occupational rigidity only stunted, but did not stifle, the technological and commercial advance spurred during the fifteenth and sixteenth centuries (Mahajan 1976: 1–2; Norman 1975).

The shock of China's defeat in the Opium War goaded the authorities of the shogunate and the forward-looking samurai to acquire knowledge of foreign affairs in the 1840s. Thus, the shogunate introduced administrative reforms and improved Japan's military preparedness within ten years of U.S. Commodore Matthew C. Perry's forced opening of Japanese ports to foreign countries in 1853–54. Moreover, the last shogun also awarded important offices on merit, contemplated abolishing the hundreds of domains (*han*) of feudal lords or *daimyo* (vassals to the shogun) and establishing modern centralized government, sent envoys abroad to study foreign technology, purchased foreign warships and merchant vessels, and had dockyards, iron works, and other industrial plants constructed on Western lines, borrowing from the United States and France. But, while the shogun helped build the foundations of modern Japan, he embarked on modernization too late. Recognizing the old system was crumbling, he barely resisted the restoration of the emperor to the throne (Allen 1964: 26–27; Han 1982: 4–5; Mahajan 1976: 7; Toyama 1966: 419–20).

Although the Tokugawa shoguns isolated Japan from foreign influence from 1638 to the 1850s or 1860s, they provided a more favorable legacy for modernization than other LDCs. The process of learning from foreigners began in Japan before the mid-nineteenth century. Despite the rigid seclusion enforced by the Tokugawa regime after 1639, the Japanese had retained a peephole on the outside world through the trade and residence of the Dutch at Deshima; many enterprising daimyo went to school with the Dutch (McCord 1973: 278–79; Nakamura 1983: 51). Mid-nineteenth-century feudal Japan had a literacy rate about as high as England, a well-integrated transport system, law and order, and guild and clan-monopoly workshops producing silk textiles, sake (rice wine), rapeseed oil, cotton cloth, candles, and other processed products for a national market, especially the large urban populations of Edo (Tokyo), Osaka, and Kyoto (Lockwood 1954: 4, 321).

The West intruded on Japan's isolation intermittently, but most devastatingly in 1863–64 when ships bombarded Satsuma and Choshu. This demonstration of modern technology's superiority convinced a dissident group from the lower ranks of the samurai that Japan had to abandon its traditional economic policies. These samurai tended to be administrators in territories (such as Satsuma, Choshu, and Tosa) located far away from Edo (Tokyo), at the fringes of the Tokugawa shogunate, that had been directly confronted with foreign threat to national security and forced to adopt modernization programs of their own (Toyama 1966: 420–26).

Most samurai lived poorly, as the low stipends eroded through inflation from currency expansion. The gap between samurai and the elite widened just before 1868. The samurai, many of whom read widely in Western literature, science, and technology and were embarrassed by the shogun's humiliating commercial treaties with the West, thought the only solution for meeting the challenge was modernization, replacing the stagnation and economic backwardness of shogun rule with emperor rule. Yet ironically, the opening of Japan by the shogun to foreign commerce brought about the downfall of the shogun, as he was charged with betraying Japan's honor (Mahajan 1976: 5–6).

The Meiji restoration, the basis for capitalist development, was led by neither a rising business class, peasants, nor workers, but by dissidents among the samurai, the court nobles, and the daimyo of Satsuma, Choshu, Tosa, and Hizen (Norman 1975: 133). Samurai dissidents, who were leaders of a reforming party from the feudal stratum alienated from the ruling clique, helped instigate peasants, with little prior unity, to revolt against the shogun in 1868.

Japan had a well-developed tax system (especially compared with sub-Saharan Africa today). Cultivators paid 40 to 50 percent of their produce as land tax (partly in kind) to the shogun. Yet the highly commercialized agriculture in the mid-nineteenth century enjoyed a productivity per hectare roughly the same as South and Southeast Asia today. Moreover, peasant average material welfare was higher than in South and Southeast Asia, and starvation deaths were practically unknown (Dore 1965a: 321; Lockwood 1954: 4; Nakamura 1983: 51; Mahajan 1976: 2–3).

Japan, a closed economy before 1868, was self-sufficient in food. Despite shogun restrictions on experimenting with new crops, the progressive daimyo introduced technical innovations (especially in rice), but no major break-throughs. Although official figures indicate an 1868 daily calorie intake per capita of only 1,350, James Nakamura's (1966) estimate of 1,600 calories is probably more accurate (Mahajan 1976: 2; T. Nakamura 1983: 2–3). This daily calorie intake was substantially lower than that of contemporary Bangladesh (1,812), Thailand (1,929), India (2,021), Sri Lanka (2,126), Indonesia (2,272), Pakistan (2,281), China (2,441), and low-income sub-Saharan Africa (2,106) (World Bank, 1983a: vol. 1., p. 101; 1986: 96).

The Tokugawa clans ruled Japan as a fief until 1868 when the Meiji rulers came to power in a relatively bloodless manner. Since many reforms pursued by the dissident samurai buttressed rather than dismantled traditions, Meiji social change was less radical than in other countries moving from feudalism to capitalism, such as late eighteenth-century France (McCord 1973: 278–81) and twentieth-century sub-Saharan Africa and South Asia. The Tokugawa period also contrasts with the premodern period in most of the rest of Asia and Africa, largely under European colonial or imperial rule (see chapter 2).

The restoration of the emperor in 1868 symbolized more a determination to modernize than worshipful respect for him. The young emperor did not enjoy power, but rubber-stamped decisions of state made in his name by a small handful of samurai administrators (Lockwood 1954: 10).[7] After the emperor assumed the throne, the clans surrendered their land registers in 1869, fiefs were abolished in 1871, the land tax was reformed in 1873, and in the early 1870s restrictions on the freedom of internal trade and movement were abolished.

In 1868, Japan lacked an industrial base comparable to Europe in 1800, Russia in 1900, or Pakistan or Nigeria today. Unlike the West, Japan could not depend on colonies for capital, resources, and markets then, and (because of Western restrictions) could not levy protective tariffs. Japan was deficient in basic minerals, and had little arable land to bring under cultivation. Per-capita income in Japan was substantially lower than in Europe (McCord 1973: 278–79).

Japan's Sustained Economic Growth

Scholars have usually rejected concepts of abrupt economic change like Rostow's takeoff or Friedrich Engels's industrial revolution. Even Simon S.

Kuznets's (1966) modern economic growth, a rapid, sustained increase in real per-capita GNP associated with capital accumulation and rapid technical change under private or state capitalism, begins so gradually that its start cannot be dated by a given year or decade. In Japan, we cannot pinpoint the beginnings of modern (or capitalist) growth more precisely than the Meiji reform era of the late nineteenth-century period.

William W. Lockwood thinks Japan's largest increases in real national income, from 1868 to 1888, were from improvements in agriculture, handicrafts, and internal commerce following the removal of feudal restrictions and unification under a strong, central government. Freedom of movement and occupation, the abolition of clan tariffs and tolls, the free transfer of land ownership, the dispersion of agricultural methods, financial unification, and improved transport slowly expanded the internal market and productivity. Factory industry and foreign trade only become leading sectors in the 1880s (Lockwood 1954: 17–18).

For more than a half century before 1936, when John Maynard Keynes discussed maintaining full employment under capitalism, Japan used financial tools for steady growth, with an economy at full capacity (Harrod 1939: 14–33; Keynes 1936; Mahajan 1976: 84). Indeed while growth fluctuated, there was virtually no negative growth, a contrast to the West. Japan's changing international market and its high saving rates (at no time falling below 9.6 percent for any four-year period between 1885 and 1935) contributed to this growth record. Japan escaped the ravages of (and even profited from) World War I. After raw silk fabrics shed their international competitiveness in the late 1920s, Japanese businesspeople switched to rayon, enjoying an expanding international demand. Production rose from 115 tons of rayon products in 1921 to 16,000 tons in 1930 and 91,000 tons in 1935. Yet at the same time Japan maintained its share of raw silk exports. During the 1929–31 world depression, Japan's growth rate was even higher than the pre-1929 rate. Japan's average real income during the world depression from 1928 to 1932, was 11 percent higher than it was during 1923–27. Furthermore, per-capita productivity of the gainfully employed increased from 360 yen in 1923–27 to 402 during 1928–32, a growth rate of 12 percent (Lockwood 1954: 138, 252, 264; Mahajan 1976: 56, 84–5; Nakamura 1983: 8–9).

Japan's growth from 1889 to 1938 was accompanied by an annual inflation (GNP deflator) of 3.8 percent, higher than DCs then but much lower than LDCs since World War II. Japanese prices rose sharply during the post–World War I boom, but fell substantially during the subsequent recession in the 1920s. While pre-1939 Japan enjoyed inflationary growth, price increases were mild compared with Africa and Asia since World War II (Minami 1986: 369–94).

Japan industrialized rapidly in the half-century before the 1920s, assisted for a quarter of a century by the division of labor which benefited from food and raw materials imports from colonies, Taiwan and Korea, and cereals, raw cotton, iron ore, and coal imports from and textile exports to subservient China. Value-added in manufacturing as a percentage of NNP (net national product) rose from 18 percent in 1883–87 to 34 percent yearly in 1918–22, before declining to 31 percent annually in 1923–27 and rising to 37 percent in 1937. By then, Japan's rising standard of living depended on its manufacturing sector for consumer goods; Japan depended less on external trade than during Meiji. Agriculture's share, which was 33 percent of NNP during 1883–87, rose to 42 percent in 1903–07 before falling to 33 percent in 1922 and 21 percent in 1937 (Duus, Myers, and Peattie 1989: xiii); Mahajan 1976: 71–73).

In contrast to Japan's fast growth, Africa and Asia grew by only a fraction of 1 percent a year from 1870 to 1950. Real growth in India, the LDC with the best estimates, was no more than 0.2 percent per year from 1900 to its independence in 1947 (Heston and Summers 1980: 96–101; Morawetz 1977: 12–14; Uppal 1977: 15–17). Moreover, despite exceptions, such as the Tata steel mill in India in 1911, African and Asian LDCs enjoyed little heavy industrialization during the period of Western suzerainty in the first half of the twentieth century.

Average Material Welfare

During the late nineteenth century, the average skilled manufacturing worker with a regular job faced harsh work conditions and a wage that barely supported his family at subsistence. In 1899, 60 to 70 percent of Tokyo's skilled machinists hardly supported their families. Even the better-paid worker could barely afford food, clothing, and cramped, dirty shelter (Gordon 1985: 26).

While real GNP per capita in Japan grew 2.1 percent annually from 1889 to 1938, personal consumption expenditure per capita grew only 1.5 percent annually, an average rate among eleven DCs (including also Russia, Sweden, Denmark, Germany, France, Italy, Ireland, the United Kingdom, the United States, and Canada) but still substantial. M.B. Bennett (1951: 648), who uses sixteen indicators for thirty-one countries from 1934 to 1938, ranks Japan's per-capita consumption level as 38 percent of that of the leading nation's, the United States (less than 20 percent in mechanical transport, telephones, and movies, and more than 60 percent in caloric diet, physicians per 1,000 population, textile fibers, and school attendance), much less than that of the United Kingdom and most other Western countries, less than Czechoslovakia, about even with Italy, but more than the USSR and other Eastern European countries, and substantially more than the levels of the rest of Asia, Africa, and the Middle East. Japan's life expectancy in 1891–1899 was forty-three to forty-four years, lower than the level of virtually all countries (except Gambia, Guinea, Guinea-Bissau, Sierra Leone, and Afghanistan) and substantially lower than the average for Africa and Asia (sixty-one) in 1993. By the 1930s, Japan's mortality rates compared with France, Spain, and Eastern Europe. Infant mortality compared favorably with Eastern Europe, and was 30 to 50 percent lower than the rate in other Asian countries. Famines, epidemics, and infanticide disappeared on a large scale; and life expectancy (halfway between the West and Asia) and nutritional levels increased much faster than in the rest of Asia. In 1993, Japan had the highest life expectancy (seventy-nine years) and lowest infant mortality rate (4.4 per 1,000) in the world (Bennett 1951: 648; Lockwood 1954: 80–81, 139–47, 272; Population Reference Bureau 1993).

With rapid agricultural technological change in the late nineteenth century and a reliance on colonies for foodstuffs beginning in 1894–95, the average food intake rose appreciably in the forty to fifty years ending in 1930, becoming more diversified, especially among the urban classes. The per-capita consumption of rice, which substituted for the inferior good, barley, increased about 25 percent, and average meat consumption soared. Food production and imports per person rose 20 percent from 1910–12 to 1925–27. By 1925–29, when Japan received foodstuffs from both colonies Taiwan and Korea, the average daily calorie intake available was 2,300, compared with 1,924 in Korea and 2,208 in Taiwan. Daily calorie intake per capita in present-day Africa, South Asia, and Southeast Asia is no more than 2,200. The widespread use of electric lighting, which replaced the kerosene lamp; the increased use of postal service, railways, buses, and bicycles; the wool clothing and leather shoes seen among middle-class men; the expansion of book and newspaper sales to a highly literate population; and the numerous cheap Western-type gadgets during the 1920s and 1930s provided evidence of increased average material welfare. The real wages of employed industrial workers rose about 33 percent between 1897 and 1914, and 65–75 percent from 1914 to the late 1930s (Minami 1985: 369–411).

In 1936, horsepower per employed factory worker was 4.8 in the United States, 2.4 in each of Britain and Germany, 2.1 in Italy, 1.4 in Czechoslovakia, and 1.7 in Japan (a figure double a generation earlier). Energy consumption per person employed in manufacturing and mining in 1937 was 34,449 kilowatt hours in the United States, 18,173 in Britain, 11,312 the Soviet Union, 19,858 Germany, 10,077 Japan, 9,466 Australia, 7,469 Chile, and 1,837 Turkey (Lockwood 1954: 180–81).

Prima facie, the meager livelihood of many in the 1930s, including the dire poverty of millions of tenant farmers and unskilled workers, challenges the evidence concerning rapid economic growth. How could such growth have left most people so close to subsistence? Some rise in per-capita income represented goods and services required for industrialization but not contributing to increased consumption. Food and raw materials, many from colonies, were hauled longer distances. In addition, Japan's high savings rate meant vast amounts were withheld from consumption. Moreover, the costs of armed forces, strategic industries, and war were a drain on living standards. Military expansion in the 1930s severely handicapped spending for education, rural development, and social welfare. Indeed, most of the substantial gain in real income per capita from 1930 to 1936 represented increased capital assets and military supply (Lockwood 1954: 74, 80–81, 139–43, 272).

Income Distribution

Ryoshin Minami and Lockwood indicate gradually increasing income inequality in Japan from the 1920s through the 1930s (especially between industry and agriculture) so that its inequality in the mid- to late 1930s was higher than in the United Kingdom, Germany, the United States, and probably all other DCs. The U.S. Department of State estimates that Japan in 1930 had a highly skewed income distribution, accompanied by large income shares by a few rich who owned most instruments of production. The top 0.2 percent of the households in 1930 received 10.4 percent of national income, while the bottom 56.5 percent received only 23.4 percent of income (table 1.2), with a Gini coefficient of concentration of 0.65, more than the household income Ginis for all thirty-seven LDCs with data in the 1950s and 1960s surveyed by the World Bank (Jain 1975). Ironically, since the post–World War II land, trade union, antimonopoly, democratic, constitutional, and demilitarization reforms (discussed below), Japan's Gini coefficient for national household income distribution is among the lowest for Organisation for Economic Cooperation and Development (OECD) countries (table 1.3).

From the 1880s to the 1930s, Japan's property incomes became more concentrated and increased relative to labor incomes. Surplus labor kept the growths of real wages (1.3 percent annually, 1883–1937) and per-capita labor consumption substantially below per-capita income and consumption growths. Moreover, the benefits from real wage growth accrued largely to workers in the formal sector (government agencies and firms with more than ten employed), while workers in the informal sector benefited little.

While the Meiji restoration destroyed much feudal income, the nobility were pensioned off and their clan debts to merchants were shouldered by government. State obligations and favors, together with prior mercantile wealth, provided a start for a new aristocracy of wealth under capitalism. The *zaibatsu*, the emerging conglomerate groups of companies, owned a substantial share of modern industry, banks, and trading firms, while land ownership was also concentrated. High salaries and bonuses were paid to the upper managerial class of zaibatsu, tax policies were regressive, favors were lavished on successful financiers and industrial magnates, and speculators acquired large profits. A high degree of income inequality contributed to upper income groups, with a lower propensity to consume being responsible for a major portion of savings invested in corporate business enterprises (Francks 1992: 63; Jain 1975; Lockwood 1954: 270–80; Mahajan 1976: 73; Minami 1985: 395–96).

Before the late 1940s, Japan modernized without the growth of political liberalism that emerged in the West. Japan's income inequality grew steadily, as the zaibatsu owned a growing share of production, land ownership became more concentrated, and profits, interest, and rents increased relative to wages.

Since 1979–80, most contemporary low-income African and Asian countries,

Table 1.2

Household Income in Japan by Income Classes, 1930*

Income bracket (yen)	Households		Aggregate income (millions of yen)	
	Number	Percent	Number	Percent
Total	12,600,276	100.0	8,740	100.0
Over 1,000,000	19	—	32	0.4
50,000–1,000,000	1,739	—	276	3.2
10,000–50,000	22,674	0.2	596	6.8
3,000–10,000	145,360	1.2	1,010	11.6
1,200–3,000	723,141	5.7	1,542	17.6
800–1,200	1,087,343	8.6	1,096	12.5
400–800	3,500,000	27.8	2,142	24.5
200–400	4,888,000	38.8	1,711	19.6
0–200	2,232,000	17.7	335	3.8

*Lockwood (1968: 272), citing U. S. Department of State (1945: 233). The State Department used figures based on the Japanese Cabinet Bureau of Statistics's (CBS's) use of income tax data in 1930 for a study of national income to estimate household incomes of 1,200 or more, and the CBS's 1931 income distribution of a representative agricultural village for household incomes below 1,200.

Table 1.3

Percentage Share of Household Income in OECD Countries, by Percentile Groups of Households (ca. 1980)

	Lowest 20 percent	Second quintile	Third quintile	Fourth quintile	Highest 20 percent	Gini coef- ficient
Netherlands	8.3	14.1	18.2	23.2	36.2	0.260
Belgium	7.9	13.7	18.6	23.8	36.0	0.265
Japan	8.7	13.2	17.5	23.1	37.5	0.270
Switzerland	6.6	13.5	18.5	23.4	38.0	0.291
Germany, Fed. Rep. of	7.9	12.5	17.0	23.1	39.5	0.295
Ireland	7.2	13.1	16.6	23.7	39.4	0.300
Norway	6.0	12.9	18.3	24.6	38.2	0.304
Finland	6.3	12.1	18.4	25.5	37.7	0.305
Sweden	7.4	13.1	16.8	21.0	41.7	0.306
Spain	6.9	12.5	17.3	23.2	40.1	0.308
United Kingdom	7.0	11.5	17.0	24.8	39.7	0.315
Denmark	5.4	12.0	18.4	25.6	38.6	0.320
United States	5.3	11.9	17.9	25.0	39.9	0.329
Canada	5.3	11.8	18.0	24.9	40.0	0.330
France	5.5	11.5	17.1	23.7	42.2	0.342
Italy	6.2	11.3	15.9	22.7	43.9	0.347
New Zealand	5.1	10.8	16.2	23.2	44.7	0.366
Australia	5.4	10.0	15.0	22.5	47.1	0.384

Source: World Bank (1989: 222–23).

largely peripheral countries within the world economy, have experienced chronic external deficits and many of these low-income countries have encountered debt overhang. As conditions for loans of last resort or debt relief (except for populous and influential China and, to a lesser extent, India and Indonesia), the World Bank, donor government, and commercial banks rely on an International Monetary Fund (IMF) "seal of approval," usually contingent on the borrower reducing spending and cutting back real wages. The IMF and World Bank macroeconomic stabilization and structural or sectoral adjustment programs usually include economic liberalization that redistributes income toward property owners, increasing inequality. In the late 1980s and 1990s, most income concentration Ginis in African and Asian LDCs have been increasing toward those in Japan before 1939 rather than falling toward figures in postwar Japan. Adjustment pressures make sweeping political and economic democratization in Africa and Asia LDCs parallel to that in post-1950 Japan unlikely for a long time.

The Focus of This Study

The Japanese development model (JDM) from the Meiji Restoration through the late 1930s is different from the JDM after 1945–47. During this early postwar period, in response to the revolutionary momentum created by a devastating military defeat and the demands of the working class, the U.S. occupational forces commanded by General Douglas MacArthur promulgated a number of reforms, changing many of the ground rules under which Japanese institutions subsequently functioned, while preserving the elite structure of Japanese state and society, including the emperor system (Selden 1983: 100). These land, educational, labor union, antitrust, and political reforms, while falling short of worker demands, made Japan more egalitarian, competitive, and peaceful.

Doubtless, South Korea, Taiwan, Hong Kong, and Singapore—newly industrialized countries (NICs) which account for more than two-thirds of total LDC manufactured exports—have learned from post–World War II Japanese development, an advanced stage of economic growth. But I limit the early JDM's application to fifty-four low-income and lower-middle income countries, less advanced economies from four world regions—sub-Saharan Africa, and South, Southeast, and East Asia (labeled low-income countries or LDCs in this study). Indeed, forty-one of the forty-three low-income countries and thirteen of the next forty-one lower-middle-income countries are from these four regions (World Bank 1993: 218–19). (Development indicators for nineteen of the major low-income countries are presented in table 1.4.)

I had initially intended to concentrate on mixed and capitalist, but not socialist (centrally directed) LDCs like China and Vietnam. But economic reform in these two countries suggests that the Japanese model may apply to them. Moreover, the interest Chinese scholars indicated when I lectured on the Japanese development model to the International Technology and Economy Institute, Research

Table 1.4

Development Indicators (by Country, LDC Regions, and Country Income Groups)

	Population (millions) mid-1991	GNP per capita 1991 ($)	Average annual growth rate of GNP per capita 1980–91 (percent)	Poorest share/richest share[a]	Percentage of population in poverty, 1985–1990 I$370 purchasing power adjustment[b]	Life expectancy at birth 1991 (years)	Adult literacy rate 1990 (%)	Human development index[c]	Human freedom index[d]
Selected countries									
China	1,150	370	7.8	0.153	20	69	73	0.566	2
India	866	330	3.2	0.213	48	60	48	0.309	14
United States	253	22,240	1.7	0.112		76	99	0.976	33
Indonesia	181	610	3.9	0.206	38	60	77	0.515	5
Brazil	151	2,940	0.5	0.031		66	81	0.730	18
Japan	124	26,930	3.6	0.232		79	99	0.983	32
Pakistan	116	400	3.2	0.212	30	59	35	0.311	5
Bangladesh	111	220	1.9	0.241	86	51	35	0.189	7
Nigeria	99	340	−2.3	0.153		52	51	0.246	13
Mexico	83	3,030	−0.5	0.114		70	87	0.805	15
Philippines	63	730	−1.2	0.136	58	65	90	0.603	10
Thailand	57	1,570	5.9	0.120	30	69	93	0.715	14
Ethiopia	53	120	−1.6	0.208	61	48	50	0.172	2
Korea, South	43	6,330	8.7		16	70	96	0.872	14
Zaïre	37	170	−2.1		83-	53	66	0.262	5
Sudan	26	240	0.0		81	51	24	0.152	
Tanzania	25	100	−0.8	0.038		51	52	0.270	10
Kenya	25	340	0.3	0.044	47	59	69	0.369	8

Malaysia	18	2,520	2.9	0.086	5	71	78	0.790	9
Ghana	15	400	-0.3	0.159	44	55	60	0.311	11
Côte d'Ivoire	12	690	-4.6	0.173	29	52	54	0.286	
Cameroon	12	850	-1.0		30	55	54	0.310	8
LDC regions									
Sub-Saharan Africa	489	350	-1.2	0.155	47	51	50		
South and Southeast Asia	1,152	320	3.1	0.288	51	59	46		
East Asia and Pacific	1,666	650	6.1	0.215	20	68	76		
Middle East	244	1,940	-2.4	0.227	31	64	55		
Latin America	445	2,390	-0.3	0.116	19	67	84		
Country income groups									
LDCs	4,528	1,010	1.0	0.198	37	64	65		
DCs	783	21,530	2.3	0.443		77	96		
Other high-income	39	11,413	2.3			77	96		
World	5,350	4,010	1.2		31	66	65		

Sources: Ahluwalia, Carter, and Chenery 1979: 302–03, 312–13; World Bank 1993b: 238–39, 296–97; World Bank 1980b; United Nations Development Programme 1991: 20, 119–120, 124–25, 160–61; and United Nations Development Programme 1993: 135–37.

Blank cells indicate data not available, except U.S., Japanese, and DC blanks for poverty rates mean virtually 0% poverty rates (by I$370 standard). LDCs comprise the low- and middle-income countries in World Bank 1993b: 238–39. DCs are Organisation for Economic Cooperation and Development (OECD) members only. Other high-income includes Israel, Hong Kong, and Singapore.

[a] Poorest 20 percent share/richest 20 percent share ca. 1990 for selected countries. Poorest 20 percent share/richest 5 percent share ca. 1970 for LDC regions and country income groups.

[b] Based on purchasing power adjustment—poverty line I$370 (i.e., 370 internationally adjusted U.S. dollars) per capita a year.

[c] United Nations Development Programme 1993: 135–37, based on life expectancy at birth (1990), educational attainment [adult literacy rate (1990) and mean years of schooling (1990)], and real GDP per capita (I$). HDI ranking varies from 0.983 in Japan to 0.045 in Guinea. HDI is not available for country groups and LDC regions.

[d] United Nations Development Programme 1991: 20, based on civil and legal rights, freedom from torture and censorship, electoral and religious freedom, ethnic and gender egalitarianism, independent media, courts, and trade unions, and related indicators. HFI ranking varies from 0 for Iraq to 38 for Sweden. HFI is not available for country groups and LDC regions.

Center of Economical, Technical, and Social Development of the State Council, Beijing, China, and at the China–U.S. Economic and Trade Exchanges Symposium, May 14–19, 1987, also suggested that I expand the scope to China.

Japan not only borrowed law, government, economic ideas, philosophy, religion, culture, art, sciences, learning, and part of its writing script (the Chinese characters or *kanji*) from China for much of the last two millennia, but it also was a major trader with, investor in, and imperial power in China for the half-century after 1895. In 1910, Japan's commodity trade with China was about five times that with Taiwan and Korea combined; these two colonies' trade only surpassed China's in 1927 (Duus, Myers, and Peattie 1989: xiii, 12). In recent years, Japan has resumed substantial trade with and investment in China.

China, India, Bangladesh, Pakistan, Myanmar (Burma), Indonesia, Thailand, the Philippines, Vietnam, Nigeria, Ethiopia, and Zaïre comprise the countries with more than 30 million population among these fifty-four countries. Other countries include Ghana, Côte d'Ivoire, Kenya, Tanzania, Sri Lanka, and Malaysia. These countries are in earlier stages of industrialization, account for over 77 percent of the LDCs' 1993 population (Population Reference Bureau 1993), and have an average real income perhaps comparable to 1868 Japan. Thus, the appropriate period for testing the JDM's application to these countries is from 1868 through the late 1930s, rather than the period after 1945.

Major Questions and Approaches

Do the economic approaches taken by Japan (1868–1939), the most successful non-Western economy, have implications for today's Third World economies? This book concentrates on unique features of the pre-1939 JDM, and how this JDM applies to today's LDCs. The major foci of chapters 2 through 6 are capital formation and technology policies that contributed to Japan's rapid industrial capitalist growth: chapter 2 looks at technological adaptation and educational policy; chapter 3 addresses state strategies of establishing industries and selling to private enterprise; chapter 4 considers government aid to private entrepreneurs; chapter 5 discusses the transfer of the agricultural surplus to industry; and chapter 6 studies wage and employment patterns. These policies benefited both modern and traditional sectors of the dual economy (discussed in chapter 7); most contemporary LDCs are also dualistic. Growth in productivity per person was increased substantially by Japan's policy of participating in the growing international specialization in the decades following 1868 (chapter 8). A key to Japan's ability to pursue favorable policies was that, unlike most non-Western countries of the time, it was not dominated by Western imperialism; indeed, its economic development benefited from its imperialist policies (see chapter 2).

In chapter 9, I will assess not only the implications of the early Japanese model for the fifty-four LDCs generally but also for the success of the Association of South East Asian Nations (ASEAN) four—Indonesia, Malaysia, the Philippines, and Thailand (excluding for our purposes the more advanced city-state, Singapore, an upper-middle- or high-income country). Three of the ASEAN four—Indonesia, Malaysia, and Thailand—comprise, with Japan and the NICs, the eight high-performing Asian economies acclaimed in the World Bank's *The East Asian Miracle* (1993a).

What is my view of the approach of dependency and world system theorists? Throughout this book, I support the dependency theorists' view that the African and Asian periphery is hurt by its dependence on decisions made at the center of the global capitalist system by the metropolitan or developed countries—North America, Western Europe, and (contemporary) Japan. In several chapters, I show how these DC decisions—about investment, aid, technology transfer, debt relief, and import liberalization—harm LDCs, and compare the damage to them with the way in which nineteenth-century and early twentieth-century Japan was able to increase the benefits and reduce the injuries from integration within the international economy.

I disagree, however, with the dependency school's policy prescription that LDCs should withdraw from the world capitalist system through reducing trade, investment flows, aid receipts, and technology transfer from the developed capitalist countries, and increasing internal controls.[8] Africa and Asia should not cut their international transactions but they should strive, like late nineteenth-century Japan, to increase the autonomy of the decisions they make to participate in international trade and receive foreign capital inflows and technology transfer. Today's developing countries need self-directed development policies that enable them to maximize their gains in efficiency and growth from international trade and investment, while providing modest protection to sectors in which the country can acquire the benefits from increasing returns to scale in new industries that require specialized management and technology, and can capture gains from external economies and technological learning gains. In chapters 8 and 9, I make my major break with the dependency theorists, supporting liberal trade and market-clearing exchange rates but advocating planning for these trade and exchange-rate adjustments (and macroeconomic stabilization) over a longer period, a view consistent with that of some modernization theorists, although not with "shock therapy" liberalizers such as Jeffrey Sachs, who was a prominent consultant to Poland and Russia during their liberalization strategies in 1990–93.[9]

I share many of the views of world systems theorists, including the explanation of Mark Selden concerning Japan's transformation in the late nineteenth and early twentieth centuries to a strong state, with a semiperipheral position in the world economy (Selden 1983: 58–120). However, I reject Wallerstein's view that continued economic growth in core and semiperipheral countries and zones depends on their superior position in the world capitalist economy relative to peripheral countries and zones. Indeed, Wallerstein explicitly states: "The key factor to note is that within a capitalist world-economy, all states cannot 'develop' simultaneously *by definition,* since the system functions by virtue of having unequal core and peripheral regions" (1975: 23). I, however, believe in the possibility of economic growth in all world regions. Positive-sum growth can be derived from innovations (that improve the practical arts in agriculture, manufacturing, mining, and services) and increased efficiency from production according to comparative advantage (chapter 8) and increased capital per worker hour that can overcome resource and environmental limitations.[10]

In writing this book, I have tried to use the language and concepts of my mainstream colleagues in economics and social science, for I have long advocated increasing the dialogue between mainstream social science and its critics.[11]

Notes

1. Readers interested in Japan's economic history should consult Allen (1964), Hane (1992), Beasley (1990), Sumiya and Taira (1979), and other sources listed in the references.

2. For critiques, see Nafziger (1990a: 82–83); and Rostow (1963).

3. This excludes high-income capital-surplus oil exporters like the United Arab Emirates and Kuwait which, despite their high per capita GNP, have illiteracy rates and infant mortality rates comparable to developing countries.

4. Seers et al. (1979) criticize "modernization" theorists.

5. McClelland (1961); McClelland and Winter (1971) advance a psychological version of modernization theory. Criticisms of this thesis include Nafziger (1988b: 129–34), Schatz (1965: 234–41), Higgins (1968: 241–49), Kilby (1971: 7–11, 15–21), Redlich (1963: 10–35), and Larrain (1989: 94–95, 99–100).

6. Frank (1969, with discussion of Japan on pp. 12, 57, 94–95). Nafziger (1990a: 89–95) criticizes Frank's and Paul Baran's (1957) theories of underdevelopment. Larrain (1989: 111–211) has some persuasive criticisms of dependency theories, despite his erroneous identification (p. 173) of the exclusion of raw materials from F.H. Cardoso's category of produced means of production (that is, capital) as a mistake!

7. The 1873 land reform recognized no hereditary feudal rights in land by the samurai (and lords). Moreover, those officials responsible for organizing Japan's modern armed forces were uncertain about whether samurai would accept the essential rules of discipline and promotion. Thus, these officials preferred a conscription army. Careers in the bureaucracy and entrepreneurial activity were, however, open to the samurai (Beasley 1990: 62–64).

8. In Nafziger (1988a) I also have been critical of African and Asian elites who use "socialism" to legitimate policies that increase urban–rural and other inequalities. I use a concept similar to that in Bettelheim (1978) to analyze class conflict under African and Asian socialism.

9. Interview with Sachs in "Jeffrey Sachs: International Boy Wonder Speaks out on Changing Global Economy," *The Margin* (Fall 1991): pp. 9–12; and Sachs (1993).

10. I elaborate on this view in Nafziger (1990a).

11. As indicated in Nafziger (1976: 31–32, reprinted in Seers et al. 1979: 45–46).

Chapter 2

Economic Autonomy and Adapting Foreign Technology

There is no doubt that without the affront to human and national dignity caused by the intrusion of more advanced powers the rate of modernization of traditional societies over the past century-and-a-half would have been much slower than, in fact, it has been. Out of mixed interests and motives, coalitions were formed in these traditional or early transitional societies which aimed to make a strong modern national government and which were prepared to deal with the enemies of this objective.

— Walter W. Rostow 1960

The 1863–64 bombardments of Satsuma and Choshu by American and British warships humiliated Japan, forcing it open to foreign commerce. To maintain independence, Meiji Japan wanted economic development and military expansion, thus requiring foreign technology. The Meiji rulers believed they could only resist Western domination by being militarily prepared, ensuring access to overseas markets and resources, and participating in the international struggle for territory and spheres of influence. Indeed, as early as the waning years of the Tokugawa shogunate, when Japan increased its military preparedness to avoid the fate of China during the Opium War, senior samurai Yoshida Shoin (1830–59) had asserted that defense required territorial expansion. "To protect [Japan] well is not merely to prevent it from losing the position it holds, but to add to the positions which it does hold" (Beasley 1987: 29).

In 1857, Hotta Masoyoshi, head of the Tokugawa council, contended that "military power always springs from national wealth" (Beasley 1987: 28). Subsequently, the slogan of the new Meiji government, dominated by the samurai, was to "enrich the nation to strengthen the army," a goal requiring the adoption of Western technology, abandonment of feudalism, and sacrifice for military spending. Meiji leaders believed that industry (especially heavy industry) was essential to provide the sinews of military power. Large business houses had no difficulty rationalizing innovation, profits, and labor repression as essential for building the nation. And the Japanese state skillfully deflected popular energies into the drive for overseas conquest.

The Meaning of Imperialism

What complicates a discussion of imperialism, whether by the West toward Japan or Japan toward its Asian neighbors, is that not every imperialistic relationship is necessarily a colonial one. Since the industrial revolution, the ability of one country to dominate another has frequently been dependent on greater economic capability rather than sheer military strength. Understanding imperialism by only examining formal empire is like inspecting the tip of an iceberg. Imperial powers eschewed territorial expansion for other methods for acquiring privileged access to overseas markets. For example, the crumbling Ch'ing empire in China was too weak to resist Western and Japanese demands for unequal trade and investment treaties, but was generally strong enough or large enough to make wide-scale conquest unthinkable. The essence of British and Japanese economic policies in the nineteenth and early twentieth centuries was, in the words of John Gallagher and Ronald Robinson, "trade with informal control if possible, trade with rule when necessary" (Duus, Myers, and Peattie 1989: xi-xix; Gallagher and Robinson 1953: 1–15).

Osterhammel indicates some features usually associated with informal imperialism (empire without colonies):

1. A power differential existing between two countries is exploited by the stronger country in pursuit of its perceived interest in the weaker country.
2. The stronger country avoids direct rule over the weaker one, but possesses an effective veto power over its domestic economic policies and imposes basic guidelines on its international economic policies.
3. The strong nation either maintains a military establishment in the weak one or is in a position to influence its armed forces through military advisors and aid.
4. Nationals from the strong country maintain a substantial economic presence in the weak country, consisting of businesses ranging from agency houses to subsidiaries of multinational corporations.
5. Foreign officials or businesspeople make major economic decisions or are monopolistically or oligopolistically entrenched in the key economic sectors of the weak country.
6. Foreign banks control much of public finance in the weaker state.
7. The stronger state invests heavily in the inferior state.

8. The stronger country's hold over the weaker country is supported by the collaboration of indigenous rulers and comprador groups partially selected by the stronger state.

9. Indigenous collaborators partly share a common ideology with the elites of the superior state (Osterhammel 1986: 295–99).

Informal imperialism encompasses not only the relationships of DCs to noncolonial African and Asian countries during the period from the mid-nineteenth century through the end of World War II (including China, Afghanistan, and Thailand during the early twentieth century), but also much of formally independent Africa and Asia in the second half of the twentieth century.

The Military, Imperialism, Industrial Power, and Foreign Technology

The government proclaimed the Conscription Ordinance in 1873, resisted initially but eventually accepted due to loyalty to the emperor. From 1895 to 1945, Japan sent troops abroad more than ten times, creating a permanent war economy dependent on maintaining and expanding imperial conquest or domination. After victory in the Sino–Japanese War in 1894–95, Japan gained control over Taiwan, strengthened its position in Korea and the adjoining Liaodong peninsula in northeast China, and received indemnity payments from China 5.4 times its annual state budget, 1895–1913. Japan then annexed the southern Sakhalin Islands and dominated Manchuria after winning the 1905 Russo–Japanese War. Subsequently, Japan annexed Korea in 1910, invaded Siberia in 1918, occupied the Pacific Mandated Islands in 1919, seized Manchuria in 1931, invaded China in 1937, and fought the Pacific War from 1941 to 1945. War also provided a powerful stimulus for centralizing and legitimating state power, and for accelerating industrialization (Selden 1983: 62–76).

One-half to one-third of government revenue from 1880 to 1937 was diverted to the military. Military victories enhanced Japan's international prestige, while giving it territories rich in minerals and agriculture. Moreover, Japan invested substantially in transport and communication, essential for defense requirements. Furthermore, despite the cost, Japanese political leaders felt Japan had no alternative to trying to match Western military might and imperial influence. Indeed, most military ruling elites believed protecting the country against the West required domination over neighboring countries. In the closing years of the nineteenth century, the writer Tokutomi Soho observed that Japan only cast off its unequal economic relationship with the West and acquired international respect with its victory over China in 1894–95 (Beasley 1987: 29–32; Inukai 1981: 80–81; Lockwood 1954: 501–5; Mahajan 1976: 105–9; Nakamura 1983: 37–38).

Rostow's epigraph about humiliation and modernization may have had some validity for Japan, as Western intrusion provided the motivation for domestic investment in infrastructure, heavy industry, and the military. But Japan, which possessed the technology and resources to undertake both military and industrial growth, was unique among mid-nineteenth-century Africa and Asia. Unlike Japan, China and other countries of Africa and Asia lacked the strength and autonomy to speed up economic and political modernization in response to the Western affront to their national dignity.

Presently, with the slow growth of low-income countries, defense expenditures are in lieu of spending on housing, slum clearance, community development, pollution abatement, water supply, sanitation, unemployment compensation, child benefits, family and maternity allowances, and payments to and services for the sick, the elderly, and the disabled. In six sub-Saharan African countries—Burkina, Kenya, Liberia, Malawi, Tanzania, and Uganda—UNICEF shows defense as a percentage of central government expenditures rose from 10 percent in 1972 to 15 percent in 1989, while social welfare spending fell from 5 percent to 2.5 percent. In 1989, LDCs spent $150 billion on the military. In Africa, one-third of all the machinery imported in 1989 was destined for the military. In LDCs generally, 1989 armament imports equaled 75 percent of economic aid received. In 1986, the forty-six least developed countries—the poorest countries of the world, primarily from sub-Saharan Africa and some from South and Southeast Asia—spent as much on the military as on health and education combined, while DCs spent only 40 percent as much on the military as on health and education (UNICEF 1992: 45–63; United Nations 1991: 157).[1] Even in the 1990s, after the end of the Cold War, the world order is sufficiently unstable so Chad, Angola, Pakistan, and Uganda spend more than twice as much on the military as on health and education. Moreover, in light of the longstanding economic hegemony of developed countries in the Third World, contemporary African and Asian regional subimperial powers such as India, Indonesia, and Nigeria lack the opportunities to acquire informal economic empire and control access to resources and markets.

Self-Directed Development

Except for Japan, in the past two centuries (especially in the late nineteenth and early to mid-twentieth centuries) most of Africa and Asia was either colonized by the West or subject in other ways to its economic dominance. Most of Latin America, though formally independent in the nineteenth century, has been subject to British and U.S. economic and political suzerainty since then. Thus, during the century or two of rapid Western economic growth, non-Western countries, aside from Japan, lacked the autonomy to plan for economic modernization.

During the early to mid-nineteenth century, the Western powers regarded China, with its resources and raw materials, as the jewel of the Far East; the scramble for China began earlier than that for Japan, which was only considered of secondary importance. China's humiliating defeat at the hands of the West in the 1840s prodded the Tokugawa shogunate to prepare militarily, to introduce administrative reforms, and to study foreign technology so as to avoid China's fate. Japan quickly moved from a peripheral nation in the international economy soon after Commodore Perry forced Japan's ports open in 1853, to a semi-peripheral nation as a regional power bolstered by political hegemony in East Asia and eventual conquest of its Asian neighbors (Selden 1983: 74).

Despite unequal treaties with the West from 1858 to 1899, Japan's economy, with a flourishing internal trade, was damaged very little. The treaties strictly confined the commercial activities of Western firms to a limited area of 15.2 kilometers around each open port. Western enterprises could only penetrate the inland market by sending Japanese employees or offering advances to Japanese merchants to obtain export items. By the last quarter of the century, Western firms wanting to trade in the inland market not only faced severe competition with Chinese merchants but also had to conduct transactions with an oligopoly of Japanese merchants or brokers. The goods Western firms bought were subject to substantial price fluctuations; in addition, the firms had to pay a heavy commission to Japanese intermediaries. Indeed, according to Shinya Sugiyama (1988: 53–54, 67–68, 74–76), the treaty port system in Japan not only failed to promote the activities of Western merchants, but actually obstructed them. In Japan, the "unequal treaties" and treaty port system had ceased to function as they were expected to function long before they formally came to an end in 1899.

During the late nineteenth century, Japan had substantial autonomy in economic affairs compared with other African and Asian countries, which became economic satellites to the West. Although the West limited Japanese import tariffs to 5 percent, Japan partially circumvented these protective limits through tax rebates, subsidies, government purchase contracts, and state industrial enterprises. Furthermore, the 1868–1912 Meiji government was committed to economic and military development. It promulgated laws encouraging joint-stock organization and freedom of enterprise. The Act of 1872, based on American and French thought, established a national system of education stressing science and technology rather than skills for the junior civil service like most colonial schools. Unlike colonial India, Japan discouraged foreign investment between the mid-1870s and 1899 but hired thousands of foreigners to adapt and improve technology under ministry or local business direction. The Meiji government invested large amounts in infrastructure—telegraphs, postal service, water supply, coastal shipping, ports, harbors, bridges, lighthouses, river improvements, railways, electricity, gas, and technical research.

Goldsmith (1983: 4–5) thinks a knowledgeable 1870 economist would have indicated India more likely than Japan to be economically and financially developed by 1970. India, a British colony, possessed a unified currency, rudiments of a Western-style banking system, access to the British capital market, and British industrial and financial technology, while Japan, just emerging from feudalism, had a negligible modern sector, a chaotic currency, and no modern financial institutions.

Yet Meiji Japan, which organized its own modern financial institutions with government initiative and assistance through the mid-1890s, had a far more developed system than either India or Siam by the end of the nineteenth century. While the British colonial government organized India's modern financial system, the Meiji government put together its own system through selective adaptation of the American, British, French, and German systems. Moreover, British civil servants, entrepreneurs, and investors owned and operated India's financial institutions, while foreign ownership or management of Japan's institutions was practically nonexistent. Furthermore, the colonial government in India intervened little in regulating banking institutions, had little contact with the few indigenous bankers, and in the half-century before World War II created few new financial institutions. In contrast, the Meiji government organized most modern financial institutions during the first two to three decades after the 1868 restoration, and cooperated with and supported local private bankers (Goldsmith 1983: 55–58).

In contrast to India, Meiji Japan's development of currency and credit institutions through the mid-1890s was "supply-leading," created before demands for industrial loans, financial services, and private saver deposits. In the last three decades of the nineteenth century Japan organized a banking system, expanded bank credit for government infrastructure and private investment, regulated banks, and stabilized the currency. In 1872 the government set up national banks, and in 1876 permitted private commercial banks. Other major financial reforms were the conversion of the rights of feudal lords to negotiable government bonds, and the land tax, which provided the revenue for the government's Reserve Fund (RF), 1873–81, and the Industrial Promotion Fund (IPF) beginning in 1878, for loans to industry. Other special banks established included the Yokohama Specie Bank (1880) for foreign exchange for importers, the Hypothec Banks (1896) at the prefectural level to make long-term loans to industry and agriculture, and the Industrial Bank (1900) to make medium- to long-term loans to industry. Then national and private banks' high ratio of currency issues to specie, as well as the RF and IPF liberal lending policies, contributed to rapid inflation from 1876 to 1881, reducing peasant and former military real incomes and increasing capitalist speculative profits, thus forming substantial initial capital accumulation for industrialists.

Finance Minister Matsukata Masoyoshi created a central Bank of Japan in 1882 (fifty-four years before the Reserve Bank of India, seventy-seven years before the Central Bank of Nigeria, and at least seventy years before most other sub-Saharan African central banks) with the power to retire the depreciated paper and liberal note issues of commercial banks, issue notes convertible to gold, control credit, and supervise private banking companies. Matsukata continued the land tax, levied new consumption taxes, restrained RF lending except to exporter industries accumulating specie, and balanced the government budget, stabilizing expectations among capitalist investors (Allen 1964: 42–55; Lockwood 1954: 14; Mahajan 1976: 24; Takeda 1965: 432–36).

All in all, the new financial institutions standardized the currency, integrated the national market, and channeled savings into industry. By 1897, Japan's credit standing had improved so it could borrow in foreign capital markets. With few exceptions, the money supply grew rapidly from 1880 to 1940, enabling rapid though fluctuating growth *rates,* but virtually avoiding recessions with negative growth (Lockwood 1954: 14; Nakamura 1983: 8–9, 60–61).

In contrast, the British colonial government of India between 1868 and 1918 supported laissez-faire policies in the domestic financial market, interfering little in private foreign-dominated banks, whose power was only gradually eroded after independence in 1947. Nor did a colonial government and foreign trading houses thwart Japanese industrial exports and import substitution, as in early twentieth-century Nigeria. Rather, Meiji Japan, unlike Siam, banned foreign ownership of land and virtually prohibited foreign direct investment. The post-1868 Japanese government, for example, helped domestic business find export opportunities, exhibit products and borrow abroad, establish trading companies, and set marketing standards. In comparison with India, where the government limited contacts with especially indigenous bankers, the Japanese enjoyed a symbiosis between bankers and government that increased over time while private banking resources were becoming more concentrated (Goldsmith 1983: 57–61; Lockwood 1954: 539–44; Yasuba and Dhiravegin 1982: I.1-I.2).

During much of the twentieth century, most LDCs suffered from at least as high financial concentration as pre–World War II Japan, but lacked the control over local financial institutions that Japan enjoyed. The rapid growth of Japan's banking and credit institutions in advance of industrial and saver demands indicates the advantage of more than a century of self-directed financial development. In contrast, the colonial powers in Africa and Asia controlled currency from the European capitals, and banks were virtually all branches of foreign institutions until years after World War II. Even after political independence, much of Africa and Asia has had an externally dependent banking system, a poorly developed securities market, and little ability to fine-tune the money supply.

Japan, which had the greatest economic success among African and Asian economies since the mid-nineteenth century, was virtually the only LDC with substantial autonomy in economic affairs. The Japanese experience indicates the advantages of domestic political and economic control. The policy implications for today's LDCs, generally formally politically independent but peripheral nations in the global capitalist economy dominated by DCs, DC commercial banks, and an International Monetary Fund and World Bank largely controlled by DCs, are greater autonomy in economic planning. Yet, cutting economic ties with DCs, while feasible for large countries with wide resource bases like Maoist China, has been costly for small countries like Ghana (1961–66) and Cuba, whose economic growth stagnated. And when resources are short, LDCs may have no choice but to solicit funds and their concomitant policy prescriptions from the Fund and Bank. In the 1980s, Zambia, Senegal, Argentina, and Brazil paid heavily for trying to resolve their debt burden outside the Bank/Fund/ OECD/commercial bank cartel.

Paul Mosley, Jane Harrigan, and John Toye refer to the Fund and Bank as a "managed duopoly of policy advice" (1991: vol. 1, pp. 54–55). Requiring IMF approval for a country's macroeconomic stabilization program before the Bank, OECD governments, or commercial banks will arrange debt writeoffs and write-downs creates an oligopolistic position that obstructs the economic development of low-income debtors. As sometime Tanzanian President Julius K. Nyerere complains, "When we reject IMF conditions we hear the threatening whisper; 'Without accepting our conditions you will not get any money, and you will get no other money'" (Parfitt and Riley 1989: 27–28). In reality, international policy enforcement is cartelized, with OECD governments—especially the United States, the European Union (EU), and Japan—largely determining policy through their control of the Bank and Fund, their domination of bilateral aid and lending, and their regulation of commercial banks.

African and Asian finance and planning officers want the Fund and Bank to place priorities on employment, growth, reducing income inequalities, and main-taining health and educational programs, rather than reducing government budget deficits, restructuring parastatals, removing food subsidies, liberalizing international trade, improving exchange rates, and encouraging exports. According to these officers, the Fund and Bank need to rely more on local research institutions and chambers of commerce and industry for policy analysis. As Dragoslav Avramovic (1991: ii) argues, "Adjustment and development pro-grammes should be prepared and seen to be prepared, by national authorities of African [and Asian] countries rather than by foreign advisors and international organizations. Otherwise commitment will be lacking."

Technical change requires a prolonged learning process embodied in indi-genes improving capital and controlling experts transferring technology and im-proving capital. Under colonialism and neocolonialism, LDCs have had little experience directing their own economic plans and technical adaptation and progress. Even today, many low-income countries face externally imposed con-ditions by the World Bank, IMF, and DC governments on technology use and other policies. Each successive piece of capital equipment is more productive since learning advances are embodied in new capital goods (Arrow 1962: 154–94; Nafziger 1990a: 259–60). Like Meiji Japan, today's Third World people must be in charge of their planning and development for them to capture techno-logical learning gains for sustained economic growth.

LDC debtors would benefit from the breaking up of the DC and Bank/Fund loan and policy cartel, strengthening independent financial power within the world economy—Middle Eastern or East Asian banking, UN Development Pro-gramme and UNCTAD funding for debtors, and EU and Japanese positions independent of the United States—and a disassociation from IMF approval of commercial bank, World Bank, bilateral, and even African Development Bank and Asian Development Bank lending. If LDC debtors can receive no funds without Bank/Fund policy conditions, developing countries may have no choice but to default and manage their own adjustments, while cooperating with other LDCs to undermine the cartel's stranglehold.

Capital Formation and Technical Progress in Economic Growth

The Japanese model has concrete lessons for how technological borrowing, capital formation, industrial policy, and banking system creation can be more self-directed.

The rapid growth of Japan, Western Europe, the United States, and Canada since the mid-nineteenth century has not been equaled by any other nonoil African or Asian country. The most important sources of this growth were capital formation (some from wealth transferred from colonies and protectorates) and increased knowledge and technology.

In the 1950s, U.N. economists considered the shortage of capital (tools, machinery, plant, equipment, inventory stocks, and the like) the major limitation to economic growth. On the basis of nineteenth- and twentieth-century Western growth, however, Cairncross, in 1955, questioned whether capital's role was central to economic growth. To be sure, he agreed with U.N. economists that capital and income grew at about the same rate. But he felt that capital increases do not explain economic growth, that, in fact, the reverse was true: the amount of capital responds to increases in demand, which depend on economic growth. Lockwood, in studying pre-1939 Japan, also stressed the increasing demand for capital in response to growth (Cairncross 1955: 235–48; Lockwood 1954: 245).

Since 1955, econometricians have tried to resolve this controversy with studies measuring how factor growth affects output growth. The studies' primary concern has been to determine the relative importance of the two major sources of economic growth—capital formation and technical progress.

Initial attempts at statistical measurement in the West and Japan in the late 1950s and 1960s indicated that capital per worker-hour explained 5 to 33 percent of growth in output per worker-hour. Scholars usually attributed the residual, 67 to 95 percent, to technical progress (Abramovitz 1956: 5–23; Aukrust and Bjerke 1959; Bruton 1967: 1099–1166; Hogan 1958: 407–11; Levine 1960: 225–28; Massell 1960: 182–88, 1962 330–35; Niitamo 1958: 30–41; Reddaway and Smith 1960: 6–37; Solow 1957: 312–20). Hagen used this evidence to argue capital formation has been stressed too much and technical progress too little (1980: 201–3).

Findings based on post–World War II Western and Japanese data are contradicted by studies of Africa, Asia, Latin America, and pre–World War II Japan, published after 1960, which point out that the contribution of capital per worker to growth is 50 to 90 percent while that of the residual is only 10 to 50 percent. Kazushi Ohkawa and Henry Rosovsky's 1973 study of Japan indicates that capital per worker-hour in 1908–18 (a period more similar to today's LDCs) explained 59 to 65 percent of growth in output per worker-hour compared with 31 percent in 1931–38 and 29 to 43 percent in 1955–64 (findings more similar to those of DCs) (Bruno 1962; Bruton 1967: 1099–1116; Gaathon 1961; Maddison 1970; Ohkawa and Rosovsky 1973: 45–48; Robinson 1971: 381–408). (Table 2.1 details the sources of growth in DCs and LDCs.)

The aggregate models used to study sources of growth are rough tools, yet they point in the same direction. First, the major source of growth per worker in Japan's early modern growth and in contemporary LDCs is capital per worker; increased productivity of each unit of capital per worker is of less significance. Second, the major source of growth per worker in DCs (including post–World War II Japan) is increased productivity, while increases in capital per worker are relatively unimportant. Accordingly, capital accumulation appears to be more important and technical progress less important as a source of growth in LDCs than in DCs.

In 1965, John R. Hicks argued that econometric studies of DC growth understate the contribution of capital formation to growth. Since many advances in knowledge are embodied in new capital, its separation from technical progress underestimates its contribution. Furthermore, accumulation of new capital is frequently offset by a decrease in value of old capital, partly from obsolescence. Thus, Hicks contended, it is wrong to give the impression to LDCs, having relatively small amounts of old capital, that capital accumulation is of minor importance. Econometric studies of early Japan and contemporary LDCs done since 1965 confirm Hicks's point. The rates of capital growth in developing countries were rapid enough to offset some of the understatement of capital in the production function. African and Asian countries concerned about rapid growth ignore capital accumulation at their peril.

Studies of DC growth find the residual is a major contributor to growth. However, to label this residual technical knowledge without explaining it is to neglect a major cause of growth. Critics object to elevating a statistical residual to the engine of growth, thus converting ignorance into knowledge (Balogh and Streeten 1963: 99–107).

Edward F. Denison (1967) indicates that sources for increased DC output per worker include advances in knowledge, economies of scale, improved resource allocation, reduction in the age of capital, and decreases in the time lags in applying knowledge. Other empirical studies have included organizational improvements, increased education and training, and learning by experience. Yuzo Yamada (1951: 152) and Lockwood (1954: 245) find that for Japan the residual encompasses science and education, improved business organization, higher-quality bureaucratic decisions, greater specialization, advances in marketing and finance, improved capital quality, simple scientific improvements, and more fertilizer and better irrigation in agriculture. Capital and technology (much borrowed) were important for Japan's pre-1939 growth and should also be for the development of contemporary LDCs.

Table 2.1

Share of Growth in Output per Worker from Increased Output per Worker

Author, year of study	Country	Measure of output per worker or person	Period	Proportion of growth in output per worker attributed to increases in capital per worker
Abramovitz 1956	U.S.	Net national product (NNP) per capita	1869–78 to 1944–53	0.05–0.20
Solow 1957, with correction by Hogan 1958 and Levine 1960	U.S.	Gross private nonagricultural output per manhour	1909–59	0.10–0.19
Massell 1960, 1962	U.S.	Manufacturing output per manhour	1919–57	0.10–0.33
Niitamo 1958	Finland	Output per manyear	1925–52	<0.50
Ankrust and Bjerke 1959	Norway	NNP per capita	1900–56	0.38
Reddway and Smith 1960	U.K.	Net manufacturing output per worker	1948–54	0.33
Gaathon 1961	Israel	GNP per capita	1950–59	0.60
Bruno 1962	Israel	GNP per capita	1958–60	0.50–0.60
Bruton 1967	U.S., Northwest Europe, Japan, Israel	Output per manhour	1940–64	0.42
Bruton 1967	Argentina, Brazil, Chile, Columbia, Mexico	Output per manhour	1940–64	0.74
Maddison 1970	22 developing countries	Output per manhour	1950–65	0.90
Robinson 1971	39 developing countries	Output per manhour	1958–66	0.88
Ohkawa and Rosovsky 1973	Japan	Output per labor input	1908–38	0.31–0.62
Ohkawa and Rosovsky 1973	Japan	Output per labor input	1955–64	0.29–0.43

Education

The 1990 literacy rate for lower and lower-middle income countries was 63
percent (World Bank 1992b: 218–19), a level reached by Japan in the first
decade of the twentieth century. Japan moved rapidly away from the early
Tokugawa philosophy of keeping the people ignorant. In 1837, the Japanese
commoner achieved about the same primary school enrollment rate as England,
one in four or five. This schooling in the *terakoya,* popular schools primarily
taught by samurai or temple priests, was prescientific but a precursor for modern
education. In 1868, Japan's literacy rate, 30 percent, was not far below Western
European rates and was above Russia's 15 percent, while primary-school enrollment as a percentage of primary-age children was about 43 percent for boys and
10 percent for girls.

Meiji gave a high priority to literacy and Western education and technology.
The Ministry of Education, established in 1871, oversaw simplifying the Japanese alphabets and improving educational quality. The Act of 1872, which de-
creed a national system of education, was greeted by a peasant uprising against
the increased economic burden. But the state, committed to the concept that all
members of the nation (regardless of class or gender) should receive an education, tried to enforce primary education as a legal duty required under the blind
compulsion of authority. The general school system was introduced in 1873;
four-year continuous schooling was compulsory in 1886 and six-year schooling
in 1900 (Hirshmeier and Yui 1975: 71; Mahajan 1976: 17; Toyama 1966: 430–31).

Yet the Act of 1872's aim of compulsory, universal primary education was
not attained for years. Japan's enrollment rates, which rose from 26.5 percent in
1868 to 28.1 percent in 1873, 41.1 percent in 1880, 48.9 percent in 1890, and
81.5 percent in 1910, only reached virtually 100 percent in 1911. As a comparison, in 1989, sub-Saharan Africa's primary enrollment rate (as a percentage of
the population of school-age children) was 69 percent, South and Southeast
Asia's 90 percent, and China's virtually 100 percent (World Bank 1992b: 274–75).

In Japan, the percentage of children aged five to fifteen years enrolled in
primary and secondary school rose from 10 percent in 1870 to 31 percent in
1880 and 63 percent by 1915. From 1880 to 1914, the percentage of those
fifteen to nineteen years enrolled in the upper secondary level (eleven to thirteen)
rose from 1 percent to 21 percent; in comparison, Africa and Asia's secondary
enrollment rate in 1989 was 40 percent (Maddison 1969: 16; World Bank 1992b:
219, 275).

In 1870, the ratio of students to population was 3.9 percent in Japan, less than
5.5 percent for England and Wales, and 17.4 percent for the United States. Japan
reached the ratio of England and Wales (15.5 percent) in 1910, surpassed them
by 18.6 percent to 15.0 percent in 1930, and surpassing the United States by 24.0
percent to 21.9 percent in 1940. By 1926, the beginning of Emperor Hirohito's
Showa era, firm managers generally had the education and training needed to run

complex industrial and financial capitalist enterprises (Allen 1982: 15; Minami 1986: 18–20).

The last decade of the nineteenth and the early part of the twentieth centuries saw much expansion of secondary and university education, as well as primary and technical education. Before World War I, Japan, with nearly two-thirds of its population educated, had among the world's highest literacy rate (Allen 1982: 13–14; McCord 1973: 281).

In Japan, the percentage of those of persons twenty to twenty-four years old enrolled in higher education rose from 0.3 percent in 1880 to 1.3 percent in 1914 to 1.6 percent in 1920. In per-capita steel and electricity, the latter year corresponded to 1965 in India, when its students in higher education as a percentage of those aged twenty to twenty-four years was 3.9 percent (Maddison 1969: 16; Okita 1981: 2–3).

In the two decades after 1872, when Asian countries like Siam were only educating elites for government service, Japan poured vast funds into primary, vocational, scientific, and (especially) technical education, but to the relative neglect of higher education. The schools were for all classes, and uniform primary education and a common language fostered national unity and cultural homogeneity while speeding up the acquisition of Western ideas and technologies. Schools were pragmatic but with no emphasis on creativity. Educational expenditures as a percentage of the total national budget were large, especially in comparison with contemporaneous Europe. While many Japanese acquired modern skills and attitudes, in 1872 the government tried to prevent modernity from disrupting tradition by ordering that all schools inculcate reverence for family and emperor as the major goal (Dore 1965a: 321; Nakamura 1983: 48; World Bank 1991b: 260–61; Yasuba and Dhiravegin 1985: 26–27).

The emphasis on "Japanese spirit and Western technology" meant that Meiji education stressed subservience to superiors and the state, superiority to other Asian countries, and acquiring Western technological expertise but not human dignity or the scientific method (Munakata 1965: 540–59; Sumiya and Taira 1979: 226–30). The Meiji Japanese experience reinforces studies indicating a high return to LDC investment in primary, science, and vocational education (World Bank 1980a: 46–51) but provides no model for using education to promote democracy, national self-determination, human rights, and female equality.

Utilizing Foreign Expertise and Techniques

Since Japan could not rely on foreign aid during early Meiji, the government and firms paid the full cost of foreign technical expertise, which, together with the introduction of universal primary education and compulsory adult male military service, caused a serious financial strain. Between 1868 and 1892 (much in the first five years), the central government spent 1.5 percent of expenditures for foreign employees, and an additional 0.4 percent for sending more than 4,000 students and government officials for training and education abroad. The Ministry of Industry, which invested in heavy and chemical industries, mining, railroads, lighthouses, ports, harbors, and telecommunications, employed almost 1,000 foreign advisors and teachers from 1870 to 1885. The Ministry of Home Affairs hired almost 250 foreigners from 1873 to 1895 to found agricultural experiment stations, introduce Western farming methods and products, and establish model factories to transfer technology to light industry. During the same period, the Ministry of Finance drew on about 125 foreign experts to help set up a modern monetary system and introduce corporate business organization. Other ministries and public enterprises hired almost 5,000, and the private sector about 12,500, foreigners from 1870 to 1899. While many foreigners were highly productive, others could not adapt to Japanese conditions.

Japan learned a lesson in the 1870s and 1880s that many contemporary LDCs have learned only recently or not at all: that importing replicas of Western institutions and capital-intensive technology may exacerbate unemployment and balance-of-payments problems if the local country lacks the necessary capital and skills. But adapting technology required a social capability acquired through painful experience. Ichirou Inukai (1981: 79–85) designates 1881 as the transition from the reckless and chaotic transplantation of Western technology and institutions to modernizing through indigenous industries:

> Only after having learned important lessons from false and confusing starts, the government and the people together began to pay serious attention to the "relevance" of Western technology and institutions to backward Japan, and an earnest effort was made to narrow the gap between "the two worlds" of people and policy-makers. [Inukai 1981: 78–79]

Foreign techniques were modified—substituting hand-powered machines in silk-reeling factories and wood for iron in Jacquard weaving machines—to save capital. Japan's Ten-Year Plan of 1884, the Kogyo Iken, advocated projects conforming to local conditions and capital, urging improvement engineering—that is, upgrading indigenous (including artisan) production—rather than importing Western replicas. For Meiji Japan, foreigners were teachers, transferring technology and other knowledge, not, as in Siam and other Asian countries, more or less permanent advisers (Inukai 1979: 6, 1981: 79–85; Nakamura 1983; 70; Yasuba and Dhiravegin 1985: 25–26). As chapter 7 indicates, many repairpeople, craftspersons, and cottage industrialists, by learning improved techniques and acquiring capital, could became small- or medium-scale manufacturers, while others expanded to become large industrialists.

Thus, Japan relied heavily on foreign engineers in the 1870s and 1880s, gradually replacing them with those from Kobu University, later Tokyo University's Department of Engineering (1877), the Tokyo Artisan School (1881), and other schools for studying industry. Engineers examined foreign treatises and imported machinery, copying and eventually modifying these techniques. Additionally, Japan's high educational levels helped the country absorb modern technology (Minami 1986: 143).

Japan, which paid for the assistance, used foreign technology effectively, unlike many LDCs today. Moreover, Japan disseminated technical learning to its population rapidly. For example, Japan's premier shipping company, the Nippon Yusen Kaisha, was organized in 1884, employing 174 foreigners in operating a modest fleet of 74 steamers totaling 60,000 tons. During the Sino–Japanese War of 1894–95, the number of foreign officers rose to 224 but subsequently declined as the Japanese learned navigation. By 1920, not a single foreign officer was employed on a Japanese vessel (Lockwood 1954: 328–9).

In contemporary LDCs, David Wheeler (1984: 1–23) shows no significant correlation between aid per capita and growth. Elliot R. Morss (1984: 465–70) argues that the effectiveness of aid to LDCs declined after 1970, as aid programs placed more burden on scarce local management skills and put less emphasis on recipients' learning by doing. After 1970, donors switched from program support (for example, to infrastructure or agriculture) to project and adjustment assistance, which entailed more specific statements of objectives and means of attaining them, more precise monitoring and evaluation, more foreign control over funds, and more local personnel and resources committed to projects. Furthermore, each of the major bilateral, multilateral, and nongovernmental organizations has competing requirements.

When donors underwrite a substantial portion of the development budget, they insist on continual, extensive project supervision and review so that recipient government agencies are more answerable to them than to their own senior policy officials. Donors frequently recommend and supervise poorly conceived projects. But even when well conceived, LDC officials fail to learn how to do something until they have the power to make their own decisions. Morss argues that the proliferation of donors and requirements has resulted in weakened institutions and reduced management capacity. For example, in 1981, Malawi, lacking the indigenous capacity to manage 188 projects from fifty different donors, hired donor country personnel (sometimes with donor salary supplements) to take government line positions to manage projects. However, Malawi has not been able to increase its capacity to run its own affairs and establish its own policies (Morss 1984: 465–70).

Other LDCs face similar costs from foreign investment—technological dependence and concentration, diversion of local entrepreneurship and investment, increased unemployment from unsuitable technology, repatriated funds, foreign political intervention, and worsened income inequalities from jobs, patronage, and final output benefiting the richest 20 percent. Frequently, foreign firms may hamper learning benefits by putting contractual limits on transferring patents, industrial secrets, and other technical knowledge to the subsidiary, which may be viewed as a potential rival.

The benefits and costs from foreign investment vary among classes and interest groups within LDC populations. Sometimes political elites welcome foreign capital because it benefits them through rake-offs on its contract, sales of inputs and services, jobs for clients, and positions on the boards of directors, even though the firm harms the interests of most of the population. Political power needs to be more widely dispersed before policies toward foreign capital represent a more general public interest.

African and Asian countries can hire foreigners, arrange apprenticeships and education abroad, establish joint ventures, contract for managers, buy or license technology, or buy machinery in which knowledge is embodied. In the 1980s, the Chinese government-owned Jialing Machinery Factory in Chongqing improved the engineering of its motorcycles substantially by buying technical advice, machines, and parts, and licensing technology from Japan's Honda Motor Company. Additional nonmarket sources of foreign knowledge include imitation, trade journals, and technical and scientific exchange, as well as feedback from foreign buyers or users of exports—all virtually costless.

Sanjaya Lall's conclusion is sensible:

> The correct strategy then must be a judicious and careful blend of permitting TNC [foreign capital] entry, licensing and stimulation of local technological effort. The stress must always be—as it was in Japan—to keep up with the best practice technology and to achieving production efficiency which enables local producers (regardless of their origin) to compete in world markets. This objective will necessitate TNC presence in some cases but not in others. [1985: 76]

Lockwood contends:

> If Japan's experience teaches any single lesson regarding the process of economic development in Asia, it is the cumulative importance of myriads of relatively simple improvements in technology which do not depart radically from tradition or require large units of new investment. The big, modern establishment with its concentration of capital in advanced forms of technology was essential in many fields, of course. . . . Much of the real substance of Japanese economic growth, however, is found in the more modest types of improvements which were more easily and pervasively adopted, more economical in cost, and often more productive of immediate returns in income. For any poor country beginning to industrialize, one of the crucial problems is to introduce and spread such innovations as widely as possible. [1954: 198–9]

Agricultural technical change in India since its independence in 1947 has been slow, despite the breakthrough in the 1960s by the Rockefeller Foundation and the Indian Ministry of Food and Agriculture in shorter and higher-yielding varieties of wheat. Ashoka Mody, Sudipto Mundle, and K.N. Raj (1985: 239–91) argue that India's new wheat technology was primarily embodied in research and development by universities and research centers and in imported fertilizers and pesticides or imported techniques for producing these inputs; the Indians, unlike the Japanese, made few learning gains through farmers improving techniques or feedback to researchers. This contrast illustrates major differences in technology acquisition between pre–World War II Japan and contemporary LDCs such as India.

For Lawrence G. Franko,

> The Japanese are without doubt the world's champion importers of "other people's" technology. Unlike other industrial nations which may have forgotten how much of their technological development was in fact based on seeking out, stumbling upon, or helping themselves to foreign discoveries and innovations, Japan has continuously sent its sons to be educated abroad and then to live or travel abroad to search out ways of catching up with or surpassing the West. [1983: 33]

Modifying Foreign Technology

Meiji Japan began by importing inappropriate capital-intensive technology. In agriculture, however, two German experts at the Komaba School of Agriculture in the early 1880s advised that Japanese farms, with a small average size, should rely on biological and chemical, not Western mechanical, innovations. Beginning in 1885, the Ministry of Agriculture and Commerce relied on local scientists (assisted by hired foreign experts) to develop technology to suit small farms and local soil, and sent veteran farmers and new Japanese agricultural school graduates as itinerant teachers to diffuse the best seed varieties used on Japanese farms through evening continuation schools for highly literate farmers. For most LDCs with high worker–land ratios (such as South, Southeast, and East Asia and parts of Africa), the Japanese biochemical emphasis is more sensible than the capital-intensive approaches of the United States, Canada, and parts of Western Europe. Yet most internationally available yield-increasing inputs for early developing Japan were labor-using while, with subsequent industrialization, most yield-increasing inputs for today's latecoming Africa and Asia are labor-saving.

In 1893, each prefecture created research institutes and experimental stations (usually with foreign help), taking over advisory responsibility from itinerant teachers. Usually these stations' research and development responded to (even small) farmer interests, spurring rapid technological diffusion. Japanese researchers and extension personnel tried to popularize innovations like artificial incubations, dry paddy cultivation for double cropping, the pedal-operated rotary thresher (invented in 1910), and a short-soled plow. Peasants who were used to paternalistic authority and had a Confucian respect for learning accepted these new techniques. Widespread literacy made written extension directives and pamphlets possible. Moreover, the government promoted meetings and associations of farmers to discuss techniques and exchange seeds. Indeed, Japan spent more on agricultural research per cultivated hectare than the United States from 1885 to 1939. From 1874 to 1913, real agricultural output grew 1.5 percent yearly, more than population growth, less than 1 percent annually.

Much Japanese labor-using, capital-saving, and land-saving agricultural technology appeared after 1903, when the central government issued to the Prefectural Farmers' Associations (*Nokai*) a recommendation to disseminate new cultivation techniques, including using better varieties, selecting better seeds by using salt water, improving the seedling bed, plowing deeper, and planting rice in a straight line (called the "Japanese method of rice cultivation" by other Asian countries). The state implemented this method through compulsion, sometimes including police force!

In 1911, the Japanese method, together with improved irrigation and new biochemical technology in rice, ushered in a Green Revolution that increased labor use per hectare in rice through multiple cropping and an increased area of cultivation, while other innovations increased labor use through more animal stock, or a switch to more intensive crops. Filipino innovations of high-yielding rice varieties and chemical fertilizers, following the Japanese method and its improvements, almost doubled labor requirements per hectare between 1966 and 1975, with increased tasks like weeding. After the 1920s, Japan usually imported foreign farm implements and machinery only to provide hints for imitative research and development rather than for actual use (Hayami 1975: 111–28; Inukai 1981: 86–87; Ishikawa 1981: 18–32, 162–64; Lockwood 1954: 194; Maddison 1969: 16–19; Mahajan 1976: 17–19).

LDC agricultural research today lags behind research on industrial technology. About 80 percent of the world's expenditure on agricultural research, technology, and capital are made in DCs. Ruttan (1972) indicates that these expenditures bear directly on the greater agricultural labor productivity in DCs. Only a small portion of this spending to increase productivity is relevant to Africa and Asia. Usually they need their own agricultural research, since many of their ecological zones are quite different from those of North America, Europe, and Japan. Much of the discovery of improved seed varieties and the improvement of agricultural methods in low-income countries is the work of an international network of agricultural research centers, the Consultative Group on International Agricultural Research (CGIAR). The principal food commodities and climate zones of LDCs have been brought into this network. Donors such as the World Bank, U.N. Development Programme, the Ford Foundation, the Rockefeller Foundation, the U.S. Agency for International Development, and agencies of other DCs and LDCs have financed the network. Prototypes of these centers are the International Center for the Improvement of Maize and Wheat (CIMMYT), the Mexican institute, founded in 1943, where a team led by Nobel Peace Prize winner Norman Borlaug developed dwarf wheats; the International Rice Research Institute (IRRI) in the Philippines, founded in 1960, which stresses research on rice and the use of multiple cropping systems; and the

International Crop Research Institute for Semiarid Tropics (ICRISAT) in India, which focuses on research on maize and millet.

The network has difficulties helping national research centers adapt its research to local conditions and encourage its adoption by farmers. Furthermore, many crop scientists in LDCs leave local research centers because of low salaries, politics on the job, government roadblocks to research, small budgets, and other grievances (Wade 1975: 91–95; World Bank 1982: 57–77).

Network research projects emphasize high-yielding grain varieties that benefit the large commercial farmers. Scientists tended to develop these varieties as part of a package, which included capital inputs, such as irrigation, fertilizers, tractors, mechanical pumps, threshers, reapers, combines, pesticides, and so on. For example, in India and Pakistan, new wheat varieties were adapted to cropland under controlled irrigation—land owned primarily by relatively affluent Punjabi farmers. The new high-yielding grain varieties did mitigate food shortages in South Asia during the 1970s and 1980s. But some negative effects of the package were increased land concentration, displacement of farm labor, rising rural unemployment and emigration, and more limited technological learning gains to local planners, researchers, administrators, and farmers.

In Japanese industry, both in firms and government training schools, foreign experts were often unsuitable, importing techniques they were acquainted with, regardless of their relevance. In the raw silk industry, imported machines and equipment were too costly and mechanically sophisticated, and their capacity was inconsistent with the inadequate storage facilities for the perishable cocoon. In flood control, Dutch experts introduced a system identical to that in the Netherlands, where flood water rises from sea level, overlooking the fact that Japan had flood water coming down the mountains. Repeated failures of Dutch technology to control floods finally convinced the Japanese government to change control measures completely. By the last two decades of the nineteenth century, the Japanese realized the necessity of questioning foreign industrial and flood control experts in light of differing local conditions (Inukai 1981: 85–88).

The Meiji government hired foreign experts directly and restricted foreign direct investment before 1890, partly through banning foreign land ownership and prohibiting the free movement of foreigners (Yasuba and Dhiravegin 1982: I.2). While the immediate financial cost of limiting investment was substantial, Japan avoided the foreign restrictions placed on the transfer of technical knowledge, continuing technological dependence on foreign sources, and associated foreign technical concentration faced by many contemporary LDCs. The Japanese learned by the 1880s the necessity of ensuring that technology introduced by foreigners be adapted and modified to fit local conditions and factor proportions. Japanese engineers and technicians would still import a foreign machine, but they would tear it apart, learn how it was put together, and modify it to fit Japanese circumstances.

Developing Appropriate Technology

Shozaburo Fujino, Shiro Fujino, and Akira Ono (1979) divide borrowed technology into (1) unmodified modern technology, (2) modern technology introduced after capital-saving modifications, and (3) older and less efficient technology from traditional sectors of DCs. The first, often with fixed capital–labor coefficients, is exemplified by English railway technology (including sleepers and tickets) borrowed in 1870–72. Beginning in 1886, Japan borrowed electric generating and transmitting technology from the United States for western Japan (which used sixty-cycle current) and from Germany for eastern Japan (which used fifty-cycle), the basis, however, for inconvenient dual electrical generation systems still existing in the 1990s!

In 1870, the Nakayama Company in Nagano Prefecture combined expensive machine filature technology from France with traditional Japanese sedentary reeling to create a new reeling technique, an example of the second type of borrowed technology. The company substituted "water wheels for steam engines, wood for iron in machinery, and ceramics for metal in cocoon-boiling basins and steam pipes" (Minami 1986). Silk reeling could not have expanded without this modification, which cut capital costs dramatically.

The third type is illustrated by silk-weaving technology. Three students brought the technology to build the hand loom with batten apparatus from France to Nishijin, Kyoto, in 1873. While Japanese carpenters could make the apparatus, local engineers lacked the capability to produce the most modern weaving technology, the power loom. In time, Japanese weaving adopted the treadle loom and eventually the power loom (Minami 1986: 138–41).

During Meiji, labor was relatively more abundant in Japan than in Western Europe and the United States. Accordingly, Japan frequently substituted more appropriate labor-intensive technology for the best-practice techniques available from the capital-abundant West.

Following are some major patterns of Japan's appropriate technology from 1868 to 1939:

1. Emphasizing the production and export of more labor-intensive goods like raw silk, silk and cotton textiles, and simple consumer goods. Capital-intensive industries like railroads and electricity only survived because they could charge high prices in semimonopolistic markets (Nakamura 1983: 71–76).

   The Japanese specialized in industrial products and processes, such as textiles, clothing, wood, and leather, which required large amounts of unskilled labor and small amounts of expensive equipment and advanced technical and managerial skills. In 1934, 41.0 percent of all factory labor in Japan was engaged in textile manufacturing, compared with only 20.5 percent in Britain and 13.4 percent in the United States (Lockwood 1954: 183–84).

In 1965–90, most expanded exports in Africa and Asia were labor-intensive manufactures, such as textiles, clothing, footwear, and simple consumer goods. In 1990, Taiwan, South Korea, Hong Kong, and Singapore (all upper-middle-income countries), comprising 2.5 percent of the population of Africa and Asia's LDCs, accounted for 54 percent of clothing and textile exports and 69 percent of total manufactured exports. The remainder of Africa and Asia, primarily low-income and lower-middle-income countries, has made little progress in emulating pre-1939 Japan's success in the growth of labor-intensive export manufactures (World Bank 1992b: 244–49). Exchange-rate policies that discriminate against exports help explain lower-income countries' slow manufacturing export expansion (see chap. 8).

2. Labor-intensive adaptation so the production process is simplified. The silk-reeling equipment that appeared in 1875 consisted of a blacksmith-made steam boiler, ceramic cocoon-boiling and silk-reeling kettles, and a frame built by a village carpenter. In addition, many Japanese manufacturing firms purchased second-hand machinery in good condition from the West. The cotton textile industry used two shifts, and substituted labor in ancillary and peripheral processes. Furthermore, many ancillary activities, like transport and machine repair, for large manufacturing units were done cheaply by small firms using simple equipment and labor-intensive processes.

3. Using manual labor instead of Western-type ancillary equipment in coal and mineral mines.

4. Adoption of technology used in an earlier stage in the West.

5. Adaptation of foreign technology to industries catering to tastes unique to the indigenous market, including traditional soybean sauce, and indigenous dyeing houses. As these enterprises learned through experience, many made the transition to technology needed for export markets.

6. Substituting labor-intensive techniques to produce goods of lower quality and performance than imported goods, like bicycles (beginning in 1890), machine tools, three-wheel trucks, and small-sized cars (Datsuns in the 1930s) (Ishikawa 1981: 355–87).[2]

Meiji Japan imitated, borrowed from, and modified techniques from the West. Can LDCs today be as successful borrowing and modifying innovations from the West and Japan?

If anything, contemporary LDCs have to be more cautious than Meiji Japan in importing foreign capital and technology. These LDCs are more peripheral in the global economy than was post-1880 Meiji Japan, which shared economic hegemony with the West in Asia, especially vis-à-vis China, Taiwan, and Korea. Since LDCs today are more technologically backward relative to DCs than Japan was relative to the West in the late nineteenth century, and since today's technology is predominantly labor-saving, it is generally more difficult today to adapt technology to indigenous conditions. For example, some foreign productivity-raising textile technologies available to early developing Japan were labor-*using* while most technologies for today's latecoming LDCs are labor-*saving*. Finally, LDCs today are less likely to directly control experts transferring technology than the Japanese did, and are more likely to face unalterable capital–labor ratios and to pursue policies creating factor-price distortions (subsidized capital and foreign exchange prices, and above-market wage costs) than the Japanese a century ago (see chaps. 6–8).

Japan was not unique in nineteenth-century Asia in trade and technology contacts with the West: India, China, the Netherlands East Indies (now Indonesia), and Siam (now Thailand) also had widespread interchange with the West. As indicated above, Japan, compared with Western colonies and China, Thailand, Afghanistan, and Ethiopia, had substantial autonomy in directing education, banking, industrial policies, and technology acquisition to increase short-term productivity and learn techniques and accumulate capital to accelerate long-term growth. Water and steam power (in the late nineteenth century), internal combustion engines (beginning at the turn of the twentieth century), and electric motors (growing rapidly after 1910) powered Japan's rapid industrialization in the half-century before World War II. If, however, acquiring production technology and technicians to supervise its use had been sufficient for rapid modernization, many other Asian countries would also have experienced rapid growth before 1939. Japan's change in industrial arts rested on broader changes in economic life on which the state focused, including the growth of the market, railways, banks, an efficient medium of exchange, new corporate forms, a division of labor, capital and labor markets, efficient civil servants, and innovative entrepreneurs (items discussed later).

The factory system, which had evolved in England for more than a century, was established in about fifty years in Japan before World War I. Japan, which had less resistance from custom, legislation, internal toll barriers, and guild restrictions than eighteenth- and early nineteenth-century Europe, borrowed from the West with few restrictions. Moreover, Japan's geographical compactness and flexible social traditions enabled the country to diffuse new ideas and skills quickly to small industry and the countryside. During Meiji, what counted was not substantial changes in production techniques but the diffusion of minor improvements such as the steel-cutting tool, the thermometer, a new chemical pigment, or the small steam engine and water wheel (Lockwood 1954: 185–89, 213–14, 326).

From the Meiji period through World War II, Japan had mastered a wide array of "know-how," the ability to adapt and improve products and processes. Not until the postwar period did Japanese business achieve "know-why"—the ability to conduct basic research and innovate beyond existing technology and its adaptation (Francks 1992: 193).

Japan as an Example of the Product-Cycle Theory

For Lockwood (1954: 331–32), the sequence of Japan's technological borrowing was: (1) imported product, (2) the copy, usually inferior in quality, and (3) slow improvement, even finer grades and specialties, which came with experience. Indeed, in some instances, Japanese emulation produced innovation, eventually generating technology superior to models on which they were once based (Westney 1987: 224). In other instances, the product, which often seemed shoddy, may have eventually been produced more efficiently with more abundant unskilled labor. By 1970, as Japan became rich in capital, skilled labor, and technology, it either became an industrial leader in fine-grade production or surrendered its leadership to other Asian countries (such as South Korea, Taiwan, Hong Kong, or Singapore).

The change in specialization in the Lockwood sequence does not result from shifts in the countries' factor proportions (as the Heckscher [1950: 272–300]–Ohlin [1933]–Samuelson theorem states), or in technological leadership, but in a product cycle that shifts comparative advantage as standardization takes place. Comparative advantage may be based on a technological advantage (as in nineteenth-century Britain, the United States, and Germany, and as in today's Japan, the United States, and Germany), perhaps a Schumpeterian innovation such as a new product or production process that gives the country a temporary monopoly in the world market until other countries imitate. The product-cycle model indicates that, while a product requires highly skilled labor in its initial development, later, as markets grow and techniques become common knowledge, a good becomes standardized, so that less-sophisticated countries can mass produce with less skilled labor. Advanced economies such as Britain and the United States from 1868 to 1939 had a comparative advantage in nonstandardized goods, while less-advanced economies like Japan had a comparative advantage in standardized goods (Schumpeter 1939, 1961; Vernon 1966: 190–207).

Product cycle is illustrated by cotton textiles. England specialized in cotton textiles from the mid-eighteenth to late-nineteenth centuries. In the 1880s and 1890s, Japan substituted the indigenous production of cotton textiles, manufactured with British machines, for imports from Britain. By 1921–39, Japan's cotton goods invaded English and other Western markets. Japan's comparative advantage in textiles was suggested by the fact that 41.0 percent of all factory labor in Japan was engaged in textiles, compared with only 20.5 percent in Britain and 13.4 percent in the United States in 1934. In the 1960s, Japan imported cotton textiles from South Korea, Taiwan, China, Hong Kong, and Singapore, and in the 1980s through the 1990s, from Thailand. Many of these countries used Japanese investment and technology to compete in Japan or third countries (Lockwood 1954: 27–31, 183–84, 332–33; Minami 1986: 238). Miyohei Shinohara (1982: 32–33, 72–75, 127–28) labels this a boomerang effect, imports in reverse or intensification of competition in third markets arising from Japanese enterprise expansion in, and technology exports to, other Asian countries.

Nineteenth-century Japanese firms initially competed as Marshallian firms, organized at the factory level, confined to a single function and a single industry, and tightly controlled by one or a few persons. In the last two decades of the nineteenth century, the United States established a second-level enterprise, the large national company, vertically integrated from production to marketing, thus benefiting from cost savings from decision coordination at various stages. An example of vertical integration is from crude petroleum marketing backward to its drilling and forward to consumer markets for its refined products. Meiji Japanese Marshallian and emerging nationally integrated firms were able to compete with companies from the United States and other advanced capitalist economies.

However, contemporary Africa and South Asia cannot compete as readily as nineteenth-century Japanese firms did at the bottom stages of the product cycle, imitation and low-level innovation. Today these countries are competing in an integrated global economy against multinational corporations (MNCs). MNCs, an outgrowth of the multidivisional corporation, established in the United States in the 1920s, gathered momentum after World War II and represented a new marketing strategy in which corporations were decentralized into several divisions, each specializing in one product and organized similarly to the second-stage national corporation of the late nineteenth-century United States. In MNCs, the function of goal determination and planning is split off from the national corporation's function of coordinating managers in Marshallian firms, and the Marshallian enterprise's function of day-to-day management (Hymer 1970: 441–53).

MNCs are important actors on the international scene. UNCTAD (1978) estimates that in 1975, MNC foreign production accounted for 20 percent of world output and that their intrafirm trade was 25 percent of international manufacturing trade. Fourth-fifths of Africa's 1983 commodity trade was handled by MNCs. Thirty-eight percent of total U.S. imports in 1977 consisted of intrafirm transactions by MNCs based in the United States.

The markets MNCs operate in today are often international oligopolies with competition among few sellers whose pricing decisions are interdependent. Large corporations invest overseas because of international imperfections in the market for goods, resources, or technology. The MNCs benefit from monopoly advantages, such as patents, technical knowledge, superior managerial and marketing skills, better access to capital markets, economies of large-scale production, and cost savings from vertical integration (ECA 1983a; UNCTAD 1978). MNCs can compete in a large range of industries with today's African or South Asian Marshallian firm or larger enterprise in the use of imitation or innovative technology, and unskilled or highly skilled labor. Today's market structures make it more difficult for indigenous firms in low-income countries to compete through technological borrowing than was the case for firms in Meiji Japan, which were competing in a more perfectly competitive market.

However, Indonesia, Malaysia, the Philippines, and Thailand—the ASEAN four—are not as peripheral to MNC production shifts in the product cycle as Africa and South Asia are. Since the devaluation of the U.S. dollar relative to the yen beginning in late 1985, Japanese companies have tried to retain their international price competitiveness in manufacturing products by organizing a borderless Asian economy. This borderless system encompasses a new international division of knowledge and function that selects the more sophisticated activities, including R&D-intensive and technology-intensive industries for the newly industrializing countries (NICs), South Korea, Taiwan, Hong Kong, and Singapore, while assigning the less sophisticated, labor-intensive, low-value-added production and assembly, which use more standardized and obsolescent technologies, to the ASEAN four and China.

According to Japanese official definitions used in the early 1990s, Japanese foreign direct investment does not necessarily depend on majority ownership, but can involve only 10 percent ownership if the Japanese corporation either has at least one part-time director, furnishes the technology, provides financial assistance, executes an exclusive agency agreement, or purchases products, raw materials, or parts from the production facility abroad. Moreover, the Japanese company does not even need any equity holding to be involved in foreign direct investment if the firm provides loans exceeding one year to a firm abroad whose management is influenced by the Japanese corporation through long-term contract (Shojiro 1992a: 11–37; Schlossstein 1991: 32, 152).[3]

Sony, an example of this global seamless network, has factories for audio, television, and video products and parts in Taiwan, Korea, Thailand, Malaysia, and Singapore, the major distribution warehouse in Singapore, and linkage of these units on-line with Japanese, U.S., European, and Southeast Asian companies as well as important cooperating firms (Shojiro 1992a: 37–38). In a similar fashion, a Pontiac Le Mans bought in the United States embodies routine labor and assembly operations in South Korea, advanced components (engines, transaxles, and electronics) from Japan, styling and design engineering from Germany, small components from Taiwan, Singapore, and Japan, advertising and marketing services from Britain, and data processing from Ireland and Barbados (Reich 1991: 113).

Despite the advantages to the ASEAN four, the borderless economy contributes to a widening gap between modern branches of industry, such as electronics, and traditional branches within the country. To be sure, ASEAN labor learns how to produce inputs and parts to precise specifications for Japanese high-tech industry. However, the ASEAN four have left technical details to their foreign business partners, so that these countries lack the ability to adapt and innovate; this latter ability is concentrated in Japan and the NICs.

Another factor limiting ASEAN's gains from the borderless system is the fact that Japanese (and other DC) MNCs raise the lion's share of their funds from the local capital market. The most successful of the fifty-four Asian and African countries in this study include Thailand, with a per-capita GNP of $1,570 in 1991 and a 5.9 percent per-capita growth rate from 1980 to 1991, and Malaysia, with a $2,520 per-capita income and a 2.9 percent growth from 1980 to 1991. Both countries have attracted high-technology industries such as computers, electronics, and semiconductors as a part of the Japanese-directed borderless economy. Indeed, in 1993, Malaysia was third to the United States and Japan in semiconductor production (primarily for Japanese companies such as Hitachi, Toshiba, and NEC) and the world's leading exporter of computer chips. But both Thailand and Malaysia pay relatively little attention to bottom–up development of indigenous manufacturing techniques. The development of indigenous technological capability requires, as in Meiji Japan, a conscious and aggressive strategy of technical innovation (Morris-Suzuki 1992: 145–48; Schlosssstein 1991: 232; Shojiro 1992c: 158–63; Takeshi 1992: 97; World Bank 1993a: 238–39).

Japan and Today's LDCs: The Relative Backwardness Hypothesis

A study of nineteenth-century Europe (France, Germany, Russia, and Italy) by Alexander Gerschenkron (1962) explaining the rapid development of latecomers can be examined for application to Japan. Gerschenkron underscores the advantages of relative backwardness in explaining the rapid development of European latecomers. In like fashion, a latecomer like Japan, relatively backward in 1870, grew faster than leaders like the United Kingdom, the United States, and Germany, because the latecomer could exploit DC technology more cheaply. In addition, relatively backward Japan, Italy, and Russia had faster structural change from agriculture to industry in GNP from 1850 to 1980 than early leaders like the United Kingdom and the United States.

Gerschenkron argues that, before industrialization, relatively backward countries experience tension between actual and potential development that spurs modern economic growth. In Japan, substantial social and political tension preceded and followed the Meiji Restoration. Moreover, the military and economic threat from the West spurred Meiji adoption of Western technology to enrich and arm Japan. With competition from advanced countries, Gerschenkron contends, relatively backward countries use the technology backlog to industrialize rapidly. Backward countries, according to him, adopt the "most modern and most labor-saving technologies" and "newer industries" like iron and steel rather than older ones like textiles.

In Meiji Japan, however, contrary to the Gerschenkron thesis, industrialization was not based on modern industry using the most up-to-date technology but on improvement engineering. Also, the moving force for Japan's development was textiles, using labor-intensive technology, rather than newer industry. And, although Gerschenkron believes that relatively backward countries industrialized through large units of production, Meiji Japan expanded both large-scale and small-scale enterprise. Chapter 7 shows how large and small enterprises complemented each other, and chapter 3 points out that Japan, following the Gerschenkron hypothesis, depended heavily on government and banks to reduce its relative backwardness (Gerschenkron 1962: 353–59; Minami 1986: 38–42, 109–12, 141–42).

The disadvantages of latecomers are greater now than in the late nineteenth and early twentieth centuries when Japan was a newly industrializing country. Best-practice technology in the United Kingdom and the United States was not far ahead of underdeveloped Meiji Japan. Today this technology is likely to be more sophisticated, highly concentrated, and less readily absorbed into peripheral economies (Ohkawa 1983: 53).

Conclusion

To avoid Western colonialism and imperialism, Meiji Japan stressed economic growth and military power. These goals required that Japan acquire and modify foreign technology, which was then available only at full cost.

During the last four decades of the nineteenth century, Japan had substantial control in economic affairs compared with other countries of Africa and Asia. Meiji Japan emphasized free enterprise, a modern financial system, science education, infrastructure investment, and foreign technology modification without sacrificing traditional values.

Japan learned in the 1870s that importing Western replicas may fail if the country lacks capital and skills, and that foreign techniques must be modified through improvement engineering and upgrading artisan production. Since labor was abundant in Meiji Japan compared with the West, Japan substituted labor-intensive technology for best-practice Western techniques. Contemporary LDCs must be more cautious in importing foreign technology than Meiji Japan was, as LDCs are more technically backward relative to DCs than Japan was vis-à-vis the DCs in the late nineteenth century.

Japan's early industrial development, especially in textiles, supports the product-cycle explanation for shifting comparative advantage. An innovation gives a DC only a temporary monopoly in the world market until less advanced countries can imitate. While a product may initially require technologies and skills available to the DC but not the LDC, later, as output becomes standardized, an LDC can compete by using less skilled labor to exploit internal economies of scale. This explanation for part of Japan's astounding pre–World War II growth could provide hope for low-income countries' industrial export expansion. On the other hand, the fact that today's global market is more oligopolistic than the market during the nineteenth and early twentieth centuries may limit the applicability of Meiji Japan's experience for contemporary LDCs.

While at the Meiji Restoration India's prospect for financial development, based on a unified currency and British institutions, appeared greater than Japan's, Japan developed more rapidly, partly because of state-directed borrowing of foreign financial institutions, including a central bank and supply-leading currency and credit institutions. This development underscores the importance of low-income economies controlling financial institutions.

Japan's high literacy rate, about the same in 1905 as Africa and Asia today, contributed to Japan's successful technology policy. The Meiji government developed uniform primary education that spurred national unity and technical progress. Meiji Japan can instruct LDCs in enhancing returns to education but not in teaching democracy and human rights.

Notes

1. The United Nations designates least developed countries on the basis of low per-capita income, low share of manufacturing in GNP, and low literacy rates.

2. Nafziger (1990a: 226–34) discusses possible LDC strategies for more appropriate technology.

3. Schlossstein (1991: 32, 152) uses the metaphor of a flying geese formation of the East and Southeast Asian economies, with Japan at the lead, the NICs toward the front, and the ASEAN four close behind.

Chapter 3

Guided Capitalism

Most contemporary LDCs, like nineteenth-century Japan, lack the strong middle-
and capitalist-class leadership for capital accumulation and technological
change. Chapter 2 discussed Japanese policies to borrow foreign technology.
This chapter examines Japan's guided capitalism, which connotes a major state
role in spurring private-sector investment and improved technology, asks
whether today's LDCs can look to guided capitalism as an alternative model to
socialism or laissez–faire capitalism, and shows how Japan facilitated private
enterprise through government policies and infrastructure investment. Chapter 4
considers the related topic of Japan creating an entrepreneurial class to spearhead
capitalist development.

The Role of the State

The late-nineteenth-century Japanese government was heavily involved in development policy in contrast to the modern West (even under mercantilism) or to
contemporaneous Siam, China, and LDC colonies. Meiji officials hoped to create the basic conditions for growth, such as infrastructure, mass literacy, and
technical education needed to increase the returns to directly productive investment. Government leaders wanted to entrust most industry and trade to private
initiative, but concentrated on developing sectors that, however, failed to attract
private capital. Thus, the Meiji government established model soap, cement,
cotton, silk, and machine-tool factories. Many model factories were equipped
with imported machinery, and some plants were even built by foreign companies. Most model enterprises, when successful, were sold to private entrepreneurs, usually samurai who supported Meiji government policies and built up
their businesses in association with these policies. In the late nineteenth century,
about half of Japan's industrial investment came from government (Beasley

1987: 38; Francks 1992: 34–35; Mahajan 1976: 10–11; McCord 1973: 279; Yasuba and Dhiravegin 1982: I.10).

Since 1868, Japan has had an extraordinary symbiosis among its elites, particularly between the government (the bureaucracy, the politicians, and pre-1946 court and armed forces) and the economic leadership, including oligopolistic cooperation among heads of the big industrial, financial, and mercantile combines. Until the end of World War II, with a few lapses like the 1920s, these elites followed a conscious policy of economic expansion throughout East Asia, with only minimal concern for the social and ecological consequences of rapid growth.

Japan's government not only was more self-directed but also contributed a larger proportion of national income than other LDCs. For the century before independence in 1947, India, for example, was governed by a fairly efficient and honest British colonial bureaucracy, which adhered to a principle of minimal interference and expense while protecting British commercial interests, often resulting in a drain of Indian resources. For colonial India, government expenditures as a share of national product was not much above 5 percent from 1870 to 1920, even lower during the 1930s, and about 10 percent in the 1940s. For Japan, ruled by a few closely cooperating elites committed to growth, government expenditure shares were higher—more than 10 percent in 1880, 16 percent in 1913, 25 percent by the end of the 1930s, and more than 30 percent in the post–World War II period (Goldsmith 1983: 18–23).

In comparison with Meiji Japan, most low-income states had little experience in the high-level technical, executive, and administrative civil service before the mid-twentieth century. These states are soft states in which the authorities who decide policies rarely enforce them (if enacted into law) and only reluctantly place obligations on people (Myrdal 1968: vol. 2, pp. 895–900).[1] These states depend on buying political support through concessions to powerful interest groups. Regime survival in the politically fragile states of Africa and Asia required the support of urban elites (businesspeople, professionals, executives, and high-ranking military officers, civil servants, and parastatal employees), landholders, and commercial farmers through economic policies that frequently sacrificed growth, income distribution, external balance, and the development of indigenous skills. And perhaps the easiest way for ruling elites to expand state largess to benefit allies and clients was by increased borrowing from abroad and joint ventures with MNCs. Yet the shortage of organizational and planning skills among the elites of LDCs has been worsened by their subsidiary role to that of the World Bank, IMF, MNCs, and bilateral lenders in planning the economy.

Infrastructure Investment

External economies are cost advantages rendered free by one producer to another, benefiting society as a whole rather than the investor concerned. Investment in infrastructure, such as power, transport, and communication, is a major source of externalities. Railroad development created externalities, providing large-scale, high-speed, cheap transport for people to work and goods to market, and establishing national labor and goods markets. Electric utilities generated externalities through increased comfort and efficiency in homes and factories. Other investments in transport and communication also reduced costs and increased markets for directly productive sectors. Growth in infrastructure investment (total gross capital stock for public works, railroads, and electric utility) from 1880 to 1940 was rapid and steady, with an annual growth each decade of 4–6 percent (Minami 1986: 119–22).

During Tokugawa, foreign trade was largely interdicted and internal trade hampered by poor transport and official restrictions. Land transport was mainly by bearer, horse, or oxcart.

Lockwood (1954: 105–6) thinks no single industry played a more essential role than transport in Japan's post-Tokugawa growth. Specialization by regions and occupations within the islands, the exchange of goods overseas, and the growth in the scale and productivity of the economy depended on improved access to wider markets (Mahajan 1976–83).

In 1870, the Ministry of Industry was established to develop railroads, bridges, lighthouses, ports, harbors, electricity, water supply, postal services, and telegraphy. In 1870–72, the first railroad was built from Tokyo to Yokohama with the aid of a small British loan. Improved land transport reduced the journey from Tokyo to Osaka from nineteen days by palanquin in 1860 to nineteen hours in 1890 (after a railroad opening) to twelve hours in 1912 (with improved locomotives), reducing cost as well. In 1884, the price of a hectoliter of grain shipped by road doubled after each additional 32 kilometers in Japan compared with each additional 160 kilometers in Germany. The 1897 opening of the Joban-Tokyo Railway Line, which transported coal, pit props, miners, and their belongings, increased coal production from 110,000 tons in 1899 to 600,000 tons in 1913 and reduced transport cost from 2.59 to 1.80–1.90 yen per ton (Minami 1986: 22–24, 120–22).

By World War I, Japan had created a nationwide transport network. Rail kilometerage nearly tripled between 1893 and 1913 to 32,008, covering most of the country. Freight traffic increased nearly sevenfold during the same period and rose threefold between 1913 and 1927. In 1937, freight traffic was comparable to France (with a 50 percent larger area) and four-fifths as much as in India (ten times the size) (Lockwood 1954: 109).

Electric light generation by the Tokyo Electric Light Company in Japan in 1886 came only four years after New York City's Edison Electric's first electric-light distribution station in the United States. Japan's generating power increased two to three times faster than that of the United States from 1903 to 1940. In 1926, electric lighting cost 0.02–0.07 sen (1 sen = 0.01 yen) per candle-power-hour, compared with 0.12 sen for kerosene lights. The real prices of electric lighting fell steadily from 1903 to 1940. In addition, by improving safety and enabling night shifts (at Osaka and other cotton-spinning companies), electric lighting increased plant productivity. Electric power stimulated electrochemical industries exporting ammonium sulphate and electrolysis soda to the United States, China, and elsewhere in the 1910s and 1920s, and had the advantages of divisibility of power, ease of operation, and reduced mechanical problems.

Electrical motors increased small-factory mechanization rapidly. Among factories with five to twenty-nine workers, the proportion mechanized increased from 21 percent in 1909 to 80 percent in 1930; 88 percent of the large factories were equipped with engines in 1909, and 99 percent in 1930. The total power capacity of manufacturing industry contributed by electric motors increased from 0 percent in 1887 to 1 percent in 1900, 22 percent in 1910, 59 percent in 1920, and 83 percent in 1930, while the share of steam engines and turbines fell from 81 percent in 1887 to 16 percent in 1930; the share of water wheels and hydro turbines also fell rapidly.

Electrification became widespread as larger factories replaced electricity from their own generating plants with electric power purchased from public utilities. Electricity's greatest contribution to larger industry was the potential of changing machine operation from group-drive (a few larger-capacity engines) to unit-drive production (small motors attached to individual machines). Unit drive resulted in reduced capital costs for shafts and belts, less power loss in transmission, more efficient factory layout and design, an absence of wasted energy from idle machines, and simpler factory expansion.

The Japanese took advantage of abundant natural energy sources; coal and falling water. By the end of the 1930s, nine of ten Japanese homes were wired for electric lighting, at least on a modest scale.

In the late nineteenth century, the state was active in constructing roads, irrigation and drainage systems, warehouses, port facilities, and other public works. Japan was one of the few non-Western countries to set up telegraph facilities when initially installed in the West; it built 6,400 kilometers of telegraph lines between 1870 and 1893, which helped people exchange information on a national scale. Postal articles grew from 2.5 million in 1872 to 100 million in 1882, reflecting an eagerness to communicate and increased mobility.

The first steamship built by the Japanese was the 32-meter, 60-horsepower *Chiyoda-gata,* completed in 1866 after four years of effort. Steamer service between Yokohama and Nagasaki, supported by government subsidies, was inaugurated shortly thereafter. By 1893, Japan had acquired its first 13,000 kilometers of operating railways (Inukai 1981: 81; Lockwood 1954: 14, 109, 126–27; Minami 1986: 120–38; Yasuba and Dhiravegin 1982a: I.10).

Marine transport was important in procuring raw materials from other countries. The government purchased ships from abroad for itself or to sell to private firms like Mitsubishi Company, and later subsidized Mitsubishi to manufacture ships commercially. The state also encouraged quality control, small-ship manufacturing, and repair consolidation, resulting in two leading shipbuilding houses, the Osaka Shoshen Kaisha (1884) and the Nippon Yusen Kaisha (1885). Foreign shipping companies were excluded from trade between the principal Japanese ports after 1894, and from all coastal trade in 1911, unless on a continuous voyage from another country. Postal subsidies and navigation bounties were awarded annually to Japanese companies under 1896 and 1909 laws. Moreover, the state remitted tariffs on imported materials going into ship construction in 1906. Wartime shortages further stimulated Japanese shipping after 1914 (Lockwood 1954: 547; Mahajan 1976: 14–16).

Paul N. Rosenstein-Rodan (1943: 202–11) argues that power, transport, communication, and other forms of infrastructure in today's LDCs are indivisible or subject to sizable jumps. To be sure, best-practice airline and power technologies used in DCs may depend on economies of large-scale production. However, electricity can be generated in small-scale coal- or oil-based steam plants, or in large-scale hydroelectric or nuclear power plants. Nor do poor countries require airports similar to Tokyo-Haneda or Chicago-O'Hare and aircraft such as jumbo jets and supersonic transport planes; indeed, some would question whether poor countries need an international air carrier at all. Before evaluating a project on the basis of a given technology and scale, the project evaluator should ask engineers and other designers if all feasible technologies and scales have been considered (Yotopoulos and Nugent 1976: 374).

The macroeconomic stabilization and adjustment policies set by the IMF, World Bank, and the cartel of international lenders as conditions for low-income countries often preclude a major role for state spending in the economy. Bangladesh and sub-Saharan Africa failed to maintain the physical infrastructure built in the 1960s. Moreover, many LDCs (mostly former colonies) lack the administrative or tax capacity to expand infrastructure substantially and the entrepreneurial skills to exploit their externalities. Yet improvement engineering or intermediate technology—techniques somewhere between DC capital-intensive processes and LDC traditional instruments—would enable low-income countries to manage social overhead investments consistent with their administrative and tax capacities.

Keynesian Employment Expansion Policies

Chapter 1 pointed out that, in the half-century before Keynes's 1936 *The General Theory of Employment, Interest, and Money,* Japan used Keynesian government spending expansion (sometimes combined with tax rate reductions) to maintain high employment and steady growth. Still, Japanese and international spending reductions in the late 1920s brought about Japan's 1929–31 depression, contributing to the rural unrest and the upheaval that destroyed parliamentary government and brought in fascism and ultranationalism. However, under Finance Minister Korekiyo Takahashi, Japan, like the United States, Germany, and Sweden, pursued Keynesian-type employment expansion policies during the early 1930s. By the mid-1930s, Japan not only regained efficiency in cotton and silk, but also expanded manufacturing, especially of machinery such as power-station equipment. Furthermore, reflation in the mid- to late 1930s helped Japan's rulers divert resources to the military (Goldsmith 1983: 10–12, 58–60; Lockwood 1954: 57–58, 62; Mahajan 1976: 80–81).

Keynesian policies, however, have little applicability to contemporary LDCs. First, the links between interest rate, investment, and output in twentieth-century Japan and DCs are questionable in low-income countries. Investment is not very sensitive to the interest rate charged by commercial banks in LDCs, partly because a lot of their money is lent by money lenders, landlords, relatives, and others outside the banking system.

Second, LDC firms cannot respond quickly to increased demand for output. Unlike earlier Japan, the LDCs' major limitations to output and employment expansion are usually on the supply side, in the form of shortages of entrepreneurs, managers, administrators, technicians, capital, foreign exchange, raw materials, transportation, communication, and smoothly functioning product and capital markets. In fact, where there are severe limitations in supply response—that is, where output or supply is price inelastic—increased spending may merely result in higher rates of inflation.

Third, LDCs may not reduce open unemployment even if spending increases labor demand. Open unemployment occurs primarily in urban areas. However, labor *supply* in urban areas responds rapidly to new employment opportunities. The creation of additional urban jobs through expanded demand means even more entrants into the urban labor force, mainly as migrants from rural areas.

Fourth, low-income countries cannot rely so much as earlier Japan on changes in fiscal policy (direct taxes and government spending) to affect aggregate demand and employment. As indicated below, Japan relied heavily on direct taxes during the Meiji period, with reliance growing during the interwar period of the 1920s and 1930s, in comparison with contemporary LDCs where direct taxes are a much smaller proportion of total taxes and GNP.

Fifth, because of the LDCs' tendency to adopt capital-intensive machines, equipment, processes, organizational methods, management systems, and technologies from capital-rich DCs discussed in chapter 2, employment growth is likely to be slower than output growth. In fact, in some instances, increasing employment may decrease output. In the 1950s when Prime Minister Nehru asked economists on the Indian Planning Commission to expand employment, they asked him how much GNP he was willing to give up. The idea of a tradeoff between output and employment, which astounded the Indian prime minister, is consistent with a planning strategy in which capital and high-level technology are substituted for labor in the modern sector. For example, milling rice by a sheller machine rather than pounding by hand increases output at the expense of employment. This tradeoff between employment and output, however, is not inevitable if LDCs adopt techniques appropriate to their factor proportions and state of arts.

Tax Ratios and Sources

Government had a major role in the Japanese economy, even in the late nineteenth century. Yet taxes as a percentage of GNP—10–11 percent for 1888–1938—were lower than the proportion for contemporary Africa and Asia—12.9 percent for low-income countries and 23.1 percent for middle-income countries. After World War II, Japan's taxation percentage remained low—22.2 percent compared with 37.7 percent for DCs (1981) in the Organisation for Economic Cooperation and Development (IMF 1984; Minami 1986: 333; Perry 1980: 91; Tanzi 1987: 205–41; World Bank 1983b: 148–49).

Wagner's Law, named for a nineteenth-century German economist Adolph Wagner, states that as real per-capita GNP rises, people demand relatively more social goods and relatively fewer private goods. A poor country spends a high percentage of its income on food, clothing, shelter, and other essential consumer goods. After these needs have been largely fulfilled, an increased proportion of additional spending is for social goods. Surprisingly, before the far-reaching Bank/Fund adjustment programs of the 1980s, Japan's taxation or government expenditure to GNP ratio was not much in excess of LDCs generally (Tanzi 1987: 205–41).

Japan relied heavily on direct taxes, even during the Meiji period, when land, income, corporation, business, and inheritance taxes comprised 44–90 percent of tax revenue. After Meiji, direct taxes as a proportion of tax revenue increased gradually from about 50 percent in 1920–40 to 75.4 percent in 1980. An elastic tax, whose coefficient exceeds one, rises more rapidly than GNP. Direct taxes are generally more elastic than indirect taxes, such as import, export, turnover, sales, and excise taxes. In the 1980s, the proportion of taxes raised from direct taxes was 75.4 percent in Japan, 65 percent in other DCs, 42 percent in middle-income countries, and 22 percent in low-income countries.

The personal and corporate income taxes are progressive, which means people with higher income pay a higher percentage of income in taxes. In addition, these taxes, especially the personal income tax, redistribute income from higher-income to lower-income groups. In the late nineteenth and early twentieth centuries, Japan made little progress in levying personal income tax because of opposition from wealthy business interests in the Diet (parliament). In 1913, with low tax rates and widespread evasion, taxes on business incomes and property accounted for less than 15 percent of total taxes collected. These rates contributed to entrepreneurs retaining large proportions of profit for investment. Japan's personal and corporate income taxes did not increase markedly until 1937. Today income and corporate taxes comprise only 39 percent of middle-income countries' revenue, and 20 percent of low-income countries' revenue, but 74 percent of high-income Japan's tax revenue (Lockwood 1954: 522; Mahajan 1976: 25–26; Minami 1986: 340; Tanzi 1987). Few LDCs rely much on the income tax because they have trouble administering them or because businesspeople and upper classes often oppose them successfully.

The following conditions must be met if income tax is to become a major revenue source for a country: (1) existence of a predominantly money economy, (2) a high standard of literacy among taxpayers, (3) widespread use of honestly and reliably maintained accounting records, (4) a large degree of voluntary taxpayer compliance, and (5) honest and efficient administration. While post–World War I Japan ranks high in these conditions, many present-day DCs, to say nothing of contemporary LDCs, have trouble fulfilling these conditions (Goode 1962: 157–71). Tanzania in the mid-1970s, under President Nyerere, was probably the only sub-Saharan African country that used its tax system to redistribute income to low-income groups, and few Asian LDCs had a tax system that could improve income distribution.

In the 1980s, Bank/Fund-sponsored adjustment programs required LDCs to reduce the little progressivity their tax structures had (Tanzania had to cease using its tax system for income redistribution) and to reduce government spending as a share of GNP. Indeed, UNICEF shows that, in the early 1980s, the reduced government spending by low-income and lower-middle income countries undertaking adjustment increased rates of malnutrition, infant mortality, and illiteracy (Cornia, Jolly, and Stewart 1987).

Summary

Early Meiji Japan, lacking a strong capitalist class, relied heavily on the government service (with strong samurai representation) to spur private ventures and start factories in lieu of private enterprise. Post-1868 Japan's economic policies have involved substantial consultation among its elites, particularly between the bureaucracy, political leadership, and private industrialists and bankers. These elites promoted domestic and imperial economic expansion through the early 1940s. Government comprised a larger proportion of national product in Japan than in other nations of Africa and Asia, peripheral countries in the global economy during most of the last two centuries. Partly as a result of this legacy of peripheralness, most contemporary LDCs lack the skilled bureaucracy for a nurturing state role similar to that of Meiji Japan.

In the early twentieth century, Japan used Keynesian-type government spending expansion to maintain high employment and steady growth. Keynesian approaches, however, are generally not applicable to contemporary LDCs because of their small commercial banking sector, their supply bottlenecks, their highly elastic labor supply from rural areas, and their lack of reliance on direct taxes.

Note

1. See, however, Migdal (1988: 18, 136), who discusses the overdeveloped postcolonial state, which is extractive, coercive, and the major employer and arena for power competition.

Chapter 4

The State and
Indigenous Capitalism

Political revolutions in Western Europe (England, France, and the Netherlands) in the seventeenth and eighteenth centuries reduced the power of the church and landed aristocracy, and eventually the industrial and commercial capitalist classes took over much of this power. These classes were less important in Japan's capitalism, where the bureaucracy, predominantly samurai, provided leadership in creating new industrial and commercial capitalists.[1] Can nineteenth-century Japan provide a model for present-day LDCs which seek to create capitalist enterprises but avoid the individualism and cutthroat competition of Western (especially U.S.) capitalism?

High Savings Rates

Japan's gross saving rates were 17 percent of national product between 1885 and 1935, at no time falling below 10 percent for a four-year period. In contrast, gross savings in India during the same period were no more than 5 percent of national product.

The savings habit was a part of the Japanese above-average-income household, which maintained family wealth intact for several generations. Japan's upper and middle classes generally saved to create capital assets, not to hoard gold, speculate on real estate, consume conspicuously, or go on pleasure tours. With poorly developed social services and consumer goods, families made provisions for training and housing, and against illness, unemployment, and old age. The age-old cultivation of nonmaterial values and personal frugality was enforced by Japanese group discipline. Moreover, the Japanese spent less on funerals, weddings, caste observances, and religious and social obligations than the Indians and other South and Southeast Asians.

The inflation of 1877–81 (when rapidly increasing rice prices provided wind-fall gains to landlords, whose taxes were fixed and rents received in kind) increased investment funds, though at the expense of tax revenues. From 1883 to 1903, a revised legal structure that facilitated land concentration and growing tenancy rates increased income concentration and savings. Unlike agriculturalists in most other LDCs, Meiji Japanese landlords invested in new banks, small industries, trading firms, agricultural land improvements, and other new enterprises, while the financial position of their farm tenants became increasingly precarious and their sons and (especially) daughters filled the ranks of the growing industrial proletariat (Gordon 1985: 82–83; Selden 1983: 63).

Japan's capital markets were well developed and not far behind Western Europe and North America by 1910–18. After World War I, Japan institutionalized savings in insurance and trust companies (Goldsmith 1983: 1, 36–37; Lockwood 1954: 14, 35, 286; Nakamura 1983: 8–9, 60–61). India, in contrast, has fragmented and poorly organized financial institutions, and has lacked a convertible currency during the twentieth century (before the 1990s).

Japan's fast growth increased capital formation rates. Meiji Japan's rapid technological innovation, by raising the returns to capital, stimulated additional savings. Furthermore, high corporate profits, reinforced by high inequality, contributed to savings. Moreover, from 1868 to 1939, Japan had a high proportion of its population self-employed (mainly small industrialist, trader, or farmer), which spurred high savings rates. In 1930, for example, 32 percent of Japan's gainfully occupied population was self-employed (Allen 1964: 97–98; Goldsmith 1983: 25; Lockwood 1954: 208, 248–64, 283–87, 301–02; Mahajan 1976: 69–70, 80–81).

In 1988, gross savings rates were 27 percent in middle-income countries, 37 percent in China, 21 percent in India, 16 percent in low-income countries other than China and India, and 11 percent in low-income sub-Saharan Africa, the last of which was substantially lower than the rate of Japan between 1885 and 1935. If we assume, as UN figures suggest, net savings rates are 60 percent of gross savings rates, then the low-income sub-Sahara's 11 percent savings rate consisted of 7 percent net new capital (4 percent replacement capital), a net rate lower than the rate Rostow indicates as the major condition for economic takeoff (Nafziger 1990a: 302–07; Rostow 1961; United Nations 1987; World Bank 1990b: 194–95).[2]

Government Policy toward Business

Following the fall of the Tokugawa shogun in 1868, none of the Meiji leaders were daimyo. Instead, the Meiji government was controlled largely by lower- and middle-ranking samurai, who had been more economically aggressive than the upper ranks because their fixed stipends proved inadequate during the inflation of the early nineteenth century (Jansen 1975: 60).

In 1868, the Meiji destroyed many Tokugawa economic barriers, disestablishing inspection stations and guardhouses, terminating wholesalers' monopolies, giving freedom of crop choice, allowing the general public to sell rice, and replacing the four-tier class system with two classes, the aristocracy and the commoner. From 1870 to 1885, the government owned and operated factories and mines, many expropriated from the shogunate and feudal lords. While the Meiji Restoration destroyed the great feudal income of the ruling classes, the nobility were pensioned off and their clan debts to merchants were shouldered by government. This pension enabled the feudal lord, who no longer was a territorial magnate receiving income from the peasant, to become a financial magnate, investing wealth in banks, stocks, industries, or landed estate, and joining a small financial oligarchy. This nobility and a mercantile class affluent from feudalism comprised a new aristocracy of wealth. Mitsui and Sumitomo had been major merchant houses of the Tokugawa period, while the merchant families Mitsubishi, Yasuda, Okura, Asano, and Furukawa expanded from cooperating with Meiji, which sold public mines and factories in the mid-1880s (Lockwood 1954: 268–80; Mahajan 1976: 103–04; Minami 1986: 148–49; Nakamura 1983: 54; Norman 1975: 201; Shishido 1983: 259).

Throughout the late nineteenth century, the Meiji regime accounted for about half the investment outside agriculture. State investment included infrastructure, such as railroads, bridges, warehouses, lighthouses, ports, irrigation, harbors, steamships, electricity, water supply, postal services, and telegraphy. The government also invested in shipbuilding, construction, cement, iron and steel, other heavy industries, and arms factories to strengthen the military, as well as mining, construction, engineering, cement, soap, silk, and chemical industries (though not textiles, the leading export sector).

After private-sector skills improved, government profits proved meager, and the state needed funds for armament, it sold most industrial properties and appropriated shogun and daimyo properties, often at bargain prices, to private businessmen, many of whom were samurai. Additionally, in 1876, the state strained its public credit to commute the pensions of 400,000 feudal lords and samurai to ¥210 million cash and public bonds, and to pay off ¥41 million debts owed to relatively privileged merchants and moneylenders (like the House of Mitsui) who had financed the 1867–68 coup restoring the emperor. The more enterprising recipients used these funds to invest in new industrial enterprise. Samurai in business, who worked closely with government, were also major recipients of other state favors, receiving subsidies and government contracts, and gaining access to scarce capital (Beasley 1987: 38–40).

From these state-assisted entrepreneurs came the *zaibatsu*, financial cliques or combines, usually family-controlled, that dominated industry and banking through World War II. The zaibatsu were hierarchical groups of companies, legally separate but linked by close personal, financial, and trading relationships. Each group was dominated by one or more major heavy industrial firms, but also included a bank, trading company, and a number of interlinked medium- and smaller-scale businesses. The four major pre–World War II zaibatsu, Mitsui, Mitsubishi, Sumitomo, and Yasuda, originated or expanded through their personal connections during Meiji rule, especially with the privatization of government-owned enterprises in the 1880s, to gain protection and patronage for establishing a diversified industrial empire. Although the zaibatsu reaped large-scale economies, managed ably, were generally frugal, invested productively, provided assistance to small industry (see below), and were partners in building national power, the zaibatsu concentration of wealth helped perpetuate high income inequalities at least seventy-five years after the Meiji Restoration (Francks 1992: 179, 227–28; Lockwood 1954: 15, 61, 234–49, 285; Takeda 1965: 437–38).

When they undertook privatization schemes, both late nineteenth-century Japan and contemporary developing countries have favored existing elites. The World Bank, IMF, and bilateral donors insisted on abrupt privatization in LDCs, which created a highly concentrated business elite from newly privatized firms falling into a few hands, similar to early Japan. In other ways, however, Meiji Japan's stress on private entrepreneurs differed substantially from that of contemporary low-income countries' privatization. Meiji Japan provided more assistance to small industrialists. Moreover, Japan's privatization was initiated by the state, whereas privatization in contemporary LDCs was thrust on them by adjustment programs initiated by the IMF, World Bank, and OECD creditors. Thus, emerging private enterprise in Japan was virtually all indigenous, while the World Bank has insisted that LDC loan recipients open investment to foreign private enterprise. For example, Nigeria, under two World Bank structural adjustment programs, 1986–88 and 1989–91, not only sold equity in public enterprises to private investors but allowed foreign investors in most manufacturing, large trade, and petroleum sectors. Foreign investors have been major contributors to high industrial concentration and factor-price distortions.

The Meiji government also aided private industry through low taxes on business enterprise and high incomes, freedom of enterprise, security for property rights, assurances against nationalization, a low wage policy, outlawing of labor organizations (1900–18), tolerance of child labor, a favorable legal climate (including corporate organization), technical research and education, development of banks and a strong currency, destruction of economic barriers between fiefs, lucrative purchase contracts, tax rebates, loans, and subsidies. (For example, the government imported spindle spinning machines in 1878–79 to sell on lenient credit terms to private enterprise in the textile industry, Japan's leading export sector.[3]) The substantial transfer of funds from the state to individuals, the high savings rates, the favorable government policies, and the acquisition of already existing enterprises facilitated private industrial enterprise.

In the early twentieth century, the state discontinued its economic leadership of the late nineteenth century. Lockwood (1954: 53, 509) contends there are few instances in modern history when so much industrial development took place within three decades with so little direct government subsidy and protection as in

Japan from 1900 to 1930. However, after the Sino–Japanese hostilities in 1937, the state again began extensive investment and direct intervention to control industrial enterprises.

Background of Businesspeople

Empirical studies on entrepreneurs indicate that landowners and wealthy farmers in contemporary developing countries rarely invest in industry. LDC landlords value highly consumption and real estate expenditure, lack a capital market and a savings habit (see below), and have little experience in managing and coordinating a production process with specialized work tasks and machinery and in overseeing secondary labor relations (Nafziger 1986: 81, 121).

Yet, perhaps as many as one-fourth to one-fifth of the farmers in the late Tokugawa and early Meiji periods managed second businesses such as small bars, rapeseed oil selling, lumber vending, eating-house management, bean-curd making, confection making, tobacco selling, sundry shopkeeping, carpentry, and plastering. Landlords, who had been the lowest rung in the Tokugawan provincial lords' administration, became fertilizer merchants, pawnbrokers, moneylenders, doctors, and dry goods merchants, but most often brewers of sake, soy sauce, and bean paste after the Meiji land reform in the 1870s which abolished the feudal fief, levied high rents on the tenant, and facilitated substantial surpluses for the owners. The landed class especially increased investment during the inflation of 1876–81, when rapidly increasing rice prices provided windfall gains when land taxes were fixed and rents received in kind (Lockwood 1954: 14, 35, 286; Nakamura 1983: 51–61).

Many economists, noting the disproportionate samurai representation among early Meiji industrialists and bankers, stress the spirit of the community-centered samurai entrepreneur, sacrificing for national economic progress (Hirschmeier 1964; Ranis 1955: 80–98; Sumiya and Taira 1979: 254–68). But Yamamura's evidence indicates that samurai status in the early Meiji period was blurred, since many from farm and merchant families purchased this status during the late Tokugawa period. The major force to establish banks and factories came from merchants and landlords motivated by profit, not from longstanding samurai motivated by nationalism (Nakamura 1983: 106–8; Yamamura 1968: 148–58). And many of these samurai received subsidies and favors from the samurai-dominated Meiji bureaucracy.

The Japanese State and the Bourgeois Class

The Meiji Revolution did not involve a rising business class demanding new political rights or overthrowing feudalism to establish a mercantile state, or a democratic revolt transferring political power to representatives of the workers and peasants. The industrialists, financiers, public officials, and landlords who shared political power with the military bureaucrats after 1868 were largely recruited from the samurai, prosperous farmers, and petty tradesmen.

After 1882, the state was less important as an entrepreneur (except in nationalizing the trunk railways), but it pursued policies to stimulate private investment: creation of big banking institutions to channel funds into private industry and trade, overseas borrowing to help provide for its needs (1897–1913), a fiscal policy relying heavily on real estate and consumption, leniency with (especially high-income) earnings from business, a broad framework of legal security, freedom of enterprise, technical research and education, and encouragement of joint-stock organization. Selective encouragement to investment included tax rebates, subsidies, and lucrative purchase contracts to industries such as steel and shipbuilding, with a high military priority (Lockwood 1954: 10, 249). Meiji Japan's policies are alternatives to the Soviet approach for accumulating capital where the bourgeois class is weak.

The Colonial State in Asia and Africa

In 1900, Lord Curzon, Britain's top colonial leader in India (comprising present-day India, Bangladesh, and Pakistan), claimed that India was prosperous. Our sketch below, however, indicates that in contrast to Japan, which benefited from directing its capitalist development, Western imperialism and colonial capitalism retarded India's economic development.

British writer William Digby, in response to Lord Curzon, declared in 1901 that the average Indian was poor, and was getting poorer every year, as a result of British rule (Johnson 1983: 22–23). Maddison (1971: 67) estimates that while the United Kingdom's per-capita income increased tenfold from 1757 to 1947, India's could not have increased by more than a third. Mukherjee's (1969) study indicates that India's growth in per-capita GNP from 1901 to 1950 was slow, 0.5 percent per annum. Uppal's (1977: 16) data for about the same period suggests negative growth, especially in the two decades or so before independence (see table 4.1). Agriculture was not only stagnant, but declined on a per-capita basis.

Beginning in the mid-eighteenth century, parts of India were controlled by a British private commercial monopoly, the East India Company, which needed forts and depots for trade and plunder. With this territorial base, company civil servants on the spot could buy pepper and indigo at harvest time when prices dropped, and store them until a ship arrived; and attain the regularity and predictability to keep indigo, opium, and jute prices under control in the hinterland. The Moghul empire was decaying, the French lost to the British at Plassey, near Calcutta, in 1757, and Portugal and France were intriguing with native rulers to oust the British, who felt it essential to counterattack and conquer for economic stability. Britain seized the revenues of conquered native rulers and zamindars

Table 4.1

Long-Term Changes in Net Output in India, 1896–1945 (1896–1906 = 100)

	1896–1906	1906–15	1916–25	1926–35	1936–45
Per-capita income[a]	100	101	104	98	91
Per-capita output growth (per decade)	1	3	–6	–7	–5
Agricultural crops[b]	100	106	108	110	112
Agricultural crops per capita[b]	100	99	100	92	84
Industry and mining[b]	100	144	185	224	313
Population[b]	100	107	108	119	134

Source: Uppal 1977: 16.
[a]In rupees, 1952–1953 prices.
[b]Index: 1896–1905 = 100.

(land owner-tax collectors), forcing India to pay largely for its own conquest (Spear 1965: vol. 2, pp. 26–29).

The Indian capitalist class was too weak to spearhead the drive for industrial development before colonialism. Moreover, British colonial policy prevented the rise of an independent Indian capitalist class. In 1750, India was as urbanized as England, France, and Italy, and as industrialized as Japan and most of Central and Eastern Europe. In the early eighteenth century, India exported manufactured products and imported primary or intermediary goods. India was the major supplier of textiles for Southeast Asia, Iran, Arab countries, and East Africa. However, as British political power grew in India after 1753, the privileged position of the East India Company and its servants set back Indian enterprise (Gadgil 1959; Raychaudhuri 1968: 77–100).

By the mid-eighteenth century, Indian merchant capital survived only under European protection and in trade or collaboration with European companies. European capital undermined independent Indian competitors, as in 1734 when the East India Company blockaded a major indigenous trading center, Surat, and established merchants there. The domination of the English increased from the end of the eighteenth century through the beginning of formal British colonization in 1857, when the company was dissolved. Colonialism coincided with the rise of Indian merchant capital that became a junior partner of British capital. These comprador entrepreneurs made profits on the East India Company's internal trade and in extracting land revenue from tenants (Davey 1975; 28–35).

By 1800, the factory system had been developed in England, and before 1825 the system had obtained a foothold in a few other Western countries. Although several English businessmen established factories in India in the first half of the nineteenth century, it was not until the middle of the century, with the expansion of the market through the development of railways and other internal transport, that such manufacturing enterprises extended beyond initial ventures in a few industries. Despite colonial obstacles, around 1850 Indian entrepreneurs, especially in the west, were instrumental in the substantial progress in modern manufacturing during the last half of the nineteenth century (Medhora 1965: 58–59). But most Indian entrepreneurs, such as Parsis (in shipbuilding and opium trade) and the Marwaris (merchants), worked in a subsidiary relationship to the British.

After a British 1813 parliamentary enquiry established that Indian textiles could be sold 50 to 60 percent cheaper than their domestic competitors, Indian cotton and textile manufacturers, which had faced a 70 to 80 percent tariff since the late seventeenth century, were excluded from the British market altogether. Soon after, Indian handicrafts, which had a long reputation, declined not only from British protection, but from new tastes, no princely patronage, and the competition of machine-made goods at home and abroad. By the mid-nineteenth century, England's textiles, in the vanguard of the industrial revolution, flooded much of the Indian countryside (Datt and Sundharam 1968: 144; Davey 1975: 45). Britain deindustrialized India in the nineteenth century. An independent India could have pursued its own "guided" capitalism and could have directed Western technology and capital inflows toward accelerating economic growth.

In 1904, India's swadeshi movement, a nationalist boycott of British goods in favor of Indian enterprise, boosted Indian manufacturing, insurance, and banks. Despite British restrictive policy, Indians even made a few beginnings in the early part of the twentieth century in heavy industry—in steel, engineering, electric power, and shipping (Lamb 1955: 105). The most spectacular of these ventures was by Jamshedjee Tata, a Parsi, who was responsible for India's first viable steel enterprise in Jamshedpur in 1911.

Although in 1916 the Indian Industrial Commission recommended that the government play an active role in the industrial development of the country, little initiative was taken by the central government. After the shortages of strategic goods during the war, however, the United Kingdom recognized its interest in selectively encouraging colonial industries that were not threatening to British manufacturers. Accordingly, the recommendation of the Fiscal Commission in 1921 led to the protection of certain industries such as iron and steel, cotton textiles, sugar, paper, matches, and heavy chemicals. Industrial development accelerated and diversified in the 1930s and 1940s, with indigenous enterprise increasingly setting the pace (Medhora 1965: 571–73).

The rate of growth in industrial output increased in the first half of the twentieth century over that of the last half of the nineteenth century. However, although industrial production doubled between 1912 and 1945 (Balakrishna 1961: 100), industrial output per capita grew only about 1 percent per annum.

Western economic and political penetration also hampered sub-Saharan Africa's use of the state to further indigenous capitalist development. Africans welcomed the exchange of ideas, inventions, cultures, and commodities, but denied that colonialism was needed. The poet Aimé Cesaire spoke of "societies emptied of themselves, of trampled cultures, undermined institutions, confiscated lands, of assassinated religions, annihilated artistic masterpieces, of extraordinary possibilities suppressed" (1970: 41). Africa would have continued its precolonial trade, technical borrowing, and internal innovations if it had been strong enough to resist European restrictions.

The majority of colonial investment was in infrastructure primarily designed to promote trade with the mother country. Most of the estimated $6 billion foreign investment (at 1978 prices) in sub-Saharan Africa up to World War II was in mineral-related industries, heavily concentrated in Southern Africa. Foreigners invested funds overwhelmingly in exports, resulting in lopsided development. In addition, the European powers expected the colonies to pay their way even though few could support the bureaucratic structures imposed on whatever forms of government existed in precolonial times, let alone a modern military establishment to guard against rebellion (Curtin et al. 1978; Markovitz 1977).

In most of Africa, colonial expenditures were niggardly. I.F. Nicolson describes colonialism in Nigeria from 1918 to 1948 as administration on a "shoestring":

> There was no more than 5s per head of population, for all the current needs of central government, for many of the purposes of local government, and for heavy interest charges on loan capital, mostly used to improve the transportation services on which the whole prospect of prosperity and increasing revenues depended. . . . [During] the upheaval of a second World War . . . the overstretched administrative machinery came very near to collapse. [1969: 216, 246]

The colonial legacy also contributed to agricultural underdevelopment after independence, discussed in chapter 5.

As European rule became expensive after World War II, far-sighted administrators sought ways to maintain influence in Africa without colonialism. The British and the French emphasized policies to meet some demands of the elite-led nationalist movements, notably by indigenizing jobs and by raising local salaries and allowances to bring them more in line with those paid to Europeans—steps that eased the colonial burden and helped create an elite that was favorable to the metropole by the date of independence. According to Peter Anyang' Nyong'o:

> the emergence of ruling classes in postcolonial Africa must be traced to their evolution in colonial times . . . . In the case of the Ivory Coast, it was the small African capitalist class, emergent in the prewar era but consciously nurtured by the colonial state in the postwar era, which . . . became the center of [the postcolonial] ruling bloc. [1987: 185–86]

The State and Postcolonial Mixed Capitalism in LDCs

In South Asia, we focus on the period after 1947, the independence and partition of India and Pakistan, and in Africa, after 1960, by which time most countries had achieved their independence. While the case studies demonstrate the harm of economic dependence, they also indicate the costs of trying to reduce dependence through domestic protection against foreign technological competition and increasing the state's extensive internal price controls.

India

At independence in 1947, India had experienced some degree of industrialization and had a more highly developed indigenous capitalism than Africa in 1960. Furthermore, educated administrators, intellectuals, and nationalist leaders, especially in the Indian National Congress, supported national autonomy in state economic planning and industrial production, and reduction in international trade and capital inflows to remove deep-seated obstacles inherited from the colonial period.

Industrial Policy

On April 6, 1948, the Indian government published the Industrial Policy Resolution, which emphasized the public and indigenous sectors. According to the Indian Constitution (1949), the state should strive to "promote the welfare of the people by securing and protecting as effectively as it may social order in which justice, social, economic and political shall inform all the institutions of national life." Yet, despite the socialist and egalitarian rhetoric of the ruling Congress and subsequent parties, these elites, to whom the British transferred power, have not placed a priority on eliminating poverty, reducing land concentration, and breaking up indigenous oligopolies.

Industries were divided into four categories: (1) the manufacture of arms, production of atomic energy, and ownership of railway transport were to be the exclusive monopoly of the central government; (2) new undertakings in coal, iron and steel, aircraft, shipbuilding, telephone, telegraph, and wireless apparatus (except radios) were to be undertaken only by the state; (3) basic industries like salt, automobiles, tractors, electrical engineering, heavy machinery, machine tools, heavy chemicals, fertilizers, electrochemical industries, nonferrous metals, rubber manufactures, power and industrial alcohol, cotton and woolen textiles, cement, sugar, paper and newsprint, air and sea defense, minerals, and industries related to defense would be planned and regulated by the central government, which could take over any industry vital for the national drive; and (4) the remainder was open to private enterprise and cooperatives. The state was to control the commanding heights of the economy, heavy industry, defense, insurance, banking, and infrastructure such as hydroelectric projects, irrigation, roads, and railways. The private sector, on the other hand, would not be allowed to develop in its own unorganized way, but was to have a well-defined place in the government's integrated plan.

While foreign capital would be needed to acquire knowledge and technology, generally the major ownership and effective control were to be in Indian hands. The government insisted that foreign companies train Indian personnel to replace foreign experts (Datt and Sundharam 1983: 112–33; Frankel 1978: 76–77).

The Growth Record

Despite the initial industrialization and a well-educated political leadership, GNP per capita the first fifteen years—1950–51 to 1965–66—grew only 1.2 percent annually, while the poverty rate rose, at least during the period's last decade. The first five-year plan of the early 1950s was only a collection of projects, rather than an integrated plan. In the second and third plans of the late 1950s and early 1960s, Prime Minister Nehru and the head of the Indian Planning Commission, P.C. Mahalanobis, tried to combine the Fel'dman-Stalin investment model with democratic socialism. The driving force was increasing the fraction of investment in steel and other capital goods. The actual pattern differed from the plan, since planning in India did not represented a binding commitment by a public department to spend funds. The Mahalanobis model completely ignored the bulk of manufacturing output in the intermediate (not capital or consumer) goods sector. Furthermore, as an indicative plan, which indicates aspirations while falling short of authorization, the planners left investment choice in a number of enterprises and industries virtually unaffected. By the late 1960s, slow growth and sectoral imbalances convinced the Indian government to abandon the Mahalanobis approach (Datt and Sundharam 1983: 290–94; India Planning Commission 1969; Nafziger 1990a: 274–76, 1990b: 8–12; Weisskopf 1973: 53–54).

Foreign Aid

The slow growth, food shortages, and external crises attributable to ill-fated planning strategies eroded India's bargaining strength vis-à-vis creditor countries and international agencies, increasing its reliance on foreign concessional aid (especially food imports under the United States's Public Law 480) and investment beginning in the late 1950s. The quid pro quo for this foreign assistance was India's relaxation of barriers to foreign private investment, especially in oil, drugs, and fertilizer (Weisskopf 1973: 54–96), and an exemption of foreign banks from the bank nationalization of 1969. India continued to depend on foreign assistance during the 1970s and 1980s, especially following the devastating impact of the fourfold increase in petroleum prices in 1973–74 on oil-importing India's trade balance.

Economic Policies

India's economic policies for its plans through 1977 suffered from the paradox of inadequate attention to programs in the public sector and too much control over the private sector. Thus, Indian planners frequently chose public-sector investments on the basis of rough, sketchy, and incomplete reports, with little or no cost–benefit calculations for alternative project locations. And the government, having selected the project, often failed to do the necessary detailed technical preparation and work scheduling related to the project. The bureaucracy was slow and rigid, stifling quick and imaginative action by public sector managers. (Even public firms had to apply for raw materials and capital import licenses a year or so in advance.) Poorly stated criteria for awarding input licenses and production quotas led to charges of bribery, influence peddling, and ethnic, caste, or political prejudice. Key public-sector products were often priced lower than scarcity prices, increasing waste and reducing savings. Furthermore, political involvement in public enterprises meant that unskilled labor overstaffed many projects.

Such planning problems led to profit rates for public enterprises that were lower than for indigenous, private operations, even when adjusted for commercial and social profit discrepancies (Bhagwati and Desai 1970). This inefficiency explains why the Indian public sector, despite its domination of large industry, contributed only 16 percent of the country's 1975 total capital formation.

Licensing and Quotas

Indian planners, on the other hand, tried to influence private investment and production through licensing and other controls. These controls were intended to regulate production according to plan targets, encourage small industry, prevent concentrated ownership, and promote balanced regional economic development.

The Indian government's award of materials and input quotas at below-market prices hampered private industrial efficiency in the following ways:

1. It subsidized some firms and forced others to buy inputs on the black market or do without.
2. Favoring existing firms discouraged new firms' entry. And inefficient manufacturers sold controlled inputs on the free market for sizable profit.
3. Businesspeople were unproductive, since they were dealing with government agencies and buying and selling controlled materials.
4. Capital was often underutilized, since government encouraged building excess capacity by awarding more materials to firms with greater plant capacity.
5. Entrepreneurs inflated materials requests, expecting allotments to be reduced by a specific percentage.
6. Businesspeople used or sold all materials within the fiscal year to avoid quota cuts the following years.

7. A shortage of controlled inputs could halt production, since the application process took several months.

8. Large companies, which were better organized and better informed than small enterprises, took advantage of economies of scale in dealing with the public bureaucracy.

9. Entrepreneurial planning was difficult because of quota delay and uncertainty (Nafziger 1978: 114–19).

The interim Janata government, 1977–79, realized the inadequacies of the bureaucracy in controlling private output and prices, and the costs of licensing and quota policies. Janata began the process of relaxing production and materials licensing, import restrictions, and other controls on private business. When Nehru's daughter, Indira Gandhi, prime minister from 1966 to 1977, returned to power following her Congress party's victory in 1979, she maintained the relaxation of economic controls begun by the Janata party. After her assassination in 1984, the liberalization she began in the early 1980s continued under her son Rajiv Gandhi's Congress government, 1984–89, and under subsequent prime ministers, resulting in increased efficiency, savings, and economic growth. The New Industrial Policy reforms, introduced under Bank/Fund pressure in 1991 mentioned below, expanded liberalization to new levels.

Protection against Foreign Capital

The Indian government maintained its restrictions on foreign capital, limiting its majority ownership and control through 1991. This policy was meant to increase local political control and gains from technological learning. The Indian leadership believed increased dependence on investment by MNCs restricted the technology transfer of subsidiaries, increased industrial and technological concentration, exacerbated foreign intervention into domestic politics, and enhanced repatriation of profits, royalties, and managerial and service fees.

Lall's study indicates that MNCs in India: (1) are agents for technology generation and diffusion, (2) export as much as indigenous firms, (3) are as likely to buy indigenous technology as local firms, and (4) are not more likely to contribute to high industrial concentration than indigenous firms. Indeed, India's industrial growth would have been faster if it would have selectively allowed foreign control initially, but gradually increased restrictions on MNCs. Newly industrialized countries (NICs) such as Taiwan, South Korea, Hong Kong, and Singapore have gained from MNC new-technology generation initially by a judicious blend of encouraging MNC foreign investment, licensing foreign technology, and stimulating local technological effort. Over time, the NICs gradually increased indigenous control as the comparative advantage of standardized manufacturing goods shifted from innovating countries to less developed countries.

The Indian government did not stress "know-how" technology, but "know-why" development without the mastery or the foreign ties essential to generate further "know-why" technology in line with developments abroad. India over-emphasized self-reliance to such a counterproductive extreme that it was a major technology exporter, but at the expense of stultifying further technological development. New Delhi's restriction of competition from the most modern technologies (through curtailing private investment expansion, protecting local production, and restricting initial foreign investment) encouraged its firms to be technologically slothful. Essentially, protective policies creating shortages, restricting markets, and curtailing foreign technologies represented a misallocation of resources saddling the Indian economy with large areas of outdated and inefficient technologies that were difficult to replace and which only found markets at home or in other LDCs (Lall 1985: 181).

Because of longstanding restrictions, Indian companies have not participated in the borderless Asian-Pacific economy, and have been at a major disadvantage in winning contracts overseas. In 1990, one year before India's liberalization program, TRP Software, Limited, a Calcutta data systems and software company, undertook a detailed study to bid to design information management services for the municipal government of a major Australian city. Foreign-exchange restrictions prevented TRP's director, J.T. Banerjee,[4] from taking more than one trip to the city to do the planning. Nevertheless, TRP took advantage of India's low-salaried professional designers, software engineers, and systems analysts to put together a highly competitive package for the Australian city. Other firms from countries without foreign-exchange restrictions sent executive officers to Australia with the design and bid. Because of the prohibitive amount of time necessary to receive Reserve Bank of India foreign-exchange permission for the trip, TRP had to rely on an express package service, which delivered the firm's bid ten minutes late, thus losing the opportunity to win the contract.

After the 1991 liberalization, TRP no longer faced these limitations in competing overseas. A number of other firms found that foreign-currency decontrol had facilitated acquiring imports to improve plant and machinery (albeit at higher rupee prices) and spurred them to seek markets overseas. The liberalized foreign-exchange regime (higher rupee price of the dollar and delicensing of many foreign purchases) was a welcome change for a Visakhapatnam, Andhra Pradesh marble products entrepreneur, who reduced his time for clearing imported machines through Indian customs from an average of one month before 1991 to two days since 1993.[5]

Policies in the Early 1990s

India faced pressure from the IMF, World Bank, the United States, and other OECD creditors, but because of its large size and international influence, it avoided the strict Fund and Bank policy conditionality that African countries faced before June 1991, when an external payments crisis resulted in rapidly dwindling foreign exchange reserves. P.V. Narasimha Rao, selected as prime minister by the ruling Congress Party in that month, just after Rajiv Gandhi's assassination, was compelled by the World Bank and IMF to devalue the rupee and move toward rupee convertibility, reduce import barriers, privatize numerous state enterprises, deregulate industry, decrease restrictions on foreign investment, liberalize capital markets, and cut income and wealth taxes.

India's policies from the early 1980s reduced price distortions, investment controls, and licensing restrictions that had impeded output and efficiency, contributing to economic growth in the 1980s in excess of that of the 1970s. However, India's increased reliance on foreign aid and investment, especially after 1991, may diminish technological learning gains from self-directed management and planning. Despite its regional political power in South Asia, postcolonial India had only limited success in shifting away from its peripheral role in the international economy.

Pakistan

British suzerainty was exercised in northwestern colonial India (Pakistan since the Bangladesh secession in 1971), under "indirect rule," an arrangement mutually advantageous to the colonial power and to the native princes. Britain economized on officers and utilized indigenous systems of tax collection and maintenance of order, while the traditional rulers obtained security through the elimination of important sources of both external and internal opposition. The maintenance of these indigenous princes hampered the development of nationalism and a strong native bourgeoisie, and strengthened the concentration of land holdings among overlords and zamindars. Princely states that joined West Pakistan maintained a semi-independent status long after independence.

Partition left Pakistan, created from the economic backwashes of India, without a major industrial or urban economic center. Traditional commercial patterns between the jute-growing areas of East Bengal and the major jute-processing center of Calcutta were broken. Trade with India dropped from more than 65 percent of Pakistan's total foreign trade in 1948–49 to about 3 percent in 1951, not rising above 6 percent for any year in the 1950s (MacEwan 1971: 42–52). A large portion of the class that had been associated with commerce and the embryonic beginnings of manufacturing was lost by its exodus to India. The vacuum was filled by a new class of Muslim industrial capitalists, whose power and influence grew during succeeding years, but who made few gains in moving Pakistan from its peripheral status in the global economy.

In Pakistan, the military intervened in 1958 to forestall a threatened loss of power by the West to the East in the upcoming elections, and in 1969 to restore order after riots occurring in both wings of Pakistan. The 1958 establishment of martial law thus consolidated the domination of the predominantly West Pakistani industrial and commercial capitalists, civil servants, army officers, and technocrats (Wright 1973: 13–15).

Although Pakistan extricated itself from the British colonial economic nexus, it replaced British with American domination. The Pakistani political leadership negotiated a long-term military and economic aid pact with the United States in 1954. The continuing political, military, and economic assistance from the United States, which provided the resources and support for a perpetuation of the West Pakistani ruling group, kept the country open to foreign investment and trade, and allied to the Western capitalist world. These ties, however, were costly to the Pakistani population at large, influencing the balance of internal political forces, affecting the shape of the class structure, making available additional means of repression against dissidents, and ultimately contributing to increased political instability.

Pakistan was highly dependent on the United States for loans, investment, and aid. The United States provided 64.3 percent of the grants, and 42.7 percent of total assistance (grants and loans) to Pakistan from 1951 through 1971. The aid consortium, representing the rich capitalist countries, contributed 93 percent of total assistance to Pakistan from 1951 to 1957. In 1969–70, Pakistan received Rs. 3.100 billion in foreign grants and loans, to compare with a balance-of-trade deficit of Rs. 2.690 billion (from exports of goods and services of Rs. 4.350 billion). Debt-service obligations (virtually all of which were owed to the Consortium of Western countries, the International Monetary Fund, and the World Bank) as a percentage of foreign-exchange earnings increased from 3.6 percent in 1960–61, to 9.9 percent in 1964–65, to 25.3 percent in 1970–71 (Pakistan 1971–72: 79–81).

Development plans and strategies, dependent on foreign aid for a large percentage of projects, were submitted to the Consortium, which frequently insisted on changes before committing funds (Hamid 1970: 132–33, 146). The United States, for example, with a contribution of 18.6 percent of the total amount of Pakistani development projects in 1966, could control most of these, as technical and financial assistance was distributed over a large number of government projects (Alavi and Khusro 1970: 64–66).

The overriding influence of the United States in the economy of Pakistan distorted its economic development, and took away potential gains in government policy and technical project development that Pakistanis could have received from experience. Foreign aid gave a major impetus to the emerging industrial capitalist elite (disproportionately migrants from India at the time of partition), allied with and overlapping with large landowners, top civil servant, and army officers in the Punjab. The severance of Pakistan from the more industrialized parts of India and the flight of the previously dominant Hindu mercantile community at the time of partition gave further impetus to the new manufacturing and commercial entrepreneurs of Pakistan. The maintenance of a coalition of the business classes with the older elite was only possible with the large injection of military, economic, and technical aid in the 1950s and early 1960s, and with the concomitant rapid economic growth, especially industrial growth (MacEwan 1971: 48). This support was needed so that enough patronage, perquisites, and resources were available to satisfy the various economic interests within the coalition, and to have sufficient access to a range of sanctions and rewards to consolidate control and to prevent restiveness among the lower elites.

Foreign assistance, primarily from the United States, then, helped in the creation of a new capitalist elite who, in coalition with other conservative forces, placed little emphasis on improving the level of living of the masses. Pakistan's rapid growth in the first two decades of independence was accompanied by a decline in real wages, and in food grains per capita. Assistance allowed the United States to have a role in the shaping of forces contributing to the rising Pakistani elite. However, military support, accounting for approximately one-fourth of U.S. aid to Pakistan from 1947 through 1968, allowed the ruling elite to maintain power despite this neglect of the population at large (Alavi and Khusro: 1970: 64–66).

Yet the support for this ruling coalition, which depended on continued military and economic support from the United States, plummeted sharply after the Indo–Pakistan War of 1965, while Pakistan's debt-servicing ratio was increasing. Total assistance by the United States declined from $964.280 million in the Second Five-Year Plan (1960–65) to $668.799 million in the Third Five-Year Plan (1965–70), while grants decreased even more drastically (Pakistan 1971–72: app., p. 89). The decline in foreign help for the coalition of elites meant that some elements in the alliance would have to be suppressed. The withdrawal of the support of the landed elite threatened the power of the capitalist class, who lacked the power to overcome this elite and its military allies (MacEwan 1971: 48).

In Pakistan, landlords, zamindars, traders, lawyers, and other professionals were formed as a part of the elite in the West in the half-century before independence, as a result of their leadership role in the movement of Muslim nationalism in India (through the vehicle of the Muslim League, in opposition to the larger nationalist movement, led by the Indian National Congress). These were joined after independence by an emerging class of Muslim industrial and merchant capitalists, the essentially newly created civil service, army officers, and white-collar workers (Maniruzzaman 1966: 84–86).

At independence, when more than one-half of the manufacturing sector was controlled by Hindus, the government, or foreigners, the percentage of national income originating in manufacturing was barely 1 percent. By 1959, this figure rose to over 6 percent. Muslims indigenous to the Indo-Pakistani subcontinent controlled two-thirds of the sector (Papanek 1962: 49). The industrial elites, with their allies in the bureaucracy, used the levers of state economic policy and planning to give their enterprises privileged protection from foreign competition, ready access to licenses for foreign exchange and domestic inputs at less than a market price, and subsidies or tax concessions. In East Pakistan, the periphera of the periphera, the petty bourgeoisie, who constituted the top of the class hierarchy, directed their discontent against the dominant feudal and business elite in the West. This elite feared that if a major bourgeoisie class were allowed to be established in East Pakistan, with a majority of the country's population, it would be dominant in national politics. In 1950–57, with Prime Minister H.S. Suhrawardy, founder of the Awami League, based in the East, the government awarded more import licenses to newcomers in import trade (particularly from the East), distributed U.S. aid for modernizing industry disproportionately to the East, gave the East parity with the West in the allocation of foreign exchange, and proposed to establish a public shipping corporation for coastal trade between the wings to compete with private shippers in the West. The vehement reaction by the coalition of landed and business interests in the West encouraged President Iskander Mirza to compel Suhrawardy's resignation, after which most of the measures that benefited aspiring business groups in the East were canceled (Ali 1970: 61; Papanek 1962: 49). The class struggle, from the viewpoint of major Bengali interests, became increasingly identified as a regional struggle against the supremacy of the Western wing.

One distinct feature of the strategy of Pakistan's Planning Commission, supported by official and foreign economists, was a conscious promotion of income inequality to achieve a high rate of domestic savings and economic growth. The concentration of income and wealth in the hands of high-income groups was a key ingredient in a strategy that used government policies with regard to taxes, subsidies, licenses, and foreign exchange to redistribute resources from agriculture to industry, and from East to West Pakistan. In the fifteen years before 1967, when this strategy was promoted, real wages in industry declined by at least 25 percent, while the real per-capita gross income of the country increased by 21 percent (Griffin and Khan 1972: 199–206; Pakistan 1971–72: app., pp. 2–3).

In Pakistan, the central government pursued projects and policies primarily oriented toward benefits for a "modernizing" elite—the capitalist and bureaucratic classes, and their allies among the landed and feudal upper classes. Planning and implementation were hamstrung by the desire of the ruling elites to keep control of the bounties distributed by government. In Pakistan, after the Six Year Development Programme initiated in 1951 was not completed because of the lack of planning machinery, the planning commissions of the next three plans (1955–70) relied heavily on foreign advisors (Waterston 1963: 13–129).

Planners in Pakistan, assisted heavily by U.S. agencies, favored an emphasis on decision making by private units, a stress on marginal governmental adjustment rather than fundamental structural change, the eschewal of increased tax rates at high income levels (to encourage private incentives), an accent on a high economic payoff from directly productive investment (as opposed to an indirect return from social overhead capital), a conservative monetary and fiscal policy with an emphasis on relatively few expenditures for social welfare measures, an economy open to foreign trade and investment, and a substantial reliance on overseas assistance. There was little coordination between the planning units, dominated by foreigners, and the government officials in the formulation of the plan. This deficiency was one reason for the lack of implementation of plan projects (Allan 1969: 219–21; Ghouse 1969: 177; Jiliani 1969: 362).

If a strong program had been designed to foster economic development among the masses, the power and privileges of the ruling elite would clearly have been threatened, especially in West Pakistan (Waterston 1963). A dispersion of economic power to the multiplicity of small businessmen without a quid pro quo would have threatened the economic interests of the political leaders— the viability and monopoly return of the large business interests influential in government. The 1965–70 Pakistan plan encountered major shortfalls in expenditures as a result of the lack of clear identification of feasible projects, and a lack of details concerning supporting government policies. The lack of preparatory work by specialized professionals resulted from the ineffective coordination, a shortage of high-level personnel, and the introduction of political criteria for determining projects. Ruling elites lacked goals and priorities that could be articulated to the masses, and—preoccupied with the preservation of their power and access to patronage—did not encourage government decision making from below.

One strategy during Japan's Meiji period (discussed in chapter 5) to increase the rate of industrialization was to force the transfer of resources from the agricultural to the industrial sector. This strategy also increased the profits and patronage of Pakistan's political leaders. In addition, the process of redistributing resources from agriculture to industry coincided with, and was an integral part of, a redistribution of income from the poor to the rich, and from East to West Pakistan.

In Pakistan, competition was increasingly viewed as being between the Eastern and Western wings, especially with the consolidation of the West into a single province in 1955. While the "problem of parity" was ostensibly one of balancing the power of two wings, in practice it meant that the majority in the East (with 55 percent of the population) was effectively neutralized so as to give dominant Western interests unbridled sway in both political and economic spheres. It was an exploitative, colonial-type relationship, with some of the Bengali elite cooperating with the West Pakistanis in order to gain position and affluence. The resentment of East Pakistan arose in part from the lack of its sharing in the economic fruits of independence and modernization. The hopes of Bengalis, stirred by the fall of President Ayub Khan in 1969 and the 1970 elections, were thwarted by the subsequent maneuvers of Western political leaders and the military.

In Pakistan, the average material level of living was probably higher in the West than in the East at independence, and these disparities increased over time. In 1949–50, GDP per capita, based on official sources, was 10 percent higher in the West than in the East. (GDP, gross domestic product, is income earned within a country's boundaries, as opposed to GNP or gross national product, income accruing to a country's residents.) This difference increased to 30–36 percent in 1959–60, and to 60 percent in 1969–70. For the West, this represented a real growth in GDP per head of 1.1 percent annually in the decade, 1949–50 to 1959–60; at the same time, this measure was declining in the East by at least 1 percent yearly. In the next decade, from 1959–60 to 1969–70, real GDP per capita grew in the East at 1.5 percent yearly, and in the West by 3.6 percent annually (Griffin and Khan 1972: 5, 29; Khan and Bergan 1966: 187).

East Pakistan resented the fact that, between 1949–50 and 1969–70, it generated the bulk of Pakistan's foreign-exchange earnings (with exports primarily of raw jute, jute goods, and tea), while the West used about 70 percent of Pakistan's foreign exchange. This policy effected a resource transfer from East to West, as the rupee was overvalued in international exchange. The East, as a price taker on its exports, received less local currency than at an equilibrium exchange rate, and still bought manufactured goods at inflated prices because of high tariffs. On the other hand, the artificially induced low price of foreign exchange encouraged an increase in the West's dollar imports of capital goods and industrial inputs, which exacerbated Pakistan's balance-of-payments problems.

In 1959–60, 58.6 percent of Pakistan's exports were from the East, compared with only 26.6 percent of the imports; in 1964–65, the corresponding figures were 52.7 percent and 31.7 percent; and even in 1969–70, 50.0 percent and 35.6 percent, respectively. This is despite the fact that exports of raw jute declined and imports of food grains increased in the East, while manufacturing exports increased and food grain imports decreased in the West during the 1960s (Pakistan 1971: 90–91), as a result partly of economic policy favoring industry and large-scale agriculture, which were concentrated disproportionately in the West.

The West was favored when it came to development plan expenditures, receiving an expenditure per head 4.9 times as much as the East in 1950–51 to 1954–55, and even 2.2 times as much in 1965–66 to 1969–70. During the last part of the 1960s, Eastern agriculture remained stagnant while Western agriculture encountered breakthroughs, especially in wheat. In the West, large subsidies were given for farm inputs such as water, fertilizers, seeds, plant protection service, and pesticides, while the East lacked government assistance in drainage, irrigation, flood control, extension service, and credit. One of the most striking instances of exacerbation of regional (and class) differences was that the high-yielding grain varieties associated with the Green Revolution were adapted to cropland under controlled irrigation—land owned primarily by rich commercial farmers in the West (Bose 1972: 69–93; Cleaver 1972: 181; Griffin and Khan 1972: 29).

One of the major grievances of East Pakistan was its substantial underrepresentation among the political elite, the bureaucracy, and the large bourgeoisie, even as late as the 1960s. In 1968, the representation of the East in the civil service of Pakistan was only 36 percent, comparable to its representation in other government services. Only in the last part of the 1960s were a few Bengalis appointed to posts as high as secretary in the central government. None, however, was secretary or minister in the crucial ministries of Defense, Home, and (except for a four-day portfolio) Finance. In the army, East Pakistanis constituted no more than 5 percent of the officers in 1963, a figure that did not change in a major way during the 1960s. While west Indian business communities, Memons, Khojas, and Bohras, which comprised only 0.5 percent of the Muslim population in Pakistan, accounted for 43 percent of industrial investment by Muslims, Bengalis, consisting of 50 percent of the Muslim population of the country, accounted for only 4 percent of industrial investment in Pakistan between 1947 and 1958 (Ayoob 1971: 202; Papanek 1962: 54).

In Pakistan, the Western governing elites utilized sentiments associated with subnational identities to transfer potential hostilities from class disparities within their own communities to differences with and antagonisms toward other ethnic groups and regions. Major political leaders pursued and implemented economic policies that served their economic advantage. These policies had the effect of increasing interregional discrepancies in Pakistan. The precipitant of the political conflict, the postponement of the Pakistan constituent assembly, was only the final step on the long road to secessionist civil war, in which the Republic of Bangladesh became independent in 1971.

The Pakistani economy, hurt by Bangladesh secession and subject to external shocks of increased oil prices and declining terms of trade, grew more slowly in the 1970s than in the 1950s and 1960s. Pakistan's related crises of a chronic balance on goods and services deficit, low savings rates, poor government budgetary performance, and slow agricultural growth compelled it to rely on IMF stabilization programs and World Bank adjustment loans during the 1980s. Under the economic reforms and inflows of emigrant worker remittances of the 1980s, economic growth recovered to rates characteristic of the period before 1970. Nevertheless, savings remained low, unemployment rose, and the balance of payments remained strained (Khan 1991: 435–39; McCleary 1991: 414–34).

Bangladesh

Although international trade as a percentage of GNP (12 percent) and net foreign direct investment (0) were low in 1989, Bangladesh, whose gross domestic savings rate was only 1 percent, is highly dependent on external technology and resources. Foreign loans and grants financed 92 percent of Bangladesh's capital formation, 65 percent of its imports, and 75 percent of its domestic development spending (most of infrastructure, health services, and family planning) in 1989 (World Bank 1991b: 204–8). Indeed, Bangladesh's suzerain changed from Britain to Pakistan (1947–71) to aid agencies and foreign companies after 1971 (with some dependence on neighboring India, especially in the early 1970s).

Since most large enterprises were foreign or West Pakistani at independence in 1971, Sheik Mujibur Rahman, president through 1975, nationalized most of the existing industrial sector. In addition, during the 1970s, multinational corporations from DCs (Philips in consumer durables, Imperial Tobacco in cigarette manufacturing, Lever Brothers in soap and detergents, British Oxygen in oxygen, and pharmaceutical companies), often jointly with the government, played a leading role in import-substitution industrialization. While most foreign trade is in Bengali hands, prices and earnings, especially for jute and jute goods, are determined by world prices.

For most of the period since independence in 1971, the majority of Bangladesh's investment, development budget, and commodity imports was financed by foreign aid. Incomes of the Bengali bourgeoisie were not linked to expanded local production but to expediting Bangladesh government access to external resources (through positions as commission agents or intermediaries for foreigners). Moreover, the state bureaucracy and political leadership have especially depended on foreign-aid-financed projects for power and patronage, including employment and contracts with suppliers and contractors, and a cushion for managerial inadequacies. Yet, in the final analysis, almost all classes—private capitalists, the rural poor, the major urban population, government employees, workers in public enterprises and large-scale industrial enterprises, school teachers, university students, and the armed forces—depend at least partly on aid (Sobhan 1983: 379–89).

In 1975–81, General Ziaur Rahman reoriented industry and commerce toward more dependence on the private sector. During the 1980s, with prodding by the World Bank, U.S. Agency for International Development, and other donors, an additional half of the country's 1975 public industrial assets were privatized (Humphrey 1990).

Country loan officers, especially for the World Bank, have been under intense pressure to meet country commitment targets for Bangladesh, the most populous least-developed country. Mosley, Harrigan, and Toye (1991: vol. 1, p. 72) report that, in the late 1980s, the Bank's Bangladesh division chief vetoed a unanimous recommendation by loan officers to curtail loans to Bangladesh, which they agreed lacked the capacity to absorb more funds. While the division chief supported the officers' analysis, he observed that if he supported slowing down lending to his director, "tomorrow you will have a new division chief." During the 1980s, the World Bank regional vice president for South Asia was under great internal pressure to lend, especially to Bangladesh.

Africa

In *The Debt Crisis in Africa* (Nafziger 1993), I show how that in the 1980s and early 1990s sub-Saharan Africa suffered from both government policies (exchange-rate, import-substitution, foreign-investment, tariff, pricing, and technology) and an unfavorable international economic environment (declining terms of trade, reduced aid and credit, and higher real interest rates) that worsened stagnation and international balance-of-payments deficits.

Many of the resources of African states were devoured by a small ruling elite of high-ranking politicians, military officers, and government administrators, managers of parastatal corporations, top professionals, and traditional authorities, as well as a few private capitalists. The public sector and its average real salaries grew steadily during the 1970s and the early 1980s, even when the growth of GNP was slow or negative.

But the crisis that struck Africa after 1973–74 was also partly linked to change in the world economy—that is, the abrupt end of a quarter-century of rapid post–World War II economic growth and the sharp reduction in Africa's commodity terms of trade and export-purchasing power. Since 1973, increased raw-materials prices, oil shocks, rise in real interest rates worldwide, cost–push inflationary wage increases, declining profit rates, reduced investment, DC exchange-rate instability, and attempts to control state spending contributed to slower growth and greater economic instability.

Africa's peripheral status in the international economy, meager economic base, and weak bourgeoisie have resulted in some built-in contradictions. Rapid expansion of output and savings undermines the hegemony of the existing political and bureaucratic elite. Yet slow growth (as in the 1980s and early 1990s), with greater ruling-class shares, threatens foreign capital, provides too few inducements for workers, or increases potential mass rebellion.

The small economic surplus, political expectations, and widespread poverty exerted revolutionary pressures. The nationalist movement before independence politicized the African masses. Nationalist leaders stressed self-determination and equality to unite against colonialism. Yet, now, the demands from the radical consciousness are directed at African rulers, who cannot meet expectations by maintaining existing productive relations. Since their stagnating economies give them little room for maneuvering, they resort to increased repression and violence to control the masses. But this increases tensions, and forces African elites to depend more on foreign economic and political support (Sklar 1979: 531–32).

By the mid-1970s, even most African countries had taken over mineral extraction, petroleum, banking, insurance, public utilities, and parts of manufacturing. But typically this control is a triangular relationship between MNCs, indigenous businesspeople and middlemen, and state officials, in which MNCs hire local citizens with privileged access to government officials as go-betweens with the state (Turner 1978: 166–97). The middleman may be a public servant or private-company employee who receives concessions, contracts, or retail outlets, or who collects bonuses, commissions, kickbacks, or bribes. In other instances, especially during stagnation, officials directly arranging joint ventures between MNCs and state enterprises may exclude the private middleman. African governments may create industrial monopolies, raise industrial relative to agricultural prices, or protect output through tariffs or quotas, providing rents for parastatal officials, political elites, middlemen, and MNCs, even with no commissions or kickbacks. Thus, in 1969, when Kenya gave Firestone a virtual monopoly of tire production for ten years, prominent Kenyans, including a former cabinet minister, were appointed managers, while the government received the right to choose distributors to share the profits (Bates 1981: 103). The World Bank (1975: 298) remarked that Kenya's protection of firms from competition was like a "license to print money." In a world economy characterized by multinational oligopolies, a national policy creating rents for middlemen, parastatals, and businesspeople in collusion with foreign capital does not create a capitalist class with the vigor of Meiji Japan or transform the country's position in the world economy.

Early Japanese and Contemporary LDC Capitalist Potentials

Before low-income states had to undertake Bank/Fund adjustment programs as a last resort in the 1980s and early 1990s, populist pressures prevented most of these states from pursuing low-wage policies, unrestricted labor rules, low welfare spending, and large subsidies used in nineteenth-century Japan. However, few of these countries have had the surplus to pursue these Meiji-type policies and reduce health, educational, and nutritional programs since 1980 without reducing the welfare of the poorest 30 to 40 percent of the population. Furthermore, few LDC societies have the Japanese nexus of community reciprocal obligation that can mitigate the destructive power of capitalist rivalries.

Yet the Meiji bourgeoisie, though weaker than that in Western Europe and the United States, was more experienced in large commercial ventures and not as far behind the DCs as are today's LDCs. The Japanese capitalist class was capable of responding to government policies to encourage private industrial ventures. Furthermore, Meiji's bureaucracy had the vision and skills to plan programs to abet private entrepreneurs.

The irony is that, while the weakness of today's bourgeoisie in developing countries indicates the need for stronger government intervention and planning skills to spur industrial entrepreneurship, investment, and technology, few LDC governments have the capabilities to facilitate these in the private sector, or to manage these in the public sector. Most civil services in contemporary LDCs lack the autonomy, expertise, freedom from politics, and commitment to economic development that late nineteenth-century Meiji bureaucrats had. And the effect of Bank/Fund post-1980 adjustment programs on the size of the government bureaucracy has reduced LDC state capabilities even further.

The Zaibatsu

In Meiji Japan, selling public-owned industrial properties to private entrepreneurs, often samurai closely associated with the government, reduced government losses as some inefficient enterprises were eliminated through bankruptcy. Many zaibatsu, or large industrial concentrations, originated as buyers of state-owned enterprises during the late 1870s or 1880s.

Those who became zaibatsu were dynamic Schumpeterian entrepreneurs—the first to introduce new goods and production methods (Schumpeter 1939, 1961). They grew stronger, especially after 1885, thriving by maintaining family wealth intact (through a unilineal system, where primogeniture, inheritance by the eldest son, kept family resources unbroken from one generation to another) (Mahajan 1976: 80; Yasuba and Dhiravegin 1985: 22), government concessions, growth consciousness, an urge to accumulate industrial assets, and a low conspicuous consumption rate. Each zaibatsu expanded beyond its initial base (textiles, coal mining, and so forth), eventually controlling a holding company dominating several operating companies. Since Japan lacked an organized capital market and public restraints on monopoly power, the zaibatsu controlled most banks in the late nineteenth century. Beginning in the 1890s, industrialists founded their own banks to raise capital; Mitsubishi and Sumitomo converted financial departments into banks in 1895. Without government favoritism, zaibatsu control of most banks, and conglomerative ability to take long-term investment risks, Japan might have avoided its high investment concentration.

After the 1905 victory in the Russo–Japanese War, the zaibatsu took the lead in promoting Japanese economic expansion overseas. The zaibatsu grew steadily during World War I and the postwar period. The great family combines, especially Mitsui and Mitsubishi, pyramided through intricate intercorporate, personal, and political ties into huge agglomerations of heterogeneous trading, banking, insurance, real estate, shipping, manufacturing, and colonial undertakings, increasingly extending indirect dominance over small-scale industries. Concentration, facilitated by close association with the military oligarchy and the civil bureaucracy, accelerated after post–World War I financial disorders like the 1920s' bank crises, when zaibatsu banks (especially Mitsui, Mitsubishi, Daiichi, Sumitomo, and Yasuda) swallowed up small and medium-sized banks. In 1937, the House of Mitsui had the most assets, ¥1,635 million (or $470 million), among the zaibatsu.

From 1920 to 1929, while aggregate bank deposits increased by one-fourth, the number of banks declined from 2,041 to 1,008. Financial power became increasingly centered in a few private (relatively free from government inspection and regulation) and semiofficial banks. The absence of a public capital market made banks the major external source of capital for firms. The zaibatsu eliminated many of their smaller bank and industrial competitors.

Small industry remaining had a symbiotic relationship to the zaibatsu as auxiliary producers (see chapter 7), while workers were rarely antagonistic to the paternalistic zaibatsu. Although the zaibatsu opposed government interference in labor relations, they often provided treatment potentially as good as under labor law. After World War I, large manufacturing companies consigned output of certain products or parts to subcontractors. Parent companies reduced costs by indirect use of cheap labor in subsidiaries, which were buffers against business fluctuations.

By the last decade of the nineteenth century through the first decade of the twentieth century, college-educated professional managers, mostly graduates of Keio University or (what became) Tokyo University, were replacing family members of the industrial pioneer as zaibatsu top managers. Management was professionalized, with hired executives (outside the family) rising step by step from a low position. The zaibatsu had the oligopolistic advantage for the outlays, risk bearing, and skill training to be innovative, setting up rayon factories in the 1920s that competed with the West. Yet from 1868 to World War I, the zaibatsu's only modest protection from international competition dampened even more monopolistic restraints. But after World War I, the strengthened zaibatsu increased state protection and weakened competition in numerous sectors (Hirschmeier and Yui 1975: 162–65; Lockwood 1954: 62; Mahajan 1976: 32–33; Minami 1986: 153–54; Schumpeter 1942: 87–106).

The Zaibatsu in the 1920s and 1930s

The zaibatsu, influential with the Diet and bureaucracy, relatively independent from central bank control, and opposed to the necessary deflationary policies, contributed to the 1920s' financial disorders. Indeed, the government and zaibatsu both generally shared support for cheap money and liberal lending through most of the post-1868 period. And financial crises concentrated zaibatsu economic control even further.

In the 1930s, the combines dominating heavy industry increased their preponderance, while being joined by newer zaibatsu (Nakajima and Nissan) producing munitions. The depression of 1930–31 spurred cartels, legally sanctioned under the Major Industries Control Law and Industrial Association Law of 1931. By 1935, the seventeen leading combines controlled companies comprising 18 percent of the paid-in capital of all Japanese corporations, while control in banking, insurance, and trust business was even greater. In 1946, before postwar occupation reforms, the four largest zaibatsu (Mitsui, Mitsubishi, Sumitomo, and Yasuda) owned one-fourth of paid-in capital of incorporated firms. The Japanese tax system, especially before 1920, was lenient toward large property incomes.

With its late-nineteenth-century advantages, the zaibatsu dominated industry and finance for fifty to sixty years. During the 1930s, the state lavished patronage on combines able to provide the capital, technical experience, and the national framework of banking, transport, and heavy industry needed for military strength. Many zaibatsu leaders, alarmed at Japanese militancy in the early 1930s, later played a leading role in the war effort.

The zaibatsu modernized technology, accumulated capital (through plowing back profits), and reaped large-scale economies for industrial development. By hampering independent economic initiative, the zaibatsu undermined the growth of a sturdy middle class, strong labor unions, and a democratic movement. In politics, the plutocratic alliance of the zaibatsu and the political parties contributed to the discrediting of parliamentary government after 1930.

While the zaibatsu were technically progressive, they weakened competition, continued the hierarchical and authoritarian control inimical to social democracy, and perpetuated inequalities of income and opportunity almost as great as under feudalism. The zaibatsu increased inequality not only between zaibatsu families and others, but also between wages and productivity of large enterprises vis-à-vis small firms and agriculture. These inequalities reduced the domestic market, putting pressure on Japan to invade other countries to create new markets. Moreover, increased inequality exacerbated dissatisfaction by farmers and workers in small enterprises who, together with low-ranking military officers, were at odds with the government and zaibatsu.

Japanese statesmen, during the seventy years before World War II, had little philosophy on the division of responsibility between public and private enterprise or on the competitiveness of private business. Public policy tended toward concentration, with business and government in close association. Japan followed the German pattern of state leadership in developing national productivity, close cooperation between the state and big business, intimate relationships between large-scale banking and industry, and self-regulation on all economic fronts except labor. Indeed, in 1938 the industrial control associations for Japan's ministries were commonly headed by a zaibatsu official (Lockwood 1954: 59–72, 214–35, 560–64; Minami 1986: 148–49).

The symbiotic relationship of the zaibatsu system with the state abetted the militarism and imperialism that brought about the devastation of the system and the state in World War II. As bankers, heavy industrialists, colonial processors, manufacturers of munitions, and exporters of silk and cotton goods, the zaibatsu stood to gain from any extension of Japanese power overseas (Beasley 1987: 39, 151–55). The zaibatsu system, while promoting growth, especially in industry, contributed to high industrial concentration, high income inequalities, and slow growth of a politically independent middle class. Japan's reforms under allied occupation established the foundation for increased income egalitarianism and (despite subsequent backtracking on antitrust policies) industrial concentration rates more comparable to those in the West.

The Zaibatsu and the Indian Managing Agency Compared

Both Japan's and British-controlled India's late nineteenth-century large enterprises were family combines. The managing agency, created by the British in the early nineteenth century, was the dominant organization for the joint-stock company in India, as the zaibatsu was the dominant corporate conglomerate in Japan.

In the managing agency system, which pervaded India's modern industry, trade, and agriculture, the administration, finance, and promotion of one or more legally separate companies were controlled by a single firm. The system's distinguishing feature was the contractual agreement between the managing agents and the board of directors of the operating company, in which the agents received commissions and fees for managing for a specified time, usually at least twenty years. In practice, the managing agency firm, which frequently controlled more than one operating enterprise, often in the same or related industry, was the basic decision-making unit.

The British established the system in India to facilitate their management and control, with business in the hands of "reputable agents." The managing agency put its holdings behind the firm. India's postindependence managing agency furthered control of the large, established industrial houses. Most agency members were relatives or members of the same caste. Generally, the managing agents and their friends comprised the board of directors of the operating company that contracted with the agency.

The major advantages of the managing agency system were large-scale economies in production, capital use, marketing, management, entrepreneurship, financial services, and vertical linkages. A small group of businesspeople could concentrate their capital in a new operating firm, arrange a contract between the firm and a managing agency, attract capital from other sources, and subsequently withdraw capital from the firm while retaining control through the managing agency firm and beginning the process again in a new operating firm.

In India, the post-1947 managing agency system helped industrial houses acquire control of other businesses, operate several enterprises in one industry, and increase the concentration of wealth in a few families. Moreover, the system hampered new indigenous managerial skills requiring "learning by doing." Economic concentration continued after the system's abolition in 1970, as industrial houses continued control of their empires through ties between family members who held management and ownership interest in the various enterprises. In fact, the separate companies frequently were controlled by one or two principals in the family who, for tax purposes or to avoid government antimonopoly measures, dispersed the ownership of enterprises in the names of other family members. Large business houses, because of their resources, organization, and skill, were more likely to receive licenses to establish enterprises or acquire materials, and could better take advantage of government schemes encouraging small industry and geographical diversification. Frequently, large houses owned a series of "small-scale" industrial enterprises, which under other arrangements would be described as branches of a large-scale firm in a major industrial city (Brimmer 1955: 554–61; Kling 1966: 37–38; Lockwood 1954: 59–60; Mahajan 1976: 29–31; Minami 1986: 148–49; Nafziger 1978: 51–53, 73–74; Rungta 1970: 223–55; Singh 1963: 57–73).

While the Japanese zaibatsu and the Indian managing systems may have initially encouraged entrepreneurship, their subsequent association with high industrial concentration probably discouraged competitive entrepreneurial activity. Moreover, the state in India and other parts of Asia and Africa had less success than the pre-1939 Japanese state in encouraging auxiliary and small-scale enterprises. Low-income countries, often dependent on foreign enterprise, have high rates of industrial concentration. For example, the industrial concentration rates of Nigeria, with greater industrial diversity than most other African countries, are twenty times those of the United States (Nafziger 1977: 57–65). So, while the Japanese government initiative in furthering private enterprise in the late nineteenth century speeded industrialization, it also gave rise to industrial concentration that few LDCs today have been able to control. Indeed, Japanese monopolistic power was only undermined during the period of crisis right after the devastating military defeat of World War II.

Summary

Most Japanese high rates of household savings maintained family wealth for many years. Samurai pensions, state obligations to financiers and supporters of the Meiji coup, state sales of model factories and mines, and state–business symbiosis, together with mercantile success from the feudal period, provided a start for new wealth under capitalism. Moreover, the state's assistance of merchant, landlord, and samurai entrepreneurs helped create the zaibatsu that dominated the economy through World War II.

In Japan, as in India, large family ventures mobilized substantial capital and unified decision making but discouraged risk, delegated authority, and secondary labor relations. Yet Meiji Japan's capitalists were more experienced in large commercial activity and not as technologically backward relative to DCs as are LDCs today.

Asian and African capitalism was hampered by colonialism, informal imperialism, and postcolonial dependence on international capitalism. In the 1980s, except for highly populated countries such as China, India, and Indonesia, most low-income countries increased their dependence on international agencies (such as the International Monetary Fund and World Bank), OECD countries, and DC commercial banks.

The cases of India and Pakistan indicate how difficult it is for contemporary LDCs to extricate themselves from a peripheral position within the global economy. To be sure, both India and Pakistan have moved from a colonial division of labor of primary-product exports and manufacturing imports to contemporary specialization in manufacturing exports and primary-commodity imports. In 1990, 72 percent of India's exports and 70 percent of Pakistan's exports were manufactures, while only 37 percent of India's imports and 44 percent of Pakistan's were food, raw materials, fuels, and other primary products (World Bank 1992b: 246–49). But the cost of the domestic industrial protection and distortion essential to achieve this transformation was substantial. In fact, tariffs, subsidies, exchange controls, and quantitative restrictions have sometimes conferred such monopoly power on protected domestic manufacturers that they subtract value from raw materials and purchased inputs! In India in the 1960s, the automobile industry had an effective rate of protection (i.e., protection as a percentage of value added by production factors at a processing stage) of 2,612 percent (Bhagwati and Desai 1970: 335–67); indeed, the foreign-exchange cost of importing an automobile was lower than the foreign-exchange cost of inputs used in producing a domestic automobile! India acquired few technical learning gains from protection, which instead supported technological sloth. Moreover, the high rates of protection discriminated against exports. Thus, few contemporary low- and lower-middle-income countries have shifted away much from their peripheral position in the international economy.

Meiji Japan became integrated within a competitive global economy while increasing its economic autonomy. Japan acquired its industrial and agricultural arts from abroad, first imitating, then modifying, then innovating, improving technology step by step. Chapter 8 demonstrates how Japan used liberal trade and market-clearing exchange rates, together with decision-making autonomy, to become the first non-Western country to graduate to a highly developed economy.

Notes

1. The samurai, who were prevalent in the Meiji bureaucracy, declined during Taisho (1912–26) and early Showa (1926–39), when graduates of the law division of Tokyo Imperial University, from a wider background, dominated (Jansen 1975: 319).

2. Lewis (1954: 139–91) also suggests a comparable rate.

3. In contrast, independent Siam, which in 1868 faced initial conditions somewhat comparable to Japan, did not establish government factories or provide assistance to private industrial entrepreneurs in the latter part of the nineteenth century (Yasuba and Dhiravegin 1985: 25–26; see also Lockwood 1954: 248; and Selden 1983: 62–88).

4. J.T. Banerjee is a pseudonym I use for the entrepreneur that I interviewed July 19, 1993; likewise, TRP Software is not the real name of Mr. Banerjee's firm.

5. I interviewed the principal of the marble products enterprise July 26, 1993.

Chapter 5

Transfer of Agricultural Surplus

Economic historians differ on the relationships between agriculture and industry in the development process, and on the timing of initial sustained growth in both sectors. As in England, where an agricultural revolution preceded the industrial revolution, in Japan late Tokugawa agricultural growth (despite the substantial output share cultivators paid to the shogun) preceded the beginning of the early industrialization spurt of the 1880s. Agricultural growth accelerated through the Meiji period before slowing down in the 1910s. During Meiji, agriculture contributed to rapid industrialization (Minami 1986).

This chapter looks at how capital, labor, and food from agriculture helped industry. I compare early Meiji Japan with contemporary LDCs; as table 5.1 indicates, their labor-force and output shares in agriculture and industry are roughly comparable.

A major concern for newly industrializing countries is the source for early industrial investment. Many economists advocate heavy reliance on a surplus in agriculture, often an LDC's largest sector. Before 1928, agriculture contributed more to net domestic product (NDP) than any other sector (Ohkawa and Shinohara 1979: 34–40). Agricultural surplus refers to an excess of savings over investment in agriculture, an amount transferred to nonagriculture (or industry). This transfer includes both private savings and taxes.

Transfer during the Tokugawa Period

Farm villages at the end of the Tokugawa period participated in a commodity economy. As indicated in chapter 4, during the late Tokugawa period, 20 to 25 percent of the farmers managed second businesses. Landlords, a part of lower Tokugawa provincial administration, were involved in trade, manufacturing, processing, and moneylending. Since landownership provided less financial security

Table 5.1

Japan in 1887 and Eleven Lower-Middle-Income and Low-Income Countries in the 1980s

	Distribution of gross domestic product (1987)(percent)		
	Agriculture	Industry	Service
Japan (1887)	41	20	39
Bangladesh	47	13	39
China	31	49	20
Egypt	21	25	54
Ethiopia	42	18	40
India	30	30	40
Indonesia	26	33	41
Kenya	31	19	50
Nigeria	30	43	27
Pakistan	23	28	49
Philippines	24	33	43
Sri Lanka	27	27	46
Tanzania	61	8	31
Average for 12 countries	33	27	40
Weighted average for all LDCs	27	37	36

	Distribution of the labor force (1980)(percent)		
	Agriculture	Industry	Service
Japan (1887)	73	13	14
Bangladesh	75	6	19
China	74	14	12
Egypt	46	20	34
Ethiopia	80	8	12
India	70	13	17
Indonesia	57	13	30
Kenya	81	7	12
Nigeria	68	12	20
Pakistan	55	16	30
Philippines	52	16	33
Sri Lanka	53	14	33
Tanzania	86	5	10
Average for 12 countries	66	12	22
Weighted average for all LDCs	62	16	22

Sources: For Japan, Ohkawa and Rosovsky (1973: 10). For other countries, distribution of gross domestic product (1987) from World Bank (1989b: 168–69), and distribution of the labor force (1980) from World Bank (1988: 282–83).

Note: Agriculture includes forestry and fisheries, and industry manufacturing, mining, public utilities, and construction.

in feudal Japan than in other societies, Japanese land holders had a higher preference for industrial investment than LDCs generally. Additionally, many merchants became landlords (Lockwood 1954: 295–96; Nakamura 1983: 51).

Land and Tax Reforms during the Early
Meiji Period

A reform to transfer land from feudal control was a precondition for modernization. During government centralization just after 1868, the bureaucracy (not landed classes) controlled policy. Bureaucrats had no interest in protecting agriculture at the cost of industrial growth. Thus, the Meiji, at a cost of more than ¥200 million (1873–76), pensioned about 400,000 landed gentry (daimyo) who had politically controlled large fiefs, giving many a fresh start as bankers, traders, or industrialists, but replacing them on the farm with smaller, capitalist village landlords who had purchased their land. While the gentry remained wealthy, they lost their land and their political power. The pressures on these feudal gentry are reminiscent of those experienced by English yeomen in the seventeenth and eighteenth centuries who were dispossessed by the enclosure movement and the disappearance of common rights. The new village landlords, on the other hand, who were often farmers during the early Meiji period, improved productive methods, employed labor to improve land and construct buildings, and maintained and improved farm irrigation and drainage systems built during the Tokugawa period.

The Meiji civil service imposed a land tax reform from 1873 to 1881 to squeeze investment capital from agriculture, partly through a moderate inflation that redistributed resources to state and private industrial ventures. This reform stabilized Meiji finances by reducing fluctuations from harvest (as new taxes were based on land value not yield), eliminating regional tax variations, and receiving payment in cash rather than in kind (rice). Land tax as a percentage of total government revenue increased from 22 percent in 1868–71 to 70 percent in 1872–75, reaching a peak in 1873 when the tax accounted for 94 percent of central revenue and appropriated one-third of the crop—nearly as much as the feudal lord appropriated before 1868. After the reform, farmers had to enter the money economy, and land became an object for investment and sale, resulting in steadily increasing tenancy and landownership concentration rates through the early 1930s, when rates jumped sharply.

The 1873–81 land reform was more conducive to concentration, investment, and growth than was a peasant smallholding system, since village landlords were frequently innovative and interested in improving tenants' production methods. Also, since a small number of landlords controlled the surplus, they could be taxed more effectively than many small peasants.

The land tax provided more than 80 percent of government revenue between 1873 and 1882, and contributed to continuing, though declining, net resource outflows from agriculture to government through 1922. Since the monetary amount of the tax was fixed annually, its real value fell with inflation. This tax had little or no effect on middle-aged and elderly farm labor and farm output, both of which had low short-run elasticities of supply and low opportunity costs.

The landowner, unable to shift the tax forward to farm-good middlemen or consumers, could only shift the tax incidence to a tenant, who rarely had alternative employment opportunities (although the sons and daughters of the increasingly precarious tenants filled the ranks of the growing industrial work force). The system whereby noncultivating landlords took a high proportion of products—well established by the end of Tokugawa—continued during Meiji. Both tenants and smallholders experienced hardships during poor harvest or low farm prices.[1] Many peasants continued the feudal cliental relationship to large landowners, who also served as moneylenders. The high and regressive land taxes required in cash, the growing burden of other taxes from 1890 to 1910, and the high rents reduced farm disposable income and consumption, especially among tenants and peasants, the last of whom faced heavy debts, frequent bankruptcies and foreclosures, and abject poverty. Yet government used only a small fraction of agricultural tax revenue for farm investment. Marxist economist Paul A. Baran (1957: 155) considered the Meiji Japanese village an internal colony, providing capital to the industrial sector. For Selden, "the Meiji state presided over a 'revolution from above' which opened the way to the formation of industrial capital while crushing the challenges from below in the form of peasant rebellion" (1983: 61; also see Hirschmeier and Yui 1975: 83).

Just before World War II, nearly two-thirds of Japanese cultivators were tenants. Yet the average noncultivating landlord held only 18.5 hectares. After the war, the Allied Occupational Authority responded to the demands of an impoverished peasantry, promulgating land reform, taking land from nonworking landlords, limiting owners to about six hectares, and giving land to former tenants; these measures increased agricultural productivity (Allen 1982: 71–72; Baran 1957: 155; Dore 1965b: 487–93; Hayami 1975: 48; Lockwood 1954: 98–99, 246, 267–68; Minami 1986: 16–17; Mody, Mundle, and Raj 1985: 272–73; Nakamura 1983: 50–56; Ohkawa and Rosovsky 1973: 10–11, 228–50; Ohkawa, Shimizu, and Takamatsu 1982: 10; Okita 1980: 7–11).

Net Capital Flows from Agriculture to Industry

From 1888 to 1937, the significant private surplus flows from agriculture to industry were concentrated during 1903–22, when cultivator-landlords were being replaced by absentee landlords who used tenant rents to accumulate capital for industries such as brewing, pawnbroking, retail shops, and village moneylending. Moreover, silk and cotton textiles attracted small-scale investment from landowners and other rural interests, as well as urban traders. But the amount of net capital private flows to industry is uncertain, since price indices to estimate the effect of changing terms of trade on net resource flows from agriculture and figures on private inflows to agriculture are not reliable (Francks 1992: 37; Ishikawa 1982: 264; Ohkawa, Shimizu, and Takamatsu 1982: 11–12).[2]

Urban Bias Policies

Meiji bureaucrats emphasized industrial versus agricultural growth, an industrial or urban bias. But as chapter 2 pointed out, agriculture was not neglected: the state was active in farm research, disseminating improved techniques to farmers. Moreover, while the land tax reduced farm income, it had little adverse effect in distorting output and price incentives.

In twentieth-century Africa, on the other hand, colonial policy toward agriculture was exacerbated by independent Africa's neglect of agriculture. This was partly due to the state leaders' political gains from market intervention to improve prices and the incomes that urban classes receive relative to farmers. African states, especially before 1980, kept farm prices far below market prices, dampened farm producer incentives, used marketing boards to transfer peasant savings to large industry, and set exchange rates that discouraged exports and encouraged import substitutes. Cleaver (1985) shows that the real exchange-rate change (domestic inflation divided by foreign inflation times the percentage change in the foreign-exchange price of domestic currency) from 1970 to 1981 was negatively related to agricultural (and overall) growth rates. Kenya and Lesotho, whose farm exports remained competitive as the real value of their currency depreciated, grew faster than Ghana and Tanzania, whose real domestic currency value appreciated (World Bank 1981). These state interventions in the price system hurt farmers, increasing industry–agricultural income differentials.

Improved rural social services, greater price incentives, effective farm cooperatives, and public spending on research, credit, rural industry, extension services, irrigation, and transport are frequently political rather than technical issues. The political survival of state leaders in fragile sub-Saharan countries has required that they marshal the support of urban elites (civil servants, private and state corporate employees, businesspeople, professionals, and skilled workers) through economic policies that sacrifice income distribution and agricultural growth. Moreover, most African countries lacked the political and administrative capability, especially in rural areas, to undertake programs to reduce poverty. Established interests—large farmers, moneylenders, and the urban classes—have frequently opposed the policy changes and spending that would be essential to improve the economic welfare of the small farmer, tenant, and landless workers.

Further, state market intervention has been an instrument of political control and assistance. Government, quasi-government corporations, and private business have pressured political elites for cheap food policies to keep down wages, and governments sometimes use troops to quell food-related riots. Unrest by urban workers over the erosion of their purchasing power has threatened Nigeria, Ghana, Kenya, and a number of other African governments. Real wage declines under Nigeria's Abubakar Tafewa Balewa government in 1964 and the Yakubu Gowon government in 1974–75, as well as Ghana's Kofi Busia government in 1971, contributed to political unrest and violence which precipitated military coups. Politicians also have helped emerging industry reduce raw material or processing costs. Market intervention provided political control for elites to use in retaining power, building support, and implementing policies.

In 1954 in Ghana, Kwame Nkrumah's Convention People's Party (CPP) passed a bill freezing cocoa producer prices for four years, anticipating using increased revenues for industry. But the CPP government undercut the newly formed opposition party in the cocoa-growing regions by selectively providing subsidized inputs (loans, seeds, fertilizer, and implements) for prospective dissidents. In addition, state farm programs in each constituency in the 1960s made public resources available to organize support for the Nkrumah government.

Market-clearing farm prices and exchange rates, whose benefits are distributed indiscriminately, eroded urban political support and secured little support from the countryside. In comparison, project-based policies allowed benefits to be selectively apportioned for maximum political advantage. Government made it in the interest of numerous individuals to cooperate with programs that harmed the interest of producers as a whole (Bates 1981; Nafziger 1988: 140–56; Rimmer 1984).

Rural dwellers, who often were politically weak and feared government reprisals, rarely organized to oppose antirural policies. While poor farmers had little tactical power, rich ones had too much to lose from protest. Moreover, the latter had less-costly options—selling in black markets, shifting resources to other communities, or migrating to urban areas.

Farmers are less prone to undertake collective action to raise prices. Generally, farm producers are numerous and scattered, so the organizing costs are high and a single unit gets few benefits. Thus, rural classes that were harmed by state market intervention rarely mobilized to oppose the urban and large-farm bias of many contemporary African political leaders.

Low-income countries undertaking Bank/Fund adjustment and stabilization programs since 1980 have reduced urban bias but at the cost of other objectives, such as wages, employment, nutrition, and income distribution.

Technical Progress in Agriculture

Japan's agricultural output (in wheat units) per hectare of agricultural land from 1878 to 1882 was 2.9, the same as that in Sri Lanka, and more than the Philippines' 1.9 and India's 1.1 in 1957–62. Even Japan's agricultural output (in wheat units) per worker from 1878 to 1882, 2.5, was higher than Pakistan's 2.4 and India's 2.1, although it was lower than the Philippines' 3.8 and Sri Lanka's 3.9 in 1957–62 (Hayami 1975: 8).

Japan's agricultural technological progress was fast, contributing to rapid annual percentage growths of 1.8 percent in agricultural gross value-added and 2.0 percent in farm productivity per worker from 1880 to 1920, which facilitated considerable surplus transfer to industry.[3] In contrast, the farm surplus in many low-income countries is too small and growing too slowly for industry to exploit it without severe human costs. Because the colonial power in Nigeria discouraged industry, Nigeria's agricultural transfer during the colonial period was small. Indeed, in 1965–66, soon after independence in 1960, 56.2 percent of Nigeria's GNP still originated in the agricultural, forestry, and fisheries sector— a share larger than Meiji Japan's 41.4 percent in 1887—and only 12.4 percent of GNP was contributed by manufacturing, mining, and public utilities—a share smaller than Japan's 13.6 percent in 1887 (International Development Center of Japan 1977b: 192–94).

Shigeru Ishikawa (1981: 184) points out that technical progress contributing more than half the growth of output in agriculture is an essential aspect of its contribution to Japan's pre–World War I industrial development. When this progress is slow, agriculture reduces the products supplied to the industrial sector and (at a given price) industry needs more resources supplied to agriculture. In Japan, the colonial production of food and raw materials helped increase the rate of technological progress by enabling Japan to become even more specialized in its domestic agriculture, thus increasing its rate of technical change.

Part of the problem of LDCs (especially in Africa) is the lack of research and development to improve technology for small farmers, who lack effective demand and political power. The concentration of the world's expenditures on agricultural research and technology in DCs contributes to their greater agricultural labor productivity. This greater productivity, particularly in Japan, has little to do with superior resource endowment (Ruttan 1972). To be sure, some agricultural innovations used in DCs can be adapted to LDCs, but these innovations must be adapted carefully. Usually LDCs need their own agricultural research, since their ecological zones are different from the DCs.

One reason why Africa lagged behind in agricultural research in the 1970s is that the benefits of research and new technology tend to be lost with urban-biased pricing policies. Technological development is more efficient when farm input and output prices are competitive. Researchers and extension agents are more likely to innovate when farm prices clear the market than when they are controlled. And farmers tend to press research institutions for technological innovations with a high payoff—for example, those that save resources with an inelastic supply (Hayami and Ruttan 1971: 56–59; Zuvekas 1979: 233–34).

Food Output Productivity and Growth

Paddy rice yields in 1878–82 Japan, 2.53 tons per hectare, were higher than post–World War II yields in Asia. According to FAO, these yields were 1.36 in India, 1.38 in Thailand, 1.74 in Indonesia, and 2.24 in Malaysia, 1953–62 (Hayami and Yamada 1969: 108).

As capital per worker and technology increased, Japan's food output per capita increased from 100 in 1875–79, to 122 in 1905–9, to 146 in 1915–19, to

151 in 1925–29, to 154 in 1935–39, while population pressure per hectare rose. Lockwood (1954: 86–87, 433) indicates that in 1938, Japan was at a midposition in food consumption per capita between countries such as India, "where productive effort had to be devoted largely to supplying the minimum essentials of life," and countries such as the United States, whose productive capacity supplied a wide margin above such essentials.

In comparison, in Asia and Africa, food output per capita increased from 100 in 1950–54, to 111 in 1958–62, to 120 in 1982–86. The growth rate in food output per capita in developing East Asia (China, Taiwan, Hong Kong, South Korea, North Korea, and Mongolia) is almost as high as Japan's growth from 1875–79 to 1925–29, and the growth rates of Latin America, South Asia, and Southeast Asia are about two-thirds as high, as these world regions benefited from capital deepening and technical change. This section concentrates on the world region whose average food output growth is lowest—sub-Saharan Africa, where food production per capita rose from 100 in 1950–54 to 101 in 1958–62 before plunging to 87 in 1982–86 and 83 in 1987–89 (FAO 1991: 167–69; U.S. Department of Agriculture 1986a, 1986b, 1988).

Africa's daily calorie consumption per capita—2,115 in the early 1960s and 2,197 in the mid-1970s—was 20 percent below the Economic Commission for Africa's (ECA's) critical minimum (set high compared with DCs because a predominantly manual work force requires more average calories). Only the 1983 daily consumption of Côte d'Ivoire, the Congo, Liberia, Senegal, and Madagascar was no less than the minimum required, according to the World Bank. Ironically, the World Bank's Berg report (1981)[4] emphasizes the marked contrast between Africa and India and Pakistan, where expanded irrigated land used new high-yielding varieties of seeds in the Green Revolution.

Illustrative of the enormity of the difference between sub-Saharan Africa and India is that, while the sub-Sahara and India both produced 50 million tons of food grains in 1960, in 1988 India produced 150 million tons (after the Green Revolution and other technological farm improvements), and sub-Saharan Africa (with faster population growth) was still stuck at little more than 50 million tons. India's yield per hectare increased by 2.4 percent yearly, while the sub-Sahara's grew at a negligible annual rate of 0.1 percent. Thus, the sub-Sahara, which was at parity with India in 1960, produced only about one-third of Indian output in 1988.

Africa's average daily calorie consumption was still below Japan's largely vegetarian, low-calorie, low-fat diet of 2,300 calorie consumption from 1926 to 1936, and of 2,270 in 1968. Although the Japanese were well nourished, the highly egalitarian distribution of food in 1968 meant they only consumed about the same calories per person as the world (Economic Commission for Africa 1983b: 9; Gavan and Dixon 1975: 49–57; Lockwood 1954: 146–48, 386, 433; Singer 1990: 178–81; World Bank 1981: 47, 1986: 88–94).

Among the lessons that Africa and Asia can learn from Meiji Japan are its emphases on self-directed technological development, learning by doing, adapting technology, and maintaining prices and exchange rates conducive to farm innovations. By spurring agricultural growth, a rapid growth in farm technology contributes to reducing food prices for industry, releasing labor for urban areas, expanding the markets for industrial goods, accumulating foreign exchange, and transferring capital to the nonagriculture sector (Johnston and Mellor 1961: 571–81). However, few LDCs today can enhance domestic agricultural specialization (and productivity) by relying on colonies or economic satellites for foodstuffs and raw materials, as Japan did.

Transfer from Colonies

For Meiji and early twentieth-century Japan, part of the intersectoral resource transfer from agriculture to industry was from colonies. One colony, Taiwan, was annexed after the 1894–95 peace settlement with China. Another, Korea, was acquired in the 1904–1905 war against Russia and was made a colony in 1910. During 1911–40, Taiwan's net resource outflow from agriculture equaled its balance-of-trade surplus (with exports predominantly agricultural) with metropolitan Japan, which received a net capital inflow. Japanese investors in the colonies (for example, sugar growers in Taiwan) acquired prime farm land for producing food exports to Japan. Cheap rice imports from Taiwan and Korea, sugar imports from Taiwan, and soybean and millet imports from Manchuria kept Japanese food prices low, keeping industrial real wages low (at least until after World War I) and increasing industrial profits until World War I (see below). Indeed, during the 1930s Japan tried to create a "Co-prosperity Sphere," consisting of Korea, Taiwan, Manchuria, and a subservient China, in which Japan would have access to privileged markets and assured raw materials (Hayami and Ruttan 1964: 218–21; Lee 1971: 92; Lockwood 1954: 526).

Clearly, few low-income countries today benefit from a Japanese-type imperial transfer. Indeed, most of these countries, especially those in the sub-Sahara, still suffer from an adverse colonial legacy and a peripheral position in the global economy.

The Colonial Roots

Sub-Saharan Africa's deteriorating food position began before the droughts in the Sahel, the Sudan, and Ethiopia in 1968–74 and 1984–85. Indeed, the roots of Africa's food crisis can be traced back to colonialism.

Colonial policy contributed to Africa's agricultural underdevelopment in several ways. First, Africans were excluded from participating in colonial development schemes, producing export crops, and improving cattle. British agricultural policy in Eastern Africa benefited European settlers and ignored African farmers; in Kenya, this meant prohibiting Africans from growing coffee until 1933. Second, colonial governments compelled farmers to grow selected crops and maintain roads. Third, colonialism often changed traditional land tenure systems from communal to individual control, creating greater inequalities from new classes of affluent farmers and ranchers, and less secure tenants, sharecroppers, and landless workers. Fourth, colonialists failed to train African agricultural scientists and managers. Fifth, research and development concentrated on export crops, plantations, and land settlement schemes, neglecting food production and small farmers and herders. And finally, Europeans reaped most of the gains from colonial land grants and export surpluses from agriculture (Eicher and Baker 1982: 20–23; Ghai and Radwan 1983: 16–21).[5] Formerly colonized Asia faced similar problems to those of Africa, although Asia's agricultural underdevelopment has been generally less severe than Africa's in the decades since 1960.

In contrast, the colonial powers did not intervene in Japan's agricultural policies. Instead, in the late nineteenth century, Meiji Japan borrowed food-crop technology overseas and improved farm techniques step by step. Subsequently, in the twentieth century, as population and per-capita food demand expanded (especially with the expansion of industrial labor force shares between the 1894–95 Sino–Japanese War and World War I), Japan relied heavily on food imports from its colonies; this strategy is not available to today's LDCs.

Meiji Japan Compared: The Soviet Union and Developing Countries

Meiji Japan, like the Soviet Union in the 1930s, accumulated industrial capital by squeezing it from agriculture. Japan has probably relied more on using agricultural savings for initial industrial capital than any other presently industrialized country, with the possible exception of the Soviet Union, where the collectivization of 1929–33 involved forcible collection of grain, confiscation of farm property, destruction of tools and livestock, class warfare between peasants and prosperous kulaks, administrative disorder, disruption of sowing and harvest, and an accompanying famine that led to the deaths of about five million people. Japan in 1868, like Europe and North America previously and Russia in the early twentieth century, and unlike many low-income countries today, enjoyed an agricultural surplus that provided resources to transfer to industry.

Near the end of the nineteenth century, the primary (mostly agricultural) sector comprised more than two-thirds of the labor force in both Japan and India, apparently not much below the share of a half-century earlier, whereas the share had fallen below one-half in the United States as early as 1850. During the next century, the share of agriculture in the U.S. labor force declined sharply and continually, falling to below 25 percent in the 1930s and below 5 percent by 1975. The decline in Japan was slower, with the share of agriculture falling from one-half in 1939 to one-eighth by 1975. In India, in contrast, agriculture continued to employ more than two-thirds of the labor force throughout the period 1939–75, and its share in national income remained near one-half until the

1960s. Factory employment accounted for less than 1 percent of the Indian population even as late as 1975 (up only slightly since 1950), compared with 12 percent in Japan and 9 percent in the United States (Goldsmith 1983: 6–17).

Both Japan and the Soviet Union grew rapidly despite the slow reduction of their labor-force shares in agriculture. In 1887, agriculture, forestry, fishing, and mining comprised 73 percent of Japan's labor force, but only 41 percent of national income (see table 5.1); by 1936, the agricultural sector accounted for 51 percent of the labor force, but no more than 20 percent of income. In the Soviet Union, agriculture's share of national income fell from 49 percent in 1928 to 31 percent in 1937, while industry's share increased from 28 percent to 45 percent and labor-force shares changed little. Economic planners in today's LDCs should bear in mind Japan's and the Soviet Union's apparent inability, despite dramatic industrialization, to take people off the farm in large numbers (Gregory and Stuart 1986: 119; Lockwood 1954: 103–4).

Other countries may find it politically difficult to extract agricultural surplus through land taxes. In England, unlike Japan, the landed aristocracy maintained political influence until an advanced stage of industrial development. Likewise, landlords in many contemporary Latin American countries are too powerful for the state to capture a farm surplus. The productivity per hectare of low-income Asian and African countries today is lower than that of Japan in 1873 (Nakamura 1983). Few of these countries have enough agrarian surplus and political tolerance to allow the squeezing of agriculture in excess of the substantial agriculture–industry transfers already being made.

Extracting Farm Surplus as a Policy for LDCs

Japan's extraction of surplus from agriculture through taxes may not be relevant for today's LDCs: a thriving agriculture is needed to produce adequate food and raw materials for other sectors. Should we not discourage the following policies LDCs frequently have used (especially before 1980) to transfer a large share of agricultural surplus to industry: (1) food price ceilings and industrial price floors to raise industrial prices relative to farm prices; (2) concentration of government investment in industry; (3) tax incentives and subsidies to pioneering firms in industry but not agriculture; (4) setting below-market prices for foreign currency, reducing domestic currency receipts from agricultural exports while lowering the price of capital goods and other foreign inputs to large industrial establishments; (5) tariff and quota protection for industry, raising its prices to farmers; and (6) spending more for education, training, housing, plumbing, nutrition, medical care, and transport in urban areas than in rural areas. These policies of urban bias have contributed to farm production disincentives and high rates of rural poverty and undernourishment in low-income countries (Lipton 1977; Nafziger 1990a: 131–62).

These disincentives in many contemporary LDCs (at least before the World Bank/IMF-imposed adjustments and price reforms favoring agriculture after 1979) have been perhaps as great as those that threatened widespread rural rebellion in Meiji Japan. Rural poverty and undernourishment rates have probably been no less and rates of surplus no more than those in Meiji Japan. Moreover, rural populist pressures in many contemporary LDCs have been greater and more politically destabilizing than peasant pressures in the 1870s' Meiji Japan. Most LDCs cannot exploit the small surplus available without incurring severe political costs.

Pakistan in the late 1950s, 1960s, and early 1970s transferred resources from agriculture to cut into subsistence more than in Meiji Japan. A below-market foreign-exchange price coupled with industrial price guarantees resulted in the transfer of about 70 percent of savings in agriculture and over 24 percent of its gross product to the nonagricultural sector in 1964 and 1965—a transfer largely from poor to rich, and from East to West Pakistan. This transfer exacerbated the East Bengali peasant discontent that contributed to the Bangladesh secession (Griffin and Khan 1972: 26, 30, 134–36; Nafziger 1983: 197–209). Few low-income Asian countries have the rural political stability sufficient to squeeze agriculture in excess of surplus transfers already being made.

In fact, some, like democratic India, faced with fast population growth, low agricultural incomes and savings, and potential farmer discontent, have no income tax on agriculture, and a net resource inflow to agriculture since independence in 1947 (Mody, Mundle, and Raj 1985: 283–91).

Summary

This chapter has examined how capital from agriculture helped industry. Because of agriculture's dominance in LDCs, many support the use of farm surplus for industrial capital. During a comparable period, Japan relied on land tax, feudal lord pensions, landlord savings and industrial activity, and colonial farm transfer. With no colonies or satellites to provide stable food supplies, however, most contemporary low-income countries have too little political latitude to squeeze agriculture more than the resource transfers already being made.

Notes

1. Mitsuru (1982: 145–63), on the Tokugawa period, and Hane (1982), on Meiji, discuss peasant uprisings.

2. Teranishi (1976) estimates savings surplus of agriculture as percentage of aggregate savings of agriculture as 0.8 percent in 1899–1902, 8.2 percent in 1903–7, 2.3 percent in 1908–12, 17.9 percent in 1913–17, 31.6 percent in 1918–22, 4.6 percent in 1923–27, and –2.7% in 1928–33. Mody, Mundle, and Raj (1985: 270–76) provide estimates of trade and savings surpluses by sector.

3. Calculations are from five-year moving averages from Ohkawa and Shinohara (1979: 86) and Hayami (1975: 228).

4. This report is sometimes named for its coordinator, Elliot Berg.

5. Nafziger (1993: 41–44) discusses ecological and climatic factors in present-day sub-Saharan Africa's low food productivity.

Chapter 6

Low Industrial Wages

While Meiji Japan lacked abundant resources, labor abundance contributed to industrialization, especially labor-intensive export manufactures, through low wage rates and high industrial profit rates. From 1868 to 1915, agricultural unskilled *real* wages remained at a subsistence level. The Lewis model (along with the Fei–Ranis model) tries to explain industrial (urban) wages as dependent on agricultural (rural) wages and rural-urban migration (Fei and Ranis 1964; Lewis 1954: 139–91; Tachi and Okazaki 1965: 497–515).

The Lewis Model

In contrast to those economists who since the early 1970s have been bothered about overurbanization, W. Arthur Lewis, writing in 1954, was concerned about avoiding possible labor shortages in the expanding industrial sector, which was also a focus in Meiji Japan. Lewis explains LDC industrial employment through the migration of people to urban areas when urban wages exceed rural wages, which stay at a subsistence level through the classical mechanism of the iron law of wages.

For Lewis, initially the economy consists primarily of a subsistence rural sector, with no reproducible capital. Growth takes place as a result of structural change. The modern urban sector expands by using surplus labor from the subsistence sector at little cost to create capital, a source of increased profits, reinvestment, and increased productivity (Lewis 1954: 139–91, summarized in Nafziger 1990a: 221–23).

Japan's Development from a Lewis–Fei–Ranis Perspective

Unlike the Lewis–Fei–Ranis models (which we shall refer to as LFR), the marginal revenue product of labor in agriculture was positive, though less than the wage, through the 1930s (Minami 1973: 200), since the village supplied subsistence to those with a marginal revenue product below the wage (closer to average productivity than marginal productivity). As in LFR, employers in the formal industrial sector paid a premium (about 30 percent more than the agricultural wage) to compensate for the migration costs, the psychological costs of city life, and the like. This premium remained low because of the large number of landless workers who could not lease land under the land reforms after 1873, and because much of industry's remaining wage laborers—women, second and third sons, or off-farm part-time workers—merely supplemented household income (Shinohara 1970: 342–44; Tsurumi 1990: 20–21).

In the 1880s, male day laborers in Japan received an average wage less than one-third that in Bangkok, while Japanese carpenters were paid two-thirds of Bangkok's unskilled wage. Even if one considers wages in Siam's hinterlands, Japan's wages were still lower than in Siam. Furthermore, in 1890, average monthly wages in cotton spinning were lower in Japan than in India for both men and women (Saxonhouse 1976: 97–125; Shinohara 1970: 342–44; Tsurumi 1990: 153; Yasuba and Dhiravegin 1985: 20–21).

Subsistence levels rose over time as the minimum maintenance expected by society increased with growth. The relatively stable agricultural (and thus industrial) real wages can be attributed partly to technical progress and increased productivity in agriculture (and cheap food from colonies after 1911), which enabled the industrial sector to buy food without declining terms of trade. These low real industrial wages increased industrial profits, business savings, and labor-intensive manufactured export competitiveness. Indeed, the large wage differential between France and Italy on the one hand and Japan on the other was a major contributor to Japan's comparative advantage in textiles, a labor-intensive commodity.

Over a normal range, where product and labor demand increase gradually, labor supply elasticities (percentage change in quantity supplied/percentage change in wage) were high (though not infinite as in LFR), benefiting from vast reserves in the rural and informal industrial sectors. But the 1915–19 increase in demand for industrial products and labor resulting from World War I was too substantial to be satisfied by labor from the elastic portion of the supply curve. Wage equilibrium could only be attained at the inelastic portion of the labor supply curve, thus increasing industrial wages and subsequently, through greater food demand by new workers, increasing agricultural product (especially rice) and labor prices. In the 1920s and early 1930s, industrial wages—rigid in the downward direction because of emerging unions—remained high, while agricultural (and informal industrial sector) wages declined from their war peak (conforming to Ohkawa and Rosovsky's [1973] rule that the ratio of traditional to modern wages increases during an upswing and falls during a downswing). Nevertheless, during the 1920s and early 1930s, Japan's rapid increase in labor productivity relative to labor remuneration increased its export competitiveness, especially in textiles. Following the war and recovery years from 1935 to 1955, the labor surplus ended and industrial formal sector labor supply turned inelastic permanently, as innovation-led demand for industrial products and labor increased rapidly, while labor supply growth from agriculture and population growth was drying up (Hayami 1975; Minami 1973; Ohkawa and Rosovsky 1973: 125–30; Shinohara 1962: 43–75).

In Japan, unlike LFR, the capitalist wage rate was raised during World War I before all surplus rural labor was absorbed. As workers with low (not zero, as in LFR) marginal productivity migrated from the subsistence agricultural sector, that sector then divided its growing output among fewer persons, resulting in a gradually increasing wage. Industrial wages then had to increase to motivate rural workers to migrate. The larger industrial labor force contributed to a growing food demand that rose more rapidly than the capacity to produce food, resulting in food price increases. Accordingly, the industrial sector had to raise wages to pay for the increased price of food. In the Japanese case, while industrial wages were low, Lewis's model overestimated the extent to which cheap rural migrant labor could stimulate industrial growth.

Japan's Low Labor Standards

In 1890, Japan had few labor standards (except general laws of property and contracts) and did not regulate hours, wages, or child labor. Factory operatives worked eleven to fourteen hours per day at a pittance. Most were girls between the ages of fourteen and twenty, hired from the countryside by practices bordering on seduction. Family paternalism gave way to the cold calculations of industrial capitalism. Labor organizations were illegal. Before 1905 there was no labor legislation, and there was little before the 1920s.

Government attempts to introduce welfare legislation were aborted because of strong opposition from businesspeople, who exercised paternalism and labor control. In 1898, a bill to prohibit child labor below the age of ten was defeated, with business arguing that such a bill would jeopardize modernization. The Mining Act of 1905 and Factories Act of 1913 to protect the interests of women and children were not effectively enforced until 1929 because the textile magnates could not tolerate an employment ban of the cheapest labor available—women and children—at night.

Government left employers free to pursue their own labor policy, thus increasing profits by paying low wages. These profits were important sources of the growth of an expanding business empire and the concentration of the zaibatsu, which militantly opposed the labor-union movement.

During the 1870s, managers of government or private silk filatures persuaded girls and women from samurai or well-to-do peasant homes to "reel for the nation." By 1887, as the demand for textile labor expanded to include work in the rapidly proliferating cotton mills, the workers, primarily female, were disproportionately from poor rural families. By the last decade of the nineteenth century, the typical industrial worker was an eleven- to twenty-five-year-old female cotton spinner or silk weaver, the daughter of a tenant or poor peasant, hired through a labor contractor (who might promise the sky) on a two- to three-year contract signed by her father with little consultation. She worked twelve hours per day, six days a week, and received a wage about 60 percent of the male wage. During the late Meiji period, the average female worker left her job (usually running away) within six months to two years, notwithstanding the contractual obligations and deposit guarantees of her father, the company dormitories (often with high walls, barbed wire, and gates locked at night), and rules forbidding her to leave the factory grounds without permission. Both labor turnover rates and labor productivity were higher in Japan than in India in 1910.[1]

From 1894 to 1909, women comprised 85 percent of the workers in the booming textile industry, and more than 60 percent of the total industrial labor force. Women continued to be a majority of the industrial labor force through the 1930s. But by 1940, men comprised almost two-thirds of this work force. This gender shift corresponded to a shift from textiles to heavy industries (and military munitions in wartime) as leading sectors of the economy.

Except for a wave of strikes in 1897–98, Japan was relatively free from strikes during the Meiji period, from 1868 to 1912. However, after almost two decades of state repression (including the outlawing of labor organizations and the fining and imprisonment of their leaders), workers finally struck and protested between 1917 and 1923. As an example, in August–September 1918, "rice riots" swept the country in response to the soaring price of rice for an expanding industrial proletariat (Selden 1983: 63–87).

In a more egalitarian setting, and with a more insistent public demand for improved living standards, Japan would not have had low wages, widespread child labor, and tenant oppression, or such rapid accumulation of business capital (Lockwood 1954: 61, 303, 556–60; Mahajan 1976: 26–34). Contemporary LDCs, committed to labor standards and social welfare policies in the 1960s and 1970s, found it difficult to institute the same type of labor policy. Under the World Bank and IMF liberalization programs of the 1980s and 1990s, however, developing countries are adopting the wage repression used by Meiji and interwar Japan to increase industrial profits. Still, ruling elites today in countries such as Nigeria, Zaïre, Zambia, and India have even less political legitimacy in enforcing low-wage policies than early twentieth-century, and sometimes even post–World War I, Japan. Indeed, the Committee for Academic Freedom in Africa (CAFA), which contends that "the most frequent violations of . . . rights occur when African governments implement World Bank and IMF policies and meet the protest they generate," even states that "the Bank's policy [toward workers and intellectuals] is unequivocally exterminist" (CAFA 1991: 2, 6).

LDC Labor Policies and Capital Formation

Since 1980, the International Monetary Fund and World Bank have provided loans and grants for LDC elites willing to undertake macroeconomic stabilization, supply-side and sectoral adjustment, and economic reform and liberalization. These changes benefited political leaders and bureaucrats (who could protect their interests and those of their clients from reform), businesspeople, commercial farmers, and an emerging economically prosperous group that was allied with foreign capital and controlled a large share of imports and exports. This benefit came at the expense of the poor, peasants, and working classes, who not only lacked voice but were generally even unaware of the political debates and struggles. In Tanzania, Nigeria, Kenya, Zambia, and Ghana, when its Fund/Bank-supported austerity policies were opposed by the popular classes, the state increasingly resorted to coercion, breaking the trade unions and expanding paramilitary repression. Even IMF Managing Director Michel Camdessus stated in 1989: "Too often in recent years it is the poorest segments of the population that have carried the heaviest burden of economic adjustment" (in Grant 1989: 17–18). Indeed, UNICEF's van der Hoeven shows that, compared with 1980, real industrial wages dropped considerably during stabilization and adjustment programs (most with the Bank/Fund)—in Tanzania by 40 percent to 1983; in Zambia, 33 percent to 1984; in Malawi, 24 percent by 1984; in Kenya, 22 percent by 1985; in Zimbabwe, 11 percent by 1984; in Mauritius, 10 percent by 1985; and in Swaziland, 5 percent by 1983 (Jamal and Weeks 1988: 273–79; Nafziger 1993: 117–77; van der Hoeven 1989: 30–31).

Yet sub-Saharan Africa and heavily indebted Asian countries did not increase investment as a result of the adjustment and reform programs. The debt overhang in these countries indicates outstanding debt so large that investment will be inefficiently low without new money or debt reductions. People's expectations of future debt burdens reduce the incentives for investment and domestically initiated adjustment, and future growth becomes less attractive as higher proportions have to be transferred abroad. When future repayments are large, these obligations act as a tax on investment because a share of returns goes to creditors. A high-debt country invests at less than the most efficient level and overconsumes or engages in capital flight (Claessens and Diwan 1989: 213–25).

Many low-income countries, having endured years of austerity and stagnation, cannot afford to reduce consumption to effect an external transfer, and thus they shift the burden to investment. For example, the sub-Sahara's gross domestic investment as a percentage of GDP fell from 23 percent in 1979 to

15 percent in 1989; the gross savings rate declined from 20 percent to 13 percent. Indeed, except for Ghana from 1984 to 1990, which had started with a low investment rate base in the 1960s and 1970s, Bank/Fund adjustment programs contributed to reduced investment rates in sub-Saharan Africa, thus wiping out the investment gains of the 1970s (Mkandawire 1991: 81; Mosley, Harrigan, and Toye 1991: vol. 1, pp. 196–98; Nafziger 1993; World Bank 1981: 147, 1991a: vol. 1, p. 221).

The Demographic Transition in Japan and Contemporary LDCs

The demographic transition is a period of rapid population growth between a preindustrial, stable population characterized by high birth and death rates (stage I) and a later, modern, stable population marked by low fertility and mortality (stage IV). The rapid natural increase takes place in the early transitional stage when fertility is high and mortality is declining.

The following indicates the stages of the transition:

Stage I—early stable. Birth and death rates are high. (Following conventional use, crude birth and death rates denote a number per 1,000, not percent.) Death rates vary widely due to famines, epidemics, and disease. The average life expectancy is thirty to thirty-five years. Japan during the later Tokugawa period (1720–1850) had virtually a stationary population of 28 to 30 million, with most pressed close to the limits of subsistence of a simple rice economy, restricted commerce and handicrafts, and the burden of feudal aristocratic exactions. Japan had a lower fertility rate, achieved through abortion and traditional contraceptives, and a higher infanticide rate than Europe during the same period. The comparable period for low- and lower-middle-income Africa and Asia is before the early twentieth century.

Stage II—early expanding. Birth rates remain high. Death rates fall rapidly as a result of advances in health, medicine, nutrition, sanitation, transportation, communication, commerce, and production. Since techniques that reduce deaths can be dispersed more quickly to some recently modernizing countries, the decline in the death rate is steeper in Africa and Asia than it was in Japan and other developed countries. Stage II, the period of most rapid population explosion, took roughly seventy years (1850–1920) in Japan, and fifteen to thirty years in Africa and Asia.

Stage III—late expanding. Death rates continue to decrease. By the end of the period, average life expectancy is at least seventy years. Birth rates fall rapidly, reflecting not only more effective contraception and more vigorous family planning programs, but also the increased cost of children, enhanced mobility, higher aspirations, and economic development. Population growth is positive, but declining. Except for LDCs such as Sri Lanka and China, which have birth rates of 24 and 19 per 1,000, respectively, most low-income countries are at the begin-

Figure 6.1. **The Demographic Transition in Developed and Developing Countries**

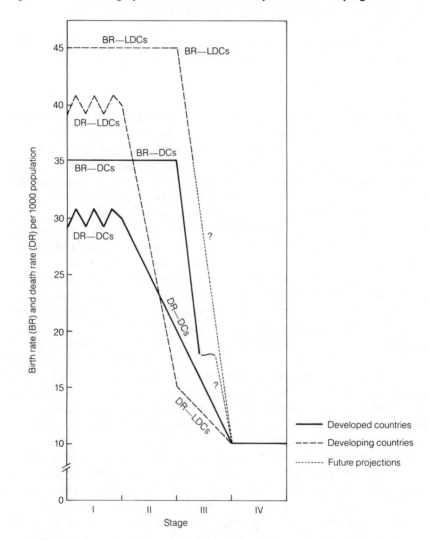

ning of stage III. Japan finished stage III in the 1980s, thus taking more than sixty years to complete the stage.

Stage IV—late stable. Both death and birth rates are low, and nearly equal. Birth rates, however, may fluctuate. Eventually the population is stationary. Only Japan and a few countries in Europe (Germany, Austria, Norway, Sweden, Denmark, Finland, Switzerland, Italy, Spain, Belgium, the Netherlands, and Britain) are close to equality in birth and death rates (Lockwood 1968: 152; Minami 1986: 261–265; Nafziger 1990: 181–212). (See fig. 6.1.)

Has Population Growth Been an Obstacle to
Development in Japan and Contemporary LDCs?

Did Japan's population growth hamper or facilitate economic growth? What lessons does Japan's experience have for today's LDCs?

Population and Food

A major tenet of the English classical economists of the late eighteenth and early nineteenth centuries was the law of diminishing returns, referring to successively lower extra outputs from adding an equal extra input to fixed land. Thomas R. Malthus used the concept of diminishing returns to land as the basis for his essay, arguing that population, which increased geometrically, would outstrip the food supply, which grew arithmetically (Malthus 1963).

Malthus failed, however, to envision the capital accumulation and technical progress that would overcome diminishing returns on land. He also underestimated the extent to which education, economic modernization, industrialization, urbanization, and improved contraception would reduce fertility rates.

In 1885, near the beginning of modern capitalist development in Japan, population was about 38,500,000 on a total land area of 382,000 square kilometers, so population density was 101 persons per square kilometer, in excess of the figure during England's early industrial revolution (43 in 1700 and 63 in 1801) and in Europe (98) in 1981. The number of male workers per square kilometer of arable land in agriculture in 1880 was ten times higher in Japan than in Germany and France and twenty times higher than the United Kingdom. This high population density hampered agricultural growth. Moreover, Japan's high labor–land ratio resulted in a farm-labor surplus that dampened urban wage increases. Furthermore, low agricultural labor productivity gave manufacturing a comparative advantage (Minami 1986: 257–59).[2]

From 1876 to 1906, Japan's food production index grew 2.14 percent annually, while population increased at 1.02 percent yearly, so that food output per capita grew 0.99 percent per annum. During these years, Japan's gains in productivity from improved technology (chapter 2) substantially outpaced losses from diminishing returns to labor applied to land. Over the sixty-year period from 1876 to 1936, Japan's food output grew 1.25 percent yearly, while population rose at 0.96 percent yearly, so that food output per capita grew only 0.29 percent per annum. The slow growth was the net effect of technical change barely overcoming reduced productivity from decreasing returns to land. Land shortages contributed to growing pressures for the imperial domination of Taiwan, Korea, and China, which provided food and raw materials for Japan's growing industrial production and labor (Lockwood 1954: 86; Minami 1986: 43, 267; Nafziger 1990: 213–25; Population Reference Bureau 1993).

From 1950 to 1990, Asia and Africa's food production per capita grew 2.48 percent annually, while population increased at an annual rate of 2.02 percent, so that food output per capita rose yearly by 0.46 percent (FAO 1991; U.S. Department of Agriculture 1986a, 1986b, 1988). As chapter 2 indicated, the major source for increased food productivity per person, agricultural research and technology, lags behind industrial technology in LDCs. Productivity gains from irrigation, multiple cropping, improved seeds, increased use of commercial fertilizer, better farm implements, and other agricultural innovations barely offset losses from diminishing returns. Moreover, the substantial gains made in food productivity since 1950 would lessen if energy supplies were to become more expensive and scarce. Also, today's LDCs lack imperial outlets for acquiring food and raw materials, and must depend on the gains from reducing population growth and from specialization according to comparative advantage to counteract diminishing returns to agricultural land. Furthermore, growth in food productivity is uneven across Asia and Africa. In chapter 5, we saw that while food output per capita has been increasing in Asia, it has been falling in Africa since the late 1960s.

Labor-Force Growth and Employment

In Japan, population grew 0.96 percent annually from 1876 to 1938, compared with Asia and Africa's 2.02 percent annual growth from 1950 to 2000 (and 2.22 percent per year in Latin America). Japan's slow population growth contributed to a slow growth in the labor force (0.53 percent annually, 1876–1920, and 0.72 percent annually, 1876–1938), compared with an annual labor-force growth of 1.89 percent in Asia and Africa from 1950 to 2000 (and 2.45 percent per year in Latin America) (Minami 1986: 43, 267; Nafziger 1990: 213–25; Population Reference Bureau 1993).

I have indicated before that Japan's excess labor supply contributed to low industrial wages. Lockwood (1954: 139–40) contends that GNP per capita in Japan would have been higher and more evenly distributed if it had been less overpopulated; indeed much the same could be said for most of contemporary LDCs. Compared with the growth rates of contemporary developing countries, Japan's slow growths in population and labor force were less deleterious to economic development:

> It is doubtful that Japan's rise as an industrial power, or her whole process of economic development, can be regarded as having been stimulated or advanced by rapid population growth in any significant fashion. Whether viewed from the standpoint of markets, of technology, or of capital accumulation, it appears to have been a decided deterrent to economic progress—certainly in per capita terms. The persistence of a high birth rate despite the steady decline in mortality increased the dependent child population just when the Japanese could ill afford the burden. It imposed a heavy drag on improvements in the

skills and equipment of the labor force. It hastened the exhaustion of natural resources at home, and required large industrial exports abroad merely to feed and clothe greater numbers. [Lockwood 1954: 167]

Growing unemployment is caused by the labor force growing faster than job opportunities. By the year 2000, the Asian and African labor force will have increased 2.5 times—from 465 million to 1,180 million—in fifty years. Asia and Africa today must contend with a much more rapid labor-force growth than Japan experienced at a similar stage of development. The labor force in Japan grew 0.5 percent annually (the rate in Western Europe and North America was 0.8 percent per year) at the turn of the twentieth century, compared with 1.9 percent per year for Asia and Africa in the last half of the twentieth century. Given Japan's 1900 rate, it takes 144 years for its labor force to double; it takes about 38 years in Asia and Africa today.

Economic growth is usually accompanied by a decline in the proportion of labor force in agriculture, and an increase in the share of labor in the more productive industrial and services sector. Yet in 1980, 68 percent of the labor force in low-income countries was in agriculture, and only 14 percent in industry (World Bank 1988: 282–83). Annual industrial employment expanded at 0.4–0.7 percent of the total labor force in Asia and Africa in 1980 compared with 3.9 percent in Japan at the turn of the twentieth century, from 1878 to 1914.

Because of fast labor-force growth, industry in Asia and Africa today absorbs only 21 to 37 percent of the increased labor force, compared with about 4.5 to 5.0 times the labor increase in Japan and 50 percent in Europe in 1900. Let us illustrate: Assume the labor force in Asia and Africa today is growing at 1.9 percent per year. Assume agricultural employment remains constant, so that employment growth is in industry and services. The nonagricultural sector in Asia and Africa employs 32 percent of the labor force. This sector would have to increase its total employment about 5.9 percent per year to absorb a labor-force growth of 1.9 percent (that is, $0.32 \times 0.059 = 0.019$). David Morawetz's (1974: 492–95) data on industrial employment growth suggest that few LDCs have been experiencing growth as rapid as 5.9 percent per year. While industrial growth often is faster than 5.9 percent per year, because of capital-intensive industrialization, industrial employment growth is much slower than industrial growth. Crucial in Japan's successful absorption was slower population growth and rural–urban migration, together with highly labor-intensive industrialization, spurred by government's low-wage and appropriate technology policies, but *not* a faster annual industrial growth rate than Asia and Africa are experiencing today.

While the unemployed are those without a job who are actively seeking one, there is no satisfactory measure of underemployment (Nafziger 1900a: 217–20). Sluggish industrial employment growth has contributed to high urban unemployment and rural underemployment, and low rural productivity. The Economic Commission for Africa estimates 1975 urban unemployment rates of 10.8 percent in Africa and 6.9 percent in Asia. The urban unemployment rates in both regions increased from 1975 to 1990 (Economic Commission for Africa 1983: 7–59; Sablo 1975: 408–17).

The Dependency Burden

Although the Asian and African labor force is growing rapidly, the number of children dependent on each worker is high. High fertility rates create this dependency burden. The dependency ratio is the population aged fourteen or less and sixty-five or over divided by population aged fifteen to sixty-four years times 100. Table 6.1 compares the dependency ratio in Japan from 1865 to 1993, and in LDCs as of 1993. From 1865 to 1900, Japan's dependency ratio, which did not exceed 62 percent, was much lower than sub-Saharan Africa, the Middle East, and South and Southeast Asia, but not East Asia, in 1993. Indeed, even in 1920, Japan's dependency ratio, at its peak, was still less than all these regions except East Asia. By 1970 and after, Japan's ratio was less than the ratio of either developing East Asia or DCs generally in 1988.

Of course, the ratio of the labor force to population is not only a function of dependency ratios. Because of crossnational differences in the participation of men, women, old people, youths, and children in the labor force, countries with similar dependency ratios may have different ratios of labor force to population. Figure 6.2 on page 115, which plots the relationships between age and service requirements, reflects the higher educational and health costs of caring for those fifteen years and under. Thus, the high dependency ratio in Bangladesh means that a substantial proportion of its resources must be diverted to provide schools, food, health care, and social services for the young. Roughly speaking, the 53 percent of the population in Bangladesh from fifteen to sixty-four years supports 47 percent of the population in the dependent age group, a substantial burden compared with Japan in 1900, where 62 percent of the population supported only 38 percent of the population in the dependent age group. Households in Bangladesh have a large number of consumers per earning member, which means a high ratio of consumption to income. Japan in 1900 had far fewer consumers per earning unit. For Bangladesh, very little is left over for savings, while Japan in 1900 had more potential for capital formation.

Japan's Population and Labor-Supply Growth

Developing Japan's labor supply grew slower than the labor supply in today's LDCs. Late nineteenth-century Japan's birth rate, 22 per 1,000, was kept down

Table 6.1

Total Population, Age Composition, and Dependent Population Ratio, Japan, 1865–1988, and Contemporary Countries

	Total population (millions)	Age composition (%)			Dependent population ratio[a] (%)
		0–14	15–64	65 or over	
Japan (year)					
1865	34.5	31.3	63.4	5.3	57.8
1880	38.2	32.4	62.2	5.3	60.7
1900	44.4	32.9	61.7	5.3	62.0
1920	56.0	36.5	58.3	5.2	71.6
1930	64.5	36.6	58.7	4.8	70.5
1940	73.1	36.1	59.2	4.7	69.0
1950	84.1	35.4	59.6	4.9	67.7
1960	94.3	30.2	64.1	5.7	55.9
1970	104.7	24.0	68.9	7.1	45.1
1975	111.9	24.3	67.7	7.9	47.6
1980	116.9	23.5	67.5	9.0	48.1
1988	122.7	21.0	68.0	11.0	47.1
1993	124.8	18.0	69.0	13.0	44.9
Country (1993)					
Egypt	58.3	39	47	4	91.5
Nigeria	95.1	45	52	3	92.3
Ethiopia	56.7	49	47	4	112.8
Kenya	27.7	49	49	2	104.1
Turkey	60.7	35	61	4	63.9
Bangladesh	113.9	44	53	3	88.7
India	897.4	36	60	4	66.7
Pakistan	122.4	44	52	4	92.3
Sri Lanka	17.8	35	61	4	63.9
Indonesia	187.6	37	59	4	69.5
Philippines	64.6	39	57	4	75.4
Malaysia	18.7	37	59	4	69.5
Thailand	56.3	34	62	4	61.2
China	1,178.5	28	67	5	49.3
South Korea	44.6	26	69	5	44.9
Taiwan	20.9	26	67	7	49.3
United States	258.3	22	65	13	53.8
Canada	28.1	22	65	13	53.8
United Kingdom	58.0	19	65	16	53.8
France	57.7	20	66	14	51.5
Germany	81.1	16	69	15	44.9
Italy	57.8	17	69	14	44.9
Russia	149.0	23	66	11	51.5

(continued)

Table 6.1 *(continued)*

Country groupings (1993)

Sub-Saharan Africa	550	46	51	3	96.1
South Asia	1,253	38	58	4	72.4
Southeast Asia	460	36	60	4	66.7
East Asia	1,275	28	66	6	51.5
Middle East	299	41	55	4	81.8
DCs	1,230	21	67	12	49.3
LDCs	4,276	36	60	4	66.7
World	5,506	33	61	6	63.9

Sources: Minami (1986: 263), Population Reference Bureau (1993).

[a]Population aged 14 or less and 65 or over divided by population aged 15–64 years x 100.

Figure 6.2. **Population Age Profile and Service Requirements: Bangladesh, 1975**

(Total population, 74 million)

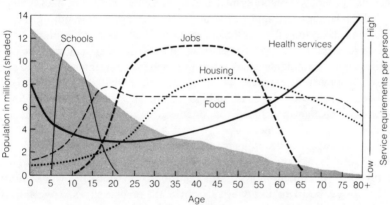

by farm land shortages, extended-family dissolution, and high literacy levels, and was lower than Asia and Africa's 1993 rate of 29 per 1,000. The Japanese death rate, 18 per 1,000, was higher than Asia and Africa's rate of 9 per 1,000, lowered by access to the nutritional, medical, health, and production techniques of the past century. Japan's annual labor growth, which never exceeded 1 percent during the nineteenth century, rose to a peak of 1.3 percent yearly by 1930, slowing to less than 1 percent by 1955. In contrast, Asia and Africa's labor-force growth was 1.7 percent annually in the 1960s, 2.0 percent annually in the 1970s, and 2.3 percent in the 1980s. (The labor forces for Japan from 1880 to 1935 and for Asia and Africa from the 1960s through the 1980s grew more slowly than the population because of increases in the ratio of dependents to workers and the rate of child survival.) Yet Meiji Japan's density of farm population per cultivated hectare of land (higher than India, Pakistan, China, Taiwan, and most other Asian LDCs today) put pressure on the nonagricultural sector.

With 51 percent of the labor force but only 20 percent of the output in agriculture, forestry, fishing, and mining, and only 20 percent of the labor force but 32 percent of output in manufacturing and construction in 1930, Japan demonstrates that a country can industrialize with a relatively slow emigration from agriculture. China, for example, which has deliberately restrained urban migration, had 27 percent of output and 74 percent of the labor force in agriculture, and 42 percent of output and 14 percent of the labor force in industry in 1990 (Lockwood 1954: 103–4, 155–56; Nafziger 1990a: 213–37; Nakamura 1983: 45–49; Ohkawa and Shinohara 1979: 104–33; Squire 1981: 44–45; Tachi and Okazaki 1965: 497–515; World Bank 1979: 46–50, 1984: 218–21, 256–57, 1988: 28–83, 282–83, 1989b: 168–69, 1992b: 222–23).

The LDCs' Labor-Force Growth and Urban Unemployment

Japan had faster food output growth and more stable food prices than contemporary LDCs because of rapid technical progress in agriculture during the Meiji period and cheap food from colonies during the early twentieth century. Low-income countries' food supply problems often result from agricultural price disincentives, bureaucratic mismanagement in supplying farm inputs, and urban bias in exchange rates, investment, tax rates, and amenities. But LDC food demand has risen relatively fast, because of high income elasticities of demand for food (percentage change in demand for food/percentage change in GNP) resulting from rapid population growth.

Until the aggressive adjustment policies of the International Monetary Fund, World Bank, and DC governments in the 1980s, trade union and political pressures in contemporary LDCs contributed to industrial wages substantially above equilibrium wages, while these pressures, together with unsuitable capital-intensive technologies, factor-price distortions (low capital and foreign-exchange costs), unrealistic job aspirations by school graduates, and rapid population growth, resulted in high open urban unemployment rates. In the midst of a large urban wage premium, the flood of urban immigrants was restrained only by high open urban unemployment rates, which keep down expected urban wages (wages times the probability of employment as in the Harris–Todaro model) but not actual urban wages (Harris and Todaro 1970: 126–42). The LFR model's unlimited long-run supply of labor to the industrial sector, roughly valid in Japan from 1868 to 1915, was replaced by relatively high wages in contemporary LDCs, reducing industrial profits and savings.

Since 1980, as argued above, while Fund/Bank adjustment and reform loans and programs have contributing to reduced wages, they have not increased investment in low-income countries because of the substantial claims from earnings earmarked for servicing the substantial external debt.

Growth, Technical Change, and
Rural–Urban Transfer

Ishikawa argues that

> The fact that [Japan's] rate of technological progress accounts for more than a
> half of the rate of growth of agricultural output is one of the most essential
> aspects of the contribution that agriculture made to the success of prewar
> industrialization. If the rate of technological progress had been very low, the
> amount of agricultural products which agriculture was able to supply to the
> emerging industrial sector under the given prices would have been much
> smaller. The amount of industrial resources which the industrial sector would
> have had to supply to the agricultural sector to prevent that event from arising
> would have been much larger. [1981: 184]

Mody, Mundle, and Raj contend that slow growth in agricultural labor
shares in postindependence India compared with Meiji Japan reflects the
tendency for increasing numbers of a rapidly growing population to remain
within agriculture without a commensurate growth of employment opportunities in the industrial sector, which takes the surplus off the land. The rapid
industrialization of Japan meant that its agricultural population did not increase in absolute terms from 1896 to World War II. These authors point out
that, except for the 1966–69 Green Revolution, independent India lacked
substantial agricultural investment and technological progress, and this made
it difficult for India to expand farm output to the industrial sector, to increase
the relative share of the labor force in the industrial sector, and to maintain
the purchasing power of food with a given urban wage (Mody, Mundle, and
Raj 1982: XII–29, 1985: 289–91).

Summary

This chapter has asked whether Japan's industrial wage determination follows
the Lewis and Fei–Ranis models. While agricultural unskilled real wages in
Japan remained at a subsistence level from 1868 to 1915, keeping industrial real
wages low, other aspects of the Japanese experience indicate the irrelevance of
Lewis–Fei–Ranis approaches. The low urban wage premium (because of the
widespread use of female, second and third son, or off-farm part-time labor), the
relatively stable wages from rapid farm technical progress, the short-run inelastic
supply of labor, the positive marginal productivity of agricultural labor, and the
wide range of the subsistence wage deviate from the Lewis–Fei–Ranis models.
Moreover, Lewis–Fei–Ranis was even less applicable to pre-1979 LDCs, where
resource-price distortions, unsuitable technologies, and rapid population growth
resulted in high urban unemployment. Since 1979, however, under adjustment

programs, LDCs have repressed industrial wages and reduced the range of the subsistence wage, providing a favorable climate for profits (as did Meiji Japan) during early stages of industrialization. However, whereas Meiji indigenous bourgeoisie did not have to divide these gains with foreigners, most African and Asian capitalists today must share—sometimes the lion's share of—these benefits with multinational corporations and their local intermediaries and collaborators.

Japan's slow population growth near 1900 was less harmful to economic growth than the fast population growth in contemporary Asia and Africa. Japan's industrial growth then was enough to absorb the growing labor force, while the industrial growth of LDCs today, though faster than that of earlier Japan, only absorbs a fraction of their rapid population growth. Moreover, Japan's lower population dependency ratio during its industrialization made the cost of supporting the nonworking population less than it is for LDCs today.

Notes

1. The first four paragraphs of this section rely on Selden (1983: 63–87), Tsurumi (1990: 3–73), Gordon (1985: 6–7), and Saxonhouse and Kiyokawa (1985: 177–211).

2. Minami (1986) discusses the possibility that Japan's official increases in birth and death rates in 1920 are inconsistent with the last part of stage III of the demographic transition theory. Some Japanese demographers believe these increases are not real, and that the apparent increases result from improved birth and death registration between 1915 and 1920.

Chapter 7

Industrial Dualism

A Dual Economy

Meiji Japan had a dual economy consisting of (1) a traditional, peasant, agricultural sector, producing primarily for family or village subsistence, with little reproducible capital, using old or intermediate technology, and a marginal productivity of labor lower than the wage (together with semisubsistence agriculture, petty trade, and cottage industry), and (2) capital-intensive modern manufacturing and processing operations, mineral extraction, and commercial agriculture, producing for the market, using reproducible capital and new technology, experiencing high and growing labor productivity (from high capital–labor ratios), and hiring labor commercially. Capital–labor ratios in the modern sector, which uses technologies borrowed substantially from abroad, are relatively rigid, while ratios in the traditional sector, using modified or indigenous techniques, are more flexible. As the Lewis model points out, transferring labor from the traditional (low labor productivity) sector to the modern sector is limited by the latter's growth in capital stock. In addition, the large firms, with their greater capital concentration, had greater monopolistic power and could limit new entry, thus increasing profits and wages (Ohkawa and Rosovsky 1973: 40; Shinohara 1970: 321–26). Japan's dualism was exacerbated by its continuing rapid growth, especially in technology, and contributed to the high income inequality that spurred expansionism and militarism.

As implied in chapter 6, the modern-sector wage was more than the traditional-sector wage for identical labor skills from 1868 to 1915. After World War I, these wage differentials widened, as the demand for industrial labor expanded faster than that for farm labor.

Wage discrepancies increased even more between skilled and unskilled labor. Post–World War I demand increased especially for skilled labor, which large firms (particularly in heavy and chemical industries) tried to retain through ratio-nalization, lifetime employment policies, seniority preference, and fringe bene-fits, while industries hiring unskilled labor still faced a surplus. At the same time, many banks went bankrupt during the financial panics; those banks that re-mained focused their loans on large enterprises, thus widening interest rates and capital–labor ratios between large and small enterprises. The large firms' price-controlling power in product markets and credit rationing in the capital market also made higher wages possible. In addition, large firms economized on un-skilled labor by hiring temporary workers, and this contributed to greater labor market dualism (Shinohara 1970: 24–25; Yasuba 1976: 224). By 1955, in the midst of the labor shortage and growing union strength of the postwar economic boom, the dual market for similar labor disappeared (although there were still wage differentials for different levels of skill and experience).

Dualism within an Industry: The Modern and Informal Sectors

In this section I go beyond industrial–agricultural dualism to discuss dualism within the industrial sector, including regional dualism. Industrial dualism is more likely to occur when economies of scale are not important. Because of geographical labor immobility, a labor market usually consisted of a village or no more than a few districts. Also, poor transport provided natural protection for regions with high wage costs. Moreover, wage dualism occurred where there was a major technological gap between firms of the same industry (Patrick 1976: 9; Shinohara 1970: 24–25). Finally, another source of dualism, especially after World War I, was the wage discrepancies between temporary and permanent workers, sometimes even in the same firm.

Most migrants from the rural areas to Tokyo and other large cities between 1909 and 1920 did not become modern wage laborers, but acquired jobs in the urban informal sector, the small-scale sector that required little capital and skill and had few entry barriers. Most males became apprentices, shop boys, small merchants, minor craftsmen, ricksha drivers, and day laborers. Female migrants, on the other hand, became operatives (for example, in spinning and silk reeling) or domestic servants (Nakamura 1983: 125–31).

The Lewis model discussed in the previous chapter does not consider why rural migration continues despite high urban unemployment. John R. Harris and Michael P. Todaro, whose model views a worker's decision to migrate on the basis of wages *and* probability of unemployment, try to close this gap in the Lewis model. They assume that migrants respond to urban–rural differences in expected rather than actual earnings. Suppose the average unskilled rural worker has a choice between being a farm laborer (or working his or her own land) for an annual income of Rs. 1,000, or migrating to the city where he or she can receive an annual wage of Rs. 2,000. Most economists, who assume full employment, would deduce that the worker would seek the higher-paying urban job. However, in low-income countries with high unemployment rates, this might be an unrealistic supposition. Assume that the probability of the worker getting the urban job during a one-year period is 20 percent. The worker would not migrate, since the expected income is Rs. 2,000 times 0.20, or Rs. 400— much less than Rs. 1,000 (1,000 times a probability of 1) on the farm. But if the probability of success is 60 percent, expected urban earnings would be Rs. 2,000 times 0.60, or Rs. 1,200. In this case, it would be rational for the farm worker to seek the urban job. And since most migrants are young (under twenty-five years old), it would be more realistic to assume an even longer time span in the decision to migrate. The migrant may consider lifetime earnings. Thus, if the present value of expected lifetime earnings in the urban job is greater than on the farm, it would be rational to migrate.

According to Harris and Todaro, creating urban jobs by expanding industrial output is insufficient for solving the urban unemployment problem. Instead, they recommend that government reduce urban wages, eliminate other resource-price distortions, promote rural employment, and generate labor-intensive technologies (Harris and Todaro 1970: 126–42).

Even without amenities, an International Labour Office study indicates that the ratio of average urban to rural income is more than 2 in Asia and 4–5 in Africa (after adjustments for living costs). Assuming a ratio of 2, urban unemployment must be 50 percent to equate urban and rural expected income. But LDC urban unemployment rarely exceeds 10 to 20 percent, indicating that migration does not close the urban and rural expected-wage gap. We can explain the gap by adding to the Harris–Todaro urban formal and rural sectors the urban informal sector, where petty traders, tea shop proprietors, hawkers, street vendors, artisans, shoe shiners, street entertainers, garbage collectors, repairpersons, artisans, cottage industrialists, and other self-employed generate employment and income for themselves in activities with little capital, skill, and few entry barriers. These small enterprisers have low startup costs and profit margins, negotiate agreements outside the formal legal system, and hire workers at less than the legal minimum wage. A substantial share of the contemporary LDC urban labor force is also relegated to the informal sector: 43 percent in Calcutta, India, and 50 percent in Lagos, Nigeria.

The informal sector's labor supply is affected primarily by wages and population growth in the rural sector. The substantial absorption of rural emigrants in the informal sector explains why migration stops long before rural expected incomes attain urban formal sector levels. Many migrants are neither unemployed nor receiving the prevailing formal sector wage but are working in informal jobs, which facilitate their entry into the urban economy (Cole and Sanders 1985: 481–94; Gills et al. 1987: 190–91; Jagannathan 1987: 57–58; Lecaillon et al. 1984: 54–57; Sethuraman 1981: 17).

In early twentieth-century Japan and contemporary South Asia and sub-

Saharan Africa, the informal urban sector served as an intermediate sector before formal sector employment for many rural emigrants to the cities. Indeed, more LDC workers are in the informal sector of craft, petty trading, and small industrial enterprises with less than ten employed than are in the government sector or the industrial sector with ten or more employed. Informal sector wages are often not much higher than farm subsistence incomes, and may undercut wage settlements in the formal sector. Production in these informal enterprises is labor-intensive, with usually no more than a few simple tools. Wages are low, as government rarely enforces minimum wages and union legislation in these firms. Indeed, in Nigeria in 1975, even the informal sector self-employed received only 62 percent of the net annual income that low-income wage earners in the small modern sector received. And these self-employed rarely expand their firm to modern sector size.

The gulf between modern and informal urban sector entrepreneurship in LDCs is wide. The movement, for example, from four workers and simple tools to twenty workers with a mechanical production line involves a major adjustment that many entrepreneurs cannot make successfully, at least not without some additional training in technique, management, or marketing. To leap over the threshold, the entrepreneur may have to change from face-to-face supervision of workers to the delegation of responsibility to submanagers or foremen, from assigning one worker several steps in the operation to designating specialized work tasks in a mass production line, and from direct consumer sales to the development of regular wholesale buyers. In addition, the entrepreneur may need to borrow additional funds, unless retained earnings from this previous operations have been high. Frequently, economies of scale result if an enterprise produces at least the minimum rate of output needed to develop an assembly line and sell regularly to wholesale buyers. However, achieving a rate of output above the threshold for a sustained period may require simultaneous increments in orders, financing, employment, materials quotas, and in some cases skills—a difficult task, especially in economies, such as pre-1979 India, that require government licenses for investment capacity and materials (Nafziger 1978: 94–95).

An extensive study of the informal sector in Dar es Salaam, Tanzania, during 1987–88 indicates that more than three-fourths of the enterprises were started during Tanzania's stagnation period, 1980–87. The number of self-employed women increased from 7 percent in 1971 to 66 percent in 1987. Two-thirds of the women began their activities because their husbands' wages were insufficient for survival. The bulk of activities were on a very small scale, such as making or selling items like tea, pastries, porridge, soup, kerosene, flour, and so forth—hardly indicating a vibrant entrepreneurial class ready to expand employment opportunities. Most income earned was for food consumption, not capital accumulation. A number of women left skilled or semiskilled occupations as instructors, nurses, and accountants, specialties emphasized by the World Bank as needing expansion, for jobs in the informal economy. The study also found children dropping out of school to assist their parents, contributing to a falling primary enrollment rate in the 1980s. Many felt that they no longer needed to attend once they could read or write, since they would end up with unskilled, informal sector jobs anyway (Fajana 1981: 193–226; Nafziger 1988b: 147–48; Stein 1991; Tripp 1989: 601–23).

During growth, the informal sector in Africa and Asia has been closely integrated with both farm and modern sector and a source of an urban starting job to help workers learn industrial discipline. Increasingly in the 1980s, however, with negative growth and restrictive adjustment programs, especially in Dar es Salaam and other parts of the sub-Sahara, the informal sector has become a sign of economic decline rather than expansion. Many informal activities arose from a lack of formal sector employment or the need to supplement formal sector wages insufficient to support a family on even the most basic diet.

Electrification and Dualism

Ironically, the rapid introduction of electric motors between 1914 and 1930 spurred industrial dualism. Manufacturing establishments with 1,000 or more employees were virtually completely electrified by 1914, and those with 30 to 99 workers by 1930 (table 7.1). The diffusion of cheap electric motors increased labor productivity in small manufacturing, and reduced economies of scale in many industries, increasing dualism in the nonagricultural sectors. Indeed, Minami (1976: 299–325) argues that Japan's high degree of dualism was largely a result of its early start in electric power.

Electricity in today's LDCs, especially in major cities, is a source of dualism. In addition, developing countries experience duality between firms with and without power.

Japan's Gradualism

Japan has stressed not large leaps to the most advanced state of industrial technology available, but step-by-step improvements in technology and capital as ministries, regions, industries, firms, and work units learn by doing. In the early Meiji period, this meant technical and management assistance and credit facilities to improve and increase the scale of small workshops, handicraft producers, and cottage industry left from before 1868; this caused less social disruption, since the small-industry environment was not alien.

Ishikawa (1981: 372, 385) mentions the bicycle industry as a successful industry where small-scale merchants and repairers adapted technology to manufacture a new product by lowering the product's quality and performance. Japan first imported bicycles in 1870. Shops that sold, repaired, and made parts for imported bicycles started to produce them domestically about 1890, a time of sharp increase in imports. Since the assembly of parts to make bicycles was

Table 7.1

Powered Factories as a Proportion of All Factories in Japan, 1909–40

		Number of workers	
	Total (5 or more)	5–29	30–99	100 or more
1909	28.2	20.5	69.7	88.4
1919	61.1	54.3	88.6	97.6
1930	82.5	80.1	95.3	99.3
1940	84.1	82.1	96.7	99.6

Source: Minami (1986: 126–27).
Note: The figures are percentages of all factories equipped with any kind of engine.

technically easy for retail shops, complete bicycles made by assembling home-made components could be sold domestically much cheaper than imported bicycles. By the 1920s, Japan exported bicycles to other parts of Asia.

The 1884 plan emphasized improving traditional technology through applied science, and favored postponing massive foreign large-scale factory transplantation until traditional enterprises could utilize new techniques (Inukai 1979: 5). Factory enterprises in Japan developed faster than in India, because Japan assisted and protected small-scale industry more than India, where small-scale firms received little credit and technological help and were hamstrung with licensing restrictions and government controls.

The Complementarity of Large and Small Industries

Large industry evolved, after state assistance and two wars (1894–95 and 1904–5) into zaibatsu concentration by 1910, but small industry, encouraged by government to take cooperative action, was retained, even in textiles, the leading manufacturing industry. Large-scale enterprises created external economies in the supply of raw materials, working capital, and markets, and (because of market power) were more innovative than small firms. In addition, large enterprises could not manufacture every item needed and found it cheaper to buy parts and components from independently run small workshops, to which large firms provided technical advice, scarce inputs, credit, and (especially after World War I) access to a large international trading company (*sogo shosha*), which economized on the scarce language skills of both Japanese and foreigners.

Japan provided a special incentive to small industry through laws enacted between 1884 and 1902 to encourage local chambers of commerce and guilds of industrialists and merchants for cooperative action. Moreover, local administration (prefectural government) had detailed knowledge about and was committed to technical assistance to small industries; the services available in the early twentieth century were far in excess of what states or districts provide in India today.

The practice of large enterprises subcontracting to smaller industrial firms was widespread in Japan, especially between World Wars I and II. Subcontractors had the following advantages: (1) superior access to large companies' technology, (2) stable prices, and (3) cheap labor not available to large firms. These principal firms benefit from ancillary firms' acting as buffers to absorb demand and employment fluctuations, and providing outlets for large firms' underused personnel (Okita 1981: 5–6; Ono and Odaka 1979: 133–34). India, which requires principal companies to help ancillary enterprises, could profit by the Japanese approach of local support and incentives for cooperative action.

The Disconnection between Large and Small Industries in Contemporary LDCs

In today's LDCs, the complementarity between large and small enterprises rarely exists; a government strategy of large enterprises frequently comes in lieu of improvement engineering and adaptive technology for entrepreneurs of small firms, who gradually increase the size of their units by learning through experience. Most large enterprises in low-income countries are state-owned enterprises (SOEs), multinational corporations (MNCs), or SOE–MNC joint ventures. Many of these large enterprises receive state support through fiscal incentives, hidden transfers, tariffs, and subsidies. R.P. Short (1983: 30–36) shows that SOEs in thirteen of fourteen countries in Asia and Africa incurred overall deficits; these deficits mean a deterioration of capital resources (or negative savings). This is despite the fact that SOEs frequently enjoy monopoly privileges, especially in mineral and energy resources.

Yet the impression of the superior performance of private enterprise in LDCs, which often originates in anecdotes of Western businesspeople and aid officials, is not necessarily supported by comparative studies. Robert Millward (1988: 143–61) indicates that the efficiency of public and private enterprises in developing countries is comparable, given a certain size of firm. However, public firms are more likely than private firms to choose an excessive scale of operations. Frequently, ruling elites in LDCs, who use public firms to dispense benefits to clients, build these enterprises beyond management capacity. Moreover, public firms have easier access to state finance to mute bankruptcy and more pressure to provide jobs and contracts to clients and relatives than do private enterprises. As the IMF points out (1986: 16), in developing countries "over the years, inefficiency has flourished in many state enterprises, its overt consequences masked by the ready availability of budgetary support." Still, as chapter 9 maintains, public enterprises can perform well in LDCs if policies on competition, management, finance, licensing, and firm size are reformed.

As indicated in chapter 4, in many African (and Asian) countries, a commercial triangle exists between MNCs, indigenous businesspeople and middlemen, and state officials, who frequently create industrial oligopolies. These oligopolies were created even when Third World states indigenized ownership, control, personnel, and technology. Claude Ake (1981) believes indigenization's prospects are poor, since, if complete, it means doing without international aid, capital, imported technology, and imported consumer goods, and making international capitalism an implacable enemy. But if indigenization means a partnership between the LDCs' political elites and foreign capitalism, it could mean continued capture of social resources by the state in the name of the people but for the primary benefit of elites and their allies.

Indigenization often increased local inequalities. In Nigeria, indigenization in the early 1970s became an instrument for a few civil servants, military rulers, businesspeople, and professionals to amass considerable wealth through manipulating state power (Ogbuagu 1983: 241–66). Ironically, an indigenization policy designed partly to reduce foreign concentration created Nigerian oligopolies, especially among those with the wealth and influence to obtain capital and government loans to purchase foreign shares.

Multinational corporations in low-income countries contribute to inequality in several ways. Foreign capital usually enters the country only if political leaders, civil servants, and private middlemen are rewarded for facilitating the joint venture. Much of this reward is for economically unproductive activity and is paid for by tariff and quota protection, higher consumer prices, or subsidies from tax revenue. In poor countries, where direct taxes such as income taxes are not well developed, the tax structure is usually regressive: people with lower incomes pay a higher percentage of income in taxes. Any subsidy to inefficiency falls disproportionately on low- to middle-income workers and farmers.

Although Kenya's policy of joint ventures increased government ownership and income, it had only limited success in the goal of Africanizing staff, decisions, and control. The Economist Intelligence Unit (1985) indicates that, although foreigners owned only 42 percent of Kenya's 1976 total issued capital of large-scale manufacturing and service firms, they controlled about 75 percent of these firms through majorities on the boards of directors. Government, if it views society as a whole, should use an efficiency criterion that balances profits with wages and savings with consumption, rather than maximizing profits (Nove 1983). Yet the Kenyan government, despite majority ownership, acquiesced in the goals of foreign private enterprises to maximize profits by keeping wages for ordinary workers low.

The weakness of indigenous capitalists in most low-income countries can be attributed largely to their dependence on foreign control. Most of these countries, in attempting to emulate the process of large-scale capital-intensive industrialization in the West, have tried to acquire capital and advanced technology through foreign investment. But Ronald Müller's (1979: 151–78) empirical evidence indicates that local individuals and financial institutions contribute a substantial share of MNC investment. Moreover, frequent contractual limits on transferring patents, industrial secrets, and other technical knowledge to the subsidiary or joint venture, which may be viewed as a potential rival, may hamper the acquisition of the skills and learning benefits on which commercial success is based. The interests of many indigenous capitalists and political leaders tend to become associated with their foreign partners or benefactors. Business intermediaries and government officials in Kenya, Malawi, the Philippines, India, and many other LDCs depend critically on external investment and assistance for state-enterprise expansion, with its income, patronage, and power.

The late nineteenth-century Japanese government, which received no foreign aid, introduced innovations by buying foreign technology or hiring foreign experts directly. Similar contemporary arrangements, such as that between Jialing and Honda discussed in chapter 2, include management contracts, buying or licensing technology, or, more cheaply, buying machinery in which knowledge is embodied (Fransman 1986: 11–14).

Small Industry's Shares

Small industry (establishments with fewer than fifty workers) increased its real output (though not output share) 2 percent annually from 1884 to 1930, contributing 45 to 50 percent of gross manufacturing output in Japan, and 65 to 75 percent of its employment in 1934 (71 percent of employment in Colombia, 70 percent in Nigeria, and 40 percent in Malaysia today). As late as 1970, small enterprises in Japan employed 43 percent of total industrial output. But most small firms were dependent—dominated by major banks, industrial companies, and trading corporations especially before the late 1940s (Lockwood 1954: 201–13, 561–62; Morawetz 1974: 524–26; Nakamura 1983: 80–86).

Small Industry in Contemporary LDCs

Many LDCs use training, extension, credit, and industrial estate programs to encourage small-scale manufacturing establishments. Since the 1950s, India has limited the expansion of large firms, and provided subsidies for the establishment of small-scale industry, especially in nonmetropolitan areas. Nigeria, since independence in 1960, has provided subsidies, tariff drawbacks, training, and extension services for the establishment of small-scale industry.

But few contemporary LDCs have developed small industry as well as did post-1868 Japan. Many low-income countries, trying to modernize industry, have emphasized capital-intensive technology representing the most advanced state of art in DCs, allowing small industry to decline (Nafziger 1990a: 213–37). These countries have not stressed gradual technical improvement and learning from experience among existing ministries and industries, together with dissemination of technology consistent with local factor endowment and culture. Creating small industry from scratch is not as effective as maintaining and upgrading workshop, handicraft, and cottage industry left from an earlier stage. Once small industry has been disrupted or destroyed, it is difficult to reconstruct.

To be sure, the technological gap between DCs and LDCs is greater today than it was during the Meiji period. But contemporary Third World countries still have many alternatives to best-practice, capital-intensive techniques.

Summary

Meiji Japan's dual economy consisted on the one hand of traditional agriculture (producing for the village, with little reproducible capital), petty trade, and cottage industry, and on the other of capital-intensive modern manufacturing and processing, mineral extraction, and commercial agriculture, producing for the market, using reproducible capital and new technology, and hiring labor commercially. In the early twentieth century, most emigrants from rural to urban areas worked in the informal or cottage industry sector, which required little capital and skill and had few entry barriers. Industrial dualism usually occurs in sectors with few economies of scale, so that the rapid introduction of electricity from 1914 to 1930 spurred dualism, reducing these economies and increasing small-industry productivity.

Japan has emphasized gradual technical and capital improvements, enabling government, business, and labor to learn through experience. After 1868, the Meiji government established industrial extension and lending agencies to improve the engineering and techniques of small industry left from the Tokugawa period. Japanese large industry grew faster, but was less disruptive to small industry, than in today's LDCs.

Chapter 8

Export Expansion and Import Substitution

Much of our analysis up to now, like Frank's dependency thesis (chapter 1), criticizes the view of modernization theorists that LDCs can only develop as they become integrated into a global economy dominated by Western Europe, North America, and Japan. Instead, we have maintained that the development of the Third World is impaired by its economic dependence on rich nations. I disagree, however, with Frank's view that low-income countries can only develop by reducing their international trade with the developed world. I agree with dependency theorists that the international trade policies of developing countries need to be autonomous. Yet, unlike the dependency school, I think that developing countries, like Japan during the Meiji and pre–World War II periods, need to be open to international trade to increase efficiency and growth, while providing modest protection to sectors in which the country can acquire the benefits from internal economies of scale in infant industries, external economies, and technological learning.

Liberal Trade and Nondiscriminatory Exchange Rates

From 1868 to World War II, the Japanese had a policy (first forced and later chosen) of multilateral, nondiscriminatory foreign trade outside their empire (1894–1945). Japan, economically isolated before 1868, became one of the world's leading trading empires just before the 1937–45 war, and its trade contributed to rapid growth.

Although nineteenth-century Meiji Japan partially circumvented the tariff restrictions imposed by Western unequal treaties by providing protection through subsidies and state undertakings (like shipping, shipbuilding, and iron and steel), it was more open to international trade than are contemporary LDCs. While foreign trade was modest by Western standards during the Meiji government's first twenty-five years, its influence stimulated scientific and technological learning. The large domestic market usually absorbed most products of this new technology. Subsequently, as the Japanese mastered and modified innovations, they began exporting, as with textiles, the leading export from 1874 to 1940 (with raw silk and silk products expanding rapidly by enjoying a high income elasticity of demand), other light manufactures, like consumer goods and simple machines that replaced primary-product exports in second place at the turn of the twentieth century (expanding from Japan's increased price competitiveness), and the leading sectors after World War II, heavy, chemical, and consumer manufactures (especially electronics, vehicles, and sophisticated consumer goods in the 1970s, 1980s, and early 1990s). The fact that Japan could not rely on foreign capital spurred it to utilize its comparative advantage between 1874 and 1940 in exports embodying cheap labor. Over time, however with technical change and capital accumulation, Japan's comparative advantage shifted from raw materials to primary-product processing and semifinished products to light manufacturing to a wide array of manufacturing items (including capital equipment) (Inukai 1979: 5; Lockwood 1954: 17, 305–9; Minami 1986: 242–46; Yamazawa and Yamamoto 1979: 135).

In the course of their economic development, a few Asian and North African countries have moved in a similar direction, if we examine the change in the division of merchandise exports into primary and manufacturing commodities over a recent twenty-five-year period. From 1965 to 1990, Singapore and the middle-income Asian countries South Korea, Taiwan, Thailand, and Turkey have shifted from exports that were predominantly primary products to exports of diverse manufactures, including capital goods, other heavy manufactures, and light manufactures. The five countries just mentioned and the middle-income Asian and North African countries Malaysia, Jordan, Morocco, and Tunisia have all shifted from primary products comprising at least 40 percent of merchandise exports in 1965 to manufactures constituting at least 40 percent in 1990. Other LDCs, the Philippines and low-income India, Pakistan, Bangladesh, Sri Lanka, and Benin, made the same shift between 1965 and 1990, but their process of reallocation to export and import substitution has been plagued by the price distortions and industrial protection indicated for India and Pakistan in chapter 4, and has been less successful in spurring economic growth (World Bank 1992b: 218–19, 248–49). While the relatively high income elasticity of demand for manufactures provides some scope for their export expansion in LDCs, the discussion in the rest of this chapter implies that this expansion needs to be coordinated with an emphasis on openness to international trade.

Arguments against Protection

During the seventy years before the start of World War II, Japan generally followed liberal trade policies, with a sprinkling of subsidies and industrial policy in the late nineteenth century and tariffs and other forms of protection in the early twentieth century. The strongest argument for free trade is the theory of comparative advantage formulated by Adam Smith and David Ricardo, English classical economists of the late eighteenth and early nineteenth centuries. This theory states that world welfare is greatest when each country exports products whose comparative costs are lower at home than abroad and imports goods whose comparative costs are lower abroad than at home (Heckscher 1950: 272–300; Ohlin 1933).[1]

International trade theory implies that (1) LDCs gain from free international trade, and (2) lose by tariffs (import taxes), subsidies, quotas, administrative controls, and other forms of protection. But theory holds that free trade has benefits other than mere efficient resource allocation. It leads to greater productivity because it disperses new ideas and innovations. It widens markets, improves division of labor, permits more specialized machinery, overcomes technical indivisibilities, utilizes surplus productive capacity, and stimulates greater managerial effort because of foreign, competitive pressures (Leibenstein 1966: 392–415; Myint 1958: 317–37).

Arguments for Protection

Despite their apparent advantage, few newly industrializing countries pursue free trade policies. This section evaluates some major arguments for tariffs. Because of a basic symmetry in argument, all subsequent arguments for tariffs except the revenue argument also constitute cases for protective devices such as subsidies (including supporting industrial policy by the state), tactics used by Japan, especially in the late nineteenth century, to partially bypass Western treaty restrictions.

The most frequent rationale for tariffs is that they protect infant industries. Alexander Hamilton, the first U.S. secretary of the treasury, criticized Adam Smith's doctrine of laissez-faire (governmental noninterference) and free trade. Hamilton supported a tariff, passed in 1789, partly designed to protect manufacturing in his young country from foreign competition. Infant industry arguments include (1) increasing returns to scale, (2) external economies, and (3) technological borrowing.

Increasing Returns to Scale

A new firm in a new industry has many disadvantages: It must train specialized management and labor, learn new techniques, create or enter markets, and cope with the diseconomies of small-scale production. Tariff protection gives a new firm time to expand output to the point of lowest long-run average cost.

An argument against this notion is illustrated by a world of two countries, each of which initially produces a different good with decreasing costs at the lowest long-run average cost. Assume that later both countries levy tariffs to start an infant industry in the good produced by the other country, so that the market is divided and both countries produce both goods well below lowest average cost output. In this case, the world loses specialization gains and economies of scale. The world would be better off if each country specialized in one decreasing-cost product, exchanging it for the decreasing-cost product of the other country.

But some may ask if infant industry protection would not be warranted for the firm in a newly industrializing country competing with firms in well-established industrial countries. In this instance, however, by distributing income from consumers to producers, tariff protection amounts to a subsidy to cover the firm's early losses. Why should society subsidize the firm in its early years? If the enterprise is profitable over the long run, losses in the early years can be counted as part of the entrepreneur's capital costs. If the enterprise is not profitable in the long run, would not resources be better used for some other investment?

Yet government might still want to protect infant industry. First, government support may cover part of the entrepreneur's risk when average expected returns are positive but vary widely. Second, the state may support local technological learning and knowledge-creating capabilities. Third, government planners may better forecast the future success of the industry than private entrepreneurs, but protect or subsidize private investment to avoid direct operation of the industry themselves. Fourth, protecting the new industry may create external economies, or promote technological borrowing.[2]

External Economies

These are production benefits that do not accrue to the private entrepreneur. One example is technological learning, measured by a learning curve that shows how much unit costs fall with the increased labor productivity from cumulative experience. This curve, which is downward sloping over time, is a source of dynamic increasing returns. Related to these, external economies also include the training of skilled labor and lower input costs to other industries, all of which cannot be appropriated by the investor but may be socially profitable even if a commercial loss occurs. Government can make a rational case for protecting or subsidizing such investment. The argument, however, can easily be abused by political leaders who discover immeasurable externalities for pet projects.

Technological Borrowing

Classical economists assumed a given technology open to all countries. In reality, much of the world's rapidly improving technology is concentrated in a few countries.

Much international specialization is based on differences in technology rather than resource endowment. Assume both Italy and Indonesia can produce corn, but only Italy has the technical capacity to manufacture transistor radios. Thus, Italy trades radios, in which it has a comparative advantage, for Indonesia's corn. Yet Indonesia has the necessary labor and materials, so that if Italy's technology could be acquired, Indonesia's comparative advantage would shift to radios. If Indonesia levies a tariff on transistor radios, Italian companies may transfer capital and technology to produce radios behind Indonesia's tariff wall. Once Indonesia acquires this technology, its average costs will be lower than those in Italy.

Critics raise one question: If Indonesia is open to foreign investment and if foreign technology gives Indonesia a comparative advantage, why is a tariff necessary to induce the foreign company to produce radios there? Should not the foreign radio manufacturer see the opportunity and bring capital and technology to Indonesia?

Tariffs may shelter inefficient technological transfers from abroad. As chapter 4 indicated, in the 1960s, India used tariffs and other barriers to protect its automobile manufacturers who were using European technology. But the foreign-exchange cost of inputs alone exceeded the foreign-exchange cost of buying automobiles directly from abroad. India obtained little technological learning from the tariffs, which made the industry technically sluggish.

Politically, it is difficult to end tariff protection for infant industries. When governments feel compelled to protect infant industry, they could instead provide subsidies, which are politically easier to remove rather than tariffs.

Changes in Factor Endowment

A government might levy a tariff so that entrepreneurs modify their output mix to match a shifting comparative advantage due perhaps to a change in resource proportions. Thus, as its frontier pushed westward and capital expanded, the United States changed from a country rich in natural resources, exporting a wide variety of metals and minerals, to a capital-rich country. Analogously, the rapid accumulation of capital and technology may alter comparative advantage from labor-intensive to capital- and technology-intensive goods. Thus, in the 1950s and 1960s, Japan's Ministry of International Trade and Industry (MITI) tried to establish capital- and technology-intensive industries, which appeared not to be in Japan's static comparative advantage but offered more long-run growth because of rapid technical change, rapid labor productivity growth, and a high income elasticity of demand (percentage change in quantity demanded/percentage change in income).

We must ask why private entrepreneurs would not perceive the changing comparative advantage and plan accordingly. Even in Japan, while MITI facilitated the output of memory chips for semiconductors, it did not encourage electronics production and tried to prevent Soichiro Honda from producing cars! Indeed, while MITI was accommodating and supportive, private entrepreneurs invested and coordinated the essential resources (Schultze 1983: 3–12). Government protection (or subsidy) is appropriate only if government foresees these changes better than private entrepreneurs.

Revenue Sources

Tariffs are often a major source of revenue, especially in young nations with limited ability to raise direct taxes. In fact, U.S. tariffs in 1789, despite Alexander Hamilton's intentions, did more to raise revenue than to protect domestic industry.

Even for a government unconcerned about the losses a tariff imposes on other people, tariffs have limits. At the extreme, a prohibitive tariff brings no revenue. And a tariff that maximizes revenue in the short run will probably not do so in the long run. In the short run, before domestic production has moved into import-competing industries, demand is often inelastic (that is, the absolute value of the percentage change in quantity is less than the absolute value of the percentage change in price). However, once productive resources adjust, demand elasticities increase, and a greater relative quantity decrease—in response to the increased price from the tariff—occurs. Thus, a government setting a maximum revenue tariff must take account of the long-run movement of productive resources.

Improved Employment and the Balance of Payments

A rise in tariff rates diverts demand from imports to domestic goods, so that the balance on goods and services (exports minus imports), aggregate demand, and employment increase.[3] The economic injury to other countries, however, may provoke retaliation. Furthermore, the effects of import restrictions and increased prices spread throughout the economy, so that domestic- and export-oriented production and employment decline. In fact, a study of the U.S. economy indicates that jobs lost by export contraction exceed jobs created by import replacement (Krause 1971: 421–25). It is more effective to use the policies discussed in chapter 2 on appropriate technology and, when possible, monetary and fiscal policies for employment and home currency devaluation to improve employment and the balance of payments.

Reduced Internal Instability

The sheer economic cost of periodic fluctuations in employment or prices from unstable international suppliers or customers may justify tariffs to reduce dependence on foreign trade. According to the World Bank (1978), commodities accounting for one-third of LDC nonfuel primary exports fluctuated in price by more than 10 percent from one year to the next from 1955 to 1976. By encouraging import substitution, tariff protection can reorient the economy toward more stable domestic production. Losses in allocative efficiency might be outweighed by the greater efficiency implicit in more rational cost calculations and investment decisions. Yet such a policy may be costly. Tariffs on goods with inelastic demand, such as necessities, increase import payments.

Policy makers should compare the costs of alternative ways of stabilizing the internal economy, such as holding reserves. An LDC with adequate foreign-exchange reserves can maintain its purchasing power during times of low demand for its exports. Moreover, a country can use reserves from import commodities to offset the destabilizing effects of sudden shortages on domestic prices and incomes (World Bank 1978: 19–29).

National Defense

An LDC may want to avoid dependence on foreign sources for essential materials or products that could be cut off in times of war or other conflict. A tariff in such a case is only worthwhile if it will take time to build the capacity to produce these goods. Otherwise, the developing country should use cheaper foreign supplies while they are available.

Policy makers will want to examine alternatives to a national defense tariff, such as stockpiling strategic goods or developing facilities to produce import substitutes without using them until the need arises. In a period of rapid technical change in military and strategic goods, a government must ask whether it is worth increasing costs through tariffs to avoid hypothetical future dangers. Would it not be better to divert these resources to investment, research, and technical education to increase the economy's overall strength and adaptability?

Extracting Foreign Monopoly or Duopoly Profit

An LDC facing a foreign monopoly supplier of a good may levy a tariff to transfer some of the monopoly profit to revenue for the LDC. While world welfare falls, the home country levying the tariff increases its welfare at the expense of the foreign producer.

Assume an LDC firm is competing against a foreign firm: (1) in a duopoly—that is, where there are two firms in an industry, (2) where price and output decisions are interdependent, and (3) where both are characterized by internal economies of scale—that is, a falling average-cost curve. A tariff can increase exports for the protected firm in any foreign market in which the firm operates. However, if the foreign country retaliates with a tariff, the two firms are likely to maintain previous market shares, with a greatly reduced volume of trade (Appleyard and Field 1992: 162–69; Brandner and Spencer 1981: 371–89; Krugman 1984: 180–93).

Antidumping

Dumping is selling a product cheaper abroad than at home. Why should a country object to it? If a foreign country is supplying cheap imports favorable to consumers, should not such action be considered as a reduction in foreign comparative costs? Yes and no. If the foreign supplier is dumping as a temporary stage in a price war to drive home producers out of business and establish a monopoly, a country may be justified in levying a tariff.

Reduced Luxury Consumption

Government may wish to levy a tariff to curtail the consumption of luxury goods. An excise tax, however, levied on the sale of luxury commodities, is probably preferable to a tariff on luxuries, which would have the unintended effect of stimulating domestic luxury goods investment and production.

From our arguments, it should now be clear that tariff protection need not necessarily be attributed to analytical error or the power of vested interests, but may be based on some genuine exceptions to the case for free trade. Yet, many of the most frequent arguments for tariffs, such as protecting infant industry, are more limited than many LDC policy makers suppose. In fact, a critical analysis of the arguments for tariffs provides additional support for liberal trade policies similar to those of early modern Japan.

Sogo Shosha

In the 1860s, when Japan opened its door to foreign trade, firms for international trade had to be newly created. Some firms, such as Mitsui Bussan, founded a modern company free from the business tradition of the Tokugawa period. Established in 1876, by 1907 Mitsui Bussan became Japan's first *sogo shosha,* with 40 foreign branches in Asia and Europe, and trading in more than 120 goods. Mitsui Bussan constituted the core company of the Mitsui business group (formed in 1874) and actively participated in the formation of a zaibatsu.

Other firms came into being after the zaibatsu was founded. For example, Mitsubishi Shoji started when Mitsubishi Goshi Kaisha established its marketing department in 1894.

The Japanese general trading company (*sogo shosha*) is a firm that trades a large variety of commodities on a global scale, in export and import trade. The *sogo shosha* in Japan contrasts to the major foreign trade organizations in other nations—the specialized trading companies and colonial traders in Britain, and the export departments of manufacturing firms in the United States.

The zaibatsu purchased substantial output directly from small manufacturers, even selling products overseas, a task usually too difficult for small firms. The great trading companies or *sogo shosha,* such as Mitsui Bussan, Mitsubishi Shoji, Okura, Sumitomo, and Yasuda, made loans to small producers (sometimes indirectly through local merchants and banks) and acquired product disposal rights. Largely because of the international trading companies, a larger share of

Japanese exports and foreign direct investment involved small and medium-sized firms than in the United States or Europe. Without these traders, many small industries would not have survived. *Sogo shosha* economized on the import of soft technologies such as accounting techniques, foreign-exchange procedures, and insurance that were essential with the opening of foreign trade; over the decades, the great trading companies also economized on information (for example, on prices) and scarce foreign-language and foreign-trade skills, and diversified to spread out risk. Moreover, the longevity of trading companies facilitated raw-material procurement, export promotion, and foreign production. To be sure, these companies charged high interest rates for loans to small units and purchased their goods at low prices. But overall, the effect of the *sogo shosha*, an institution unique to Japan, was probably positive (Allen 1982: 60–64; Lockwood 1954: 210–11; Mahajan 1976: 35–36; Yonekawa and Yoshihara 1987: ix–35, 347).

Replacing Western Imports, Financing, and Shipping

The Western trader pioneered early modern Japan's foreign trade, Western banks provided much of the financing, and Western shipping lines carried most of the cargoes. But by 1876, with government help, Japanese trading companies such as Mitsui Bussan (Mitsui Trading Company) began international operations. In addition, Tokyo Marine Insurance Company (1879), Yokohama Specie Bank (1880), and Japan Mail Steamship Company (1885), with state assistance, pioneered marine insurance, foreign exchange, and marine transport organizations. As the Japanese acquired knowledge of Western markets and the skills of large-scale trade and finance, they steadily replaced the Westerner. Thus, while in 1885 only 9 percent of Japan's export trade was in Japanese hands, by 1913 Japanese firms handled most overseas commerce, Japanese ships moved half of that commerce, and Japanese general trading companies were involved in some way in more than two-thirds of Japan's foreign trade. In the late nineteenth and turn of the twentieth centuries, Americans sold electric light plants, streetcars, phonographs, taxis, and so forth to Japan, but by the 1910s, U.S. manufacturers distributed directly to capture the Japanese market or the Japanese learned to copy the product. This era of economic liberalism meant that, in contrast to today, advanced nations made many machines and techniques freely available, providing opportunity for Japanese innovation and modification. During World War I, Japan sacrificed internal demand to expand exports to new markets. Also, by 1930, Japan was carrying two-thirds of its foreign trade in its own ocean vessels (partly because of bans on foreign shipping companies in principal Japanese ports after 1894 and on foreign companies' coastal trade after 1911), and was financing trade through Japanese banks and trading companies (Lockwood 1954: 329–30, 544–49; Minami 1986: 238–39; Nakamura 1983: 244–55).

Like Meiji and early twentieth century Japan, today's low-income countries need to facilitate the creation of new international trade institutions, including specialized trading services, foreign-exchange banks, insurance establishments, marine transport agencies, and the like. While in the short run many of these institutions can be foreign, in the long run LDCs may want to capture some of the gains from learning to establish and operate these institutions.

Japan's Rapid Export Growth

Early modern Japan did not discriminate against exports (through overvalued domestic currency and farm price ceilings) as late twentieth-century Asia and Africa have. Increased tariff protection in the first quarter of the twentieth century reduced the price of foreign exchange, but government export promotion through a bank to finance trade, the study and development of foreign trade techniques, exhibiting Japanese products overseas, sales bureaus abroad, official inspection for quality control, chambers of commerce and commodity guilds for cooperative export activity, merchant-marine subsidies, and business privilege in the new empire brought export inducements near that of an equilibrium exchange rate through 1937 (except for the 1920s). An equilibrium rate results in an international current-account balance (exports minus imports of goods and services plus net grants, remittances, and unilateral transfer received) of zero over the long run without undue trade and payments restrictions and without financial policies that sacrifice the optimal tradeoff between growth and price stability.

Japan's annual real average growth rates in export receipts were 8.4 percent between 1880 and 1913 (compared with 2.6 percent for Britain, 4.2 percent for the United States, and 3.2 percent for the world generally), and 5.2 percent between 1913 and 1937 (compared with 0.4 percent for Britain, 1.4 percent for the United States, and 1.4 for the world). The fast growth from 1913 to 1937 occurred despite a decline in the commodity terms of trade (price index of exports/price index of imports). Overall, on the average, Japan's export volume doubled every decade from 1880 to 1937. Many contemporary LDCs overvalue their domestic currency (the Indian rupee, the Indonesian rupiah, the Thai baht, the Philippine peso, and the Nigerian naira at least through the early 1980s) relative to foreign currency, discouraging domestic producers from exporting and substituting imports unless protected by massive subsidies (Lockwood 1954: 104, 531; Mahajan 1976: 57–58; Minami 1986: 174–77, 222–23; Nakamura 1983: 4–5; Power 1979: 44–45).

Export expansion stimulates economic growth by creating effective demand and allowing increased imports without a balance-of-trade deficit. In the late nineteenth century, exports included textiles (with raw silk accounting for one-third of Japan's commodity export earnings between 1870 and 1930), marine products (state-sponsored), tea, rice, copper, coal, pottery, paper, lacquer, and bronze.

During the first three decades of the twentieth century, Japan depended heavily on exports of raw materials and semifinished product, gradually switching to the export of metal, machinery, electrical equipment, and chemicals. Japan's initial boom in shipping, munitions, and other manufactures during World War I, especially in China and the United States, continued in the postwar period. Its industry quickly adapted to the exacting demand of foreign consumers, especially from American women. Textile and fiber exports reoriented from silk to cotton, woolen, and rayon goods in the 1930s. After raw silk fabrics had begun to shed their international competitiveness in the late 1920s, Japanese businessmen switched to rayon, becoming the second largest producer (to the United States) in 1935 and benefiting from the expanding international demand for rayon. Production rose from 115 tons of rayon products in 1921 to 16,000 tons in 1930, and 91,000 tons in 1935. Yet, at the same time, Japan maintained its share of raw silk exports (Lockwood 1954: 65–83; Mahajan 1976: 55–57).

The value of exports—6–7 percent of GNP in the early Meiji period—gradually rose to 15–20 percent of GNP from the middle of Meiji through the 1930s. The *marginal* propensity to export (ratio of increased real exports to increased real GNP) from 1888 to 1938 was 25 percent. Indeed, the value of textile exports (f.o.b.) as a percentage of the total value of textile manufacturing output was 50.2 percent in 1909, 59.9 percent in 1919, and 33.9 percent in 1934.

Rapid export growth reduced resource-poor Japan's import constraint on raw materials and fuels for industrialization. Japan's imports of goods and services as a percentage of GNP increased gradually from 7.6 percent in 1888 to 13.6 percent in 1900 to 16.8 percent in 1910 to 21.7 percent in 1938. While *merchandise* imports exceeded exports from 1885 to 1938, much of this deficit was offset by invisibles (mostly shipping), net grants, remittances, unilateral transfers, and net capital inflows. Indeed, the net current-account balance was positive during the period 1885–1938.

Imports encouraged modern science, technology, and management, as the Japanese dismantled and analyzed promising products and began to produce them, sometimes after modification. Technological learning from imports was especially important for twenty-five years after the country opened in 1859. Exports also spurred increased capital formation, technology, management improvement, employment, and scale economies. Overall, Japan's international trade contributed more to industrialization than trade statistics indicate (Lockwood 1954: 15–17, 38–39, 189–90; Mahajan 1976: 56–57, 109–21; Minami 1986: 223–29).

In the 1930s, Japan's exports diversified to consumer goods (toys, pottery, brushes, hat braids, rubber tires, shoes, electric lamps, canned fish, and so forth), and increasing machinery and equipment. Japan's role as a rising industrial power required a steady rise of imports—raw materials (cotton, wool, pulp, petroleum, iron, steel, and nonferrous metals), vehicles, food, and fertilizer.

On the eve of World War II, Japan occupied an intermediate position in the international economy between the West and Africa, Asia, and Latin America. Japan exported textiles, silk products, consumer manufactures, semimanufactures, and some machinery to and imported raw materials from China and other parts of Asia, and imported advanced industrial equipment from the West.

Japan's exports grew from 2.9 percent of world exports in 1929 to 3.6 percent in 1935 and 1936, increasingly threatening finished manufactures in Britain, the United States, and other leading industrial nations. This "flooding" of foreign markets by Japanese goods after 1931, during the height of the Great Depression, brought frantic outcries in the West, resulting in increased trade barriers against Japan and arousing Japan's fear and resentment. With colonial trade shares having fallen, Japan was shut out from much of the world market through tariffs and quotas; these and other restrictions were a major factor driving Japan into global war in the late 1930s and early 1940s. No country had a greater stake in liberal multilateral trade than Japan: by 1936 it depended on foreign sources for 20 percent of rice and beans, 35 percent of oils and fats, 60 to 80 percent of iron and steel, 90 percent of superphosphate fertilizer, and all cotton, wool, and rubber. To escape its dependence on the world economy, Japan became highly aggressive, seizing Manchuria in 1931 and using violence to carve out a self-sufficient economic empire in East Asia. Japan's remarkable ability to hold out for so long during World War II resulted from its devotion of an estimated 80 percent of its resources to war during 1940–44. The civilian population suffered many hardships, paying heavily for the war. In World War I, by contrast, Japan could afford to be neutral and less aggressive because of the West's low trade barriers (Allen 1964: 151; Lockwood 1954: 65–68, 75–76, 81–83, 94, 306).

During the seven decades before World War II, colonialism and informal imperialism usually inhibited export expansion or import substitution in other LDCs in Asia and Africa. For example, the Nigerian participation in the colonial commercial economy consisted primarily of peasants producing export crops and mining workers employed by oligopolistic foreign companies. Nigerian exports (mainly primary products) stagnated as the commodity terms of trade declined between 1913 and 1945 (especially during two world wars and the Great Depression). Furthermore, the indigenous middle classes had a high propensity to emulate foreigners' import of luxury consumer goods, while monopolistic foreign trading houses discouraged competition from Nigerian import-substitution industry (International Development Center of Japan 1977: 164–79).

Japan's Borrowing and Capital Inflows

The growing export earnings by Japan during the last three decades of the nineteenth century enabled it to finance its bulging import bill with a minimum of foreign borrowing before 1900—two small railroad loans totaling ¥30 million during 1870 and 1873. Lockwood believes that Japan's wariness of Western financial imperialism and the West's reluctance to lend were responsible for the small borrowing. Japan's borrowing in the early twentieth century encouraged exports and import substitution in key industries (Lockwood 1954: 253; Mahajan 1976: 54, 83–84).

Japan's ratio of foreign capital to GNP from 1887 to 1896 was 0.2 percent, and rose to a high of 4 percent from 1897 to 1906. This is compared with peaks of ratios of 2 percent from 1880 to 1913 in Russia, and 1 percent in the United States in the 1880s. Japan, a debtor nation in 1914, began exporting capital (with an international balance of goods and services surplus) in World War I and became a large creditor in 1919 (Gregory and Stuart 1986: 43–44; Kuznets 1966: 332–334).

Export Promotion and Import Substitution Strategies

A newly industrializing country usually needs to increase its access to the inputs needed for the expansion of manufacturing. The country can either expand exports to increase the capacity to import or substitute the domestic production of essential inputs purchase overseas. Most studies indicate that the Japanese emphasis on export expansion is a more efficient strategy.

For example, a National Bureau of Economic Research (NBER) study of fifteen LDCs indicates that the Japanese approach, with its emphasis on foreign-exchange rate equilibrium and export promotion, is generally more effective than highly protected import substitution in expanding output and employment in contemporary LDCs (but see the next section on today's disadvantageous international economic environment). NBER empirical data confirm the Heckscher–Ohlin theorem, in which LDCs in early stages of growth are most likely to have a comparative advantage in exporting labor-intensive goods and importing capital- or skilled-labor-intensive commodities. A strategy that substitutes domestic output for imports, then, emphasizes the production of goods more likely to use considerably more capital per unit of labor. Export promotion includes the following advantages: (1) international competition, which encourages quality control, new products and techniques, and good management; (2) cost to society is more visible than protection, and (3) efficient firms are not limited by domestic demand growth. Export promotion relies on pricing incentives, such as market exchange rates, export subsidies, and concessional credit, which provide a uniform bias among export activities.

As an example, during most of the 1980s, Mexico provided incentives for import substitutes and implicitly discouraged export development. During the same period, on the other hand, South Korea, generally pursued a policy consistent with the Japanese model, providing few incentives for import substitution while encouraging export activity through capital subsidies, depreciation allowances, import duty exemptions, and exchange rates near equilibrium. From 1980 to 1991, Mexico's real annual growth rates were 1.3 percent in industry and –0.5 percent overall, compared with Korea's 12.1 and 8.7 percent—spurred by scale economies, international competition, price flexibility, and no agricultural and foreign-exchange shortages associated with export promotion. Like Japan from 1868 to 1939, the major strategy for LDCs expanding exports today is to increase domestic productivity (Krueger 1978, 1983; Krueger et al. 1981, vol. 1; World Bank 1993b: 238–41).

The International Economic Environment for Meiji Japan and LDCs Today

Meiji Japan's exports also benefited from favorable international economic conditions in the late nineteenth century. The demand for light industrial exports, such as textiles, was not saturated, nor did Japan face competition (as today's LDCs do) from numerous other newly industrializing countries seeking to take advantage of their labor abundance in specializing in labor-intensive manufactures. Moreover, from 1868 to 1897, the yen chronically depreciated vis-à-vis the pound sterling and dollar, making exports more competitive and imports less alluring. Indeed, from 1882 to 1897, the yen was on a de facto silver standard, as silver declined relative to gold.

Although the immediate postwar and early Great Depression trade balance was in deficit due to yen overvaluation and the resulting slow growth of exports, exports grew well after 1931, when Japan reversed its ill-timed return to the gold standard in 1930–31 and followed England's abandonment of the standard, depreciating the yen and stimulating industrial exports (food processing, chemical, and machinery industries) and import substitution (steel and electric motors) for the rest of the 1930s. In contrast, India, whose rupee was pegged to sterling during most of the 1860s to the 1930s, was prevented from devaluing its rupee to stimulate exports and import replacements (Goldsmith 1983: 36–37; Lockwood 1954: 46–47, 63–64).

Contemporary Asian countries are not hampered as much by the low income and demand of neighboring countries as was Meiji Japan. Still, today's international economic conditions are less favorable to LDC export expansion. The most rapidly expanding LDC manufactured exports during the 1970s and 1980s were textiles, clothing, footwear, and simple consumer goods, which required labor-intensive technology that was widely available. Yet, the substantial development of manufactured exports in developing countries was concentrated in a relatively few middle-income countries. While in 1990, the four leading newly industrialized countries—South Korea, Taiwan, Hong Kong, and Singapore—which comprised less than 3 percent of the LDC population, accounted for 54 percent of LDC clothing and textile exports and 69 percent of LDC manufactured exports. China, with 28 percent of the LDC population, had 15 percent of manufactured exports; South and Southeast Asia, with 38 percent of the population, had 5 percent of total manufactured exports; and sub-Saharan Africa, with 12 percent of the LDC population, had 1 percent of total manufactured exports.

The competition from other aspiring newly industrial exporting countries is more severe than it was for Meiji Japan (Lockwood 1954: 398–401; Population Reference Bureau 1993; World Bank 1988: 244–45, 1992b: 244–49).

One sign of the peripheralness of many LDCs is their international trade vulnerability, which is exacerbated by a high export commodity concentration ratio, the four leading commodities as a percentage of total merchandise export earnings. From 1973 to 1985, these ratios included Zambia at 96 percent (with copper 90 percent), Somalia at 94 percent (with livestock 90 percent), Ethiopia at 87 percent (coffee, oilseeds, and hides and skin), Liberia at 85 percent (iron ore, rubber, and wood), Malawi at 84 percent (tobacco, tea, peanuts, and oilseeds), Ghana at 82 percent (cocoa, wood, and aluminum), Côte d'Ivoire at 73 percent, Sudan at 65 percent, Kenya at 63 percent, Bangladesh at 59 percent, Sri Lanka at 59 percent, Tanzania at 55 percent, the Philippines at 50 percent, and Pakistan at 47 percent. Oil-exporting countries such as Nigeria and Indonesia are in a similar position; their major export is petroleum, of course. In 1985, tropical beverages (coffee, cocoa, and tea) accounted for 24 percent and six primary commodities for more than 70 percent of sub-Saharan Africa's export earnings. Meiji Japan's export commodity concentration ratios (45 percent in both 1900 and 1920) were much lower than these contemporary LDC ratios. However, several Asian countries had figures even lower than early twentieth-century Japan: a diversified and industrially oriented South Korea had a ratio of 4 percent, Malaysia had 34 percent, and Thailand 35 percent (El Samhouri 1989, calculated from United Nations 1973–85; Bank of Japan 1966: 280–83; Nafziger 1988a: 55).[4]

The high commodity concentration of contemporary LDCs is associated with volatile export prices and earnings. Developing countries are vulnerable to relative international price instability not only because of their dependence on volatile primary product exports but also because exports are highly concentrated in a few commodities and directed to a few countries. The resulting wide swings in export prices have had a disastrous effect on government budgets and external balances.

The predominantly nonoil primary products that LDCs export and the manufactured products exported by DCs and a few newly industrializing countries are not priced the same way. Although global marketing for most primary products is oligopolistic, the LDC farmer is a price taker, with no influence on market price; however, widespread commodity productivity gains can result in lower prices. On the other hand, most industrial production and marketing are monopolistic, with productivity gains leading to higher prices.

From 1970 to 1990, Africa and Asia, especially sub-Saharan Africa, disproportionately producing and exporting primary products, suffered from both fluctuating and declining prices of exports relative to imports, which were predominantly industrial goods. African and Asian commodity terms of trade (the price index of exports divided by the price index of imports) changed from 100 in 1970 to 103 in 1980 to 79 in 1990. The sub-Sahara's commodity terms of trade plummeted from 100 in 1970 to 77 in 1980 to 53 in 1990, a 47 percent reduction in twenty years! Indeed, from 1985 through 1991, the sub-Saharan terms of trade declined every year, falling 34 percent (fig. 8.1). Export volume fell from 100 in 1970 to 86 in 1980, only recovering to 100 for the first time in 1990. Export purchasing power (or income terms of trade), the commodity terms of trade times export volume, dropped from 100 in 1970 to 66 in 1980 to 53 in 1990, indicating, again, a reduction of 47 percent during the twenty-year period. These declines contributed to a falling goods and services balance and a continually worsening external crisis during the 1980s. In contrast, Japan from 1871 to 1938 did not experience sharp swings downward in terms of trade until they fell 29 percent from 1921–30 to 1931–38 (IMF 1989: 98, 102, 1990: 139, 141, 1991: 114; Minami 1986: 239–42).

The fall in Asian and sub-Saharan African commodity terms of trade over a period of two decades is consistent with the Prebisch–Singer thesis that the terms of trade of countries specializing in primary goods (food, raw materials, minerals, and organic oils and fats) decrease in the long run. This thesis, based on declining primary-product prices from the 1870s to 1938, states that the terms of trade deteriorate because of differences in the growth of demand for, and the market structure in, primary and manufacturing production. Engel's law indicates that as income increases, the proportion of income spent on manufactured goods rises and the proportion spent on primary products, falls. If resources do not shift from primary to manufacturing output, there will be an excess supply of and declining relative price in primary products, and an excess demand for and increasing relative price in manufactured goods. Moreover, primary production is relatively competitive, so the productivity gains result in lower prices, but manufacturing is relatively monopolistic, with productivity gains leading to higher prices (IMF 1987: 68, 1991: 114; Prebisch 1962: 1–2; Singer 1950: 473–85; United Nations Department of Economic Affairs 1949).[5]

Is the Prebisch–Singer thesis adequate? The bulk of the extensive evaluation of this thesis during the 1950s through 1970s (summarized in Nafziger 1990a: 396–99) indicated the inadequacy of the data sources used by Raul Prebisch and Hans Singer. However, John Spraos's (1985) careful statistical study for the United Nations in 1983 showed that, when we adjust for biases, these data sources would still indicate a deterioration of primary producers' terms of trade, although by a smaller magnitude than Prebisch and Singer thought. Figure 8.2 on page 146 shows a declining trend for the price of *nonoil* commodities relative to exports of manufactures since 1948.

In 1956, Charles P. Kindleberger, while not supporting deteriorating long-run terms of trade for *primary product exporters,* observed that LDCs are especially vulnerable to declining terms of trade because they cannot easily shift resources as patterns of comparative advantage change. The primary-product export concentration mentioned above, the dependence of LDC primary exports on foreign multinational corporations for processing, marketing, and financing, and limita-

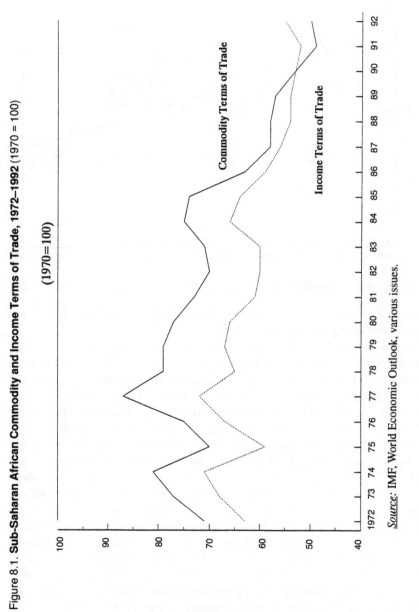

Figure 8.1. Sub-Saharan African Commodity and Income Terms of Trade, 1972–1992 (1970 = 100)

(1970=100)

Commodity Terms of Trade

Income Terms of Trade

Source: IMF, World Economic Outlook, various issues.

Source: IMF, World Economic Outlook, various issues.

Figure 8.2. **Nonoil Commodity Prices Relative to Unit Value of Manufactures Exports, 1948–1990**

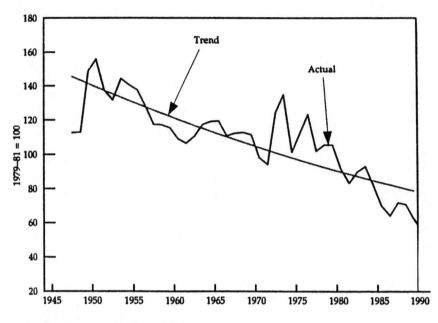

Source: World Bank (1991a: 46).

tions on the expansion of processing indicate the LDCs' inability to shift resources with changing demand and technologies.

A *single country,* such as Meiji Japan, exporting agricultural and light manufacturing goods, would often be a price taker with substantial scope in expanding export receipts alongside a long-run elastic supply curve. Could not a single primary-producing country today assume that it can expand export volume without adversely affecting price? The World Bank admonishes African and Asian governments to "get prices right," allowing prices to reach a market-clearing rate, rejecting past policies of setting minimum prices for industrial goods, fixing price ceilings on food, and setting low prices for foreign currency, all of which discourage primary product exports. Today, however, this single-country analysis suffers from a fallacy of composition: What is true of the individual case is not necessarily true of all cases combined. Thus, while policies promoting domestic-currency prices favorable to primary-product exporters might help a given country (whose global market share is probably too small to affect world price adversely), the adoption of these policies by numerous LDCs under pressure to improve external balances results in a market glut from increased export volume, which reduces total export receipts when the price elasticity of demand (the absolute value of the percentage change in quantity demanded divided by the percentage change in price) is less than one (inelastic). Inelastic demand can be illustrated by the doubling of cocoa exports (in tons), thereby reducing their prices per ton 75 percent so that total export receipts fall by 50 percent.

Given the slow growth of exports, many LDC governments have tried to industrialize and improve their international balance of payments by import substitution. Replacing imports with domestic production, as an exception to resource allocation by comparative advantage, can be justified on the grounds of increasing returns, external economies, technological borrowing, and internal stability. However, as indicated above, arguments for protection are more limited in effect than many Third World leaders suppose. Studies indicate that most LDCs have carried import substitution to the point at which gains to local industrialists are less than losses to consumers, merchants, input buyers, and taxpayers. Indeed, import substitution in Africa and South Asia has generated self-reliant but socially wasteful technology that would have been written off with lower protection rates.

Inward-looking policies have been costly to Africa and South Asia, increasing their dependence on just a few exports and on the protection and monopoly power of foreign capital. Moreover, protection reduces the domestic-currency price (shilling or rupee) of foreign exchange, thus discouraging exporters. Import restrictions increase local demand for import-competing sectors' production and use of domestic resources, increasing the price of domestic inputs and foreign-exchange (dollar) price of domestic currency, thus reducing exports. Indeed, Dean DeRosa argues that this fall in exports matches the protection-induced fall in imports in the sub-Sahara. The mean tariff, customs surcharge, surtax, stamp tax, other fiscal charges, and tax on foreign-exchange transactions in sub-Saharan countries are 33 percent of value. Since nontariff barriers (quantitative restrictions, foreign-exchange restrictions, minimum price systems, and state trading monopolies) affect 81 percent of tariff line items, the total protective and exchange-rate distortions caused by the sub-Sahara's import barriers are substantial. DeRosa (1991: 42–45) estimates that sub-Saharan Africa loses 15 to 32 percent of its potential export revenue because of import protection. Emphases on export expansion activities have the following advantages: (1) competitive pressures tend to improve quality and reduce costs; (2) information provided by DC users can improve export technology and product quality; (3) cost economies develop from increased market size, and (4) increased imports of productive inputs result from the greater availability of foreign-exchange earnings (Fransman 1986: 75–93).

Yet, DeRosa and other Bank/Fund liberalizers fail to realize that Africa's emphasis on import substitution rather than export expansion is a result of an export trap: declining export purchasing power is due to rapid LDC primary-product export growth and a DC tariff structure biased against LDC expansion in primary-product processing and light manufactures. For African industrial export expansion to be successful, DCs must reduce protectionist policies. If DCs had

Table 8.1

Simulated Effects of a 5 Percent Reduction in DC Manufacturing Tariffs on Africa in 1989

	1990	1991	Average 1992–95
Current account balance/export	+1.0%	+0.8%	0.0%
Debt/export	−9.2%	−11.3%	−9.5%
Debt service/export	−1.5%	−1.7%	−1.4%
Real GNP	+1.2%	+1.6%	+1.6%
Export volume	+2.6%	+3.4%	+3.3%
Import volume	+3.0%	+4.1%	+4.5%

Source: IMF (1990: 74–75).

dropped manufacturing tariffs on Africa in 1989 by 5 percentage points, an IMF simulation model estimates the effects presented in table 8.1.

In the late nineteenth century, Japan faced U.S. and European tariffs at least as high as contemporary DC tariffs levied against African and Asian exports. Late nineteenth-century protection in the West, however, did not discriminate so systematically against the early stages of processing primary products, such as textiles, as contemporary DC protection does.

Most LDC policy makers perceive the International Monetary Fund and World Bank strategies as focusing on a narrow range of agricultural and light industrial exports. Countries adopting Bank/Fund structural adjustment, including agricultural export expansion through currency devaluation and price decontrol, face severe competition from other LDCs whose adjustment programs require similar policies (Mills 1989: vii–2; World Bank 1981, 1991b). Although expanding primary-product and light-manufacturing exports and achieving market-clearing exchange rates were successful strategies in Meiji Japan from 1868 to 1912, where there was little competition from other LDCs, today's low-income countries face export expansion limitations from numerous LDC competitors producing commodities in markets with low income and price elasticities.

For Asia and Africa, industrial comparative advantage may lie in the processing of natural-resource-based goods. For example, Pakistan might export textiles and yarn, Zambia might export refined copper, and Tanzania might export coffee essences or extracts. DC nominal tariff rates appear low (5–6 percent of value after the General Agreements on Tariffs and Trade's 1974–79 Tokyo Round trade negotiations); however, on processing and manufacturing, DC effective rates of protection, which are a measure of protection as a percentage of value added by production factors at each processing stage, have been high. Tokyo Round effective protection on LDC commodities according to processing state, not lowered during GATT's Uruguay Round, 1986–94, was 3 percent on stage 1 (the raw material, for example, raw cotton), 23 percent on stage 2 (low-level processing, as of cotton yarn), 20 percent on stage 3 (high-level processing, as of cotton fabrics), and 15 percent on stage 4 (the finished product, for example, clothing). DC effective rates of protection, which are highest at low levels of processing where poor countries concentrate their industrial activities, have encouraged the importing of raw materials at the expense of processing, especially at lower levels. Fifty-four percent of DC imports from LDCs are at stage 1, 29 percent at stage 2, 9 percent at stage 3, and 8 percent at stage 4. Zambia, which had the largest nonagricultural share (85 percent) of 1989 GDP in the low-income sub-Sahara and a high elasticity of employment growth with respect to nonagricultural output growth, expanded from consumer goods to intermediate and capital goods. But high effective protection rates on processing have diverted Zambia's industrial growth from exports to import substitution. Indeed, until the late 1980s, MNCs with subsidiaries in Zambia, Zaïre, Botswana, and Namibia built most of the fabricating and processing plants in South Africa and in the West. High protection rates on processing have also diverted India, Pakistan, Sri Lanka, and Indonesia, each of which has a nonagricultural sector with a share in 1989 GDP of at least 70 percent, from exports to import substitution (World Bank 1991b: 208). Moreover, since the Tokyo Round, DCs have promulgated new trade restrictions—"voluntary" export restraints (often imposed in anticipation of more severe restrictions levied by DC parliaments) including Multifiber Arrangements (MFA) that limit India and Nigeria, trigger price mechanisms, antidumping duties, industrial subsidies, and other nontariff barriers, especially on labor-intensive goods such as textiles, clothing, and food, in which LDCs are more likely to have a comparative advantage, as well as iron and steel and chemicals. The share of OECD imports from LDCs subject to nontariff barriers climbed from 20.5 percent in 1981 to 21.8 percent in 1990. Manufactures increased from 26.5 percent to 28.0 percent (Nafziger 1990a: 403–4; World Bank 1981: 23, 1987b: 136–38, 1988: 16–17, 1991b: 234–35, 1992b: 15–26; World Bank and U.N. Development Programme 1989: 15–16).

The MFA allows bilateral agreements—often arising from economic pressures brought by rich countries—and unilateral ceilings on any product category to limit "disruptive" textile and clothing imports. While the NICs like South Korea, Taiwan, and Singapore have been the chief losers under MFA, low-income countries have also been affected, including Nigeria, which has been subject to U.S. textile quotas since 1991. Even little Mauritius was forced to conclude a "voluntary" export restraint agreement, restricting its textile exports to the European Union (then the European Community), even though exports from Mauritius comprise less than 0.1 percent of the EU's textile imports (Parfitt and Riley 1989: 46).

In 1987, DC use of nontariff barriers affected about 25 percent of nonfuel imports from LDCs, compared with 21 percent of those from other DCs. Beginning in 1989, the Super 301 provision of the U.S. Omnibus Trade and Competitiveness Act directed the president to identify unfair trade sanctions against LDCs for trade, foreign-exchange, and investment restrictions. Indeed, international trade agreements with the United States and other DCs represent attempts to reregulate markets in response to changing economic and political conditions. In 1990, the net producer subsidy equivalents for the United States were 44 percent in wheat, 49 percent in rice, and 62 percent in milk; for the European Union, 46 percent for wheat, 60 percent for rice, and 69 percent for milk; and for Japan, 99 percent for wheat, 87 percent for rice, and 69 percent for milk (*IMF Survey* (December 21, 1988): 386–89; Ray 1989: 145–46; UNCTAD 1991: 152; World Bank 1987b: 136–37).

Many low-income countries, especially in sub-Saharan Africa, are caught in an export trap: as numerous LDCs face pressure from Bank/Fund adjustment programs to expand primary-product export supply, relative prices fall substantially. In the 1970s and 1980s, the purchasing power of exports, which comprise 20 to 25 percent of GNP in the sub-Sahara, fell more than one-half, spreading negative multiplier and linkage effects to other sectors of the economy. Primary-product export expansion encountered competition from other economies requiring export expansion for adjustment. Furthermore, DC tariff structure limits growth in processing and agroindustry exports in Africa. Indeed, international economic factors, such as low and falling export relative to import prices, increased economic pressures on Nigeria's Second Republic (1979–83) and on the Mohammed Buhari military government (1983–85), both of which were overthrown; and on the Ibrahim Babangida regime (1985–93), which faced discontent evidenced by several aborted coups. (In Nigeria, if 1980 = 100, commodity terms of trade were 76 in 1982, 81 in 1983, 78 in 1985, and 36 in 1990, while income terms of trade were 28 in 1982, 40 in 1983, 43 in 1985, and 21 in 1990 [Nafziger 1993: 69].) In addition, declining relative export prices added to the pressures on political leaders in African countries with high export commodity concentration ratios (especially in primary products): Mobutu Sese Seko (Zaïre), Kenneth Kaunda (Zambia), Jerry Rawlings (Ghana), Hastings Kamuzu Banda (Malawi), Daniel arap Moi (Kenya), and the late Felix Houphouet-Boigney (Côte d'Ivoire) and Samuel K. Doe (Liberia).

Part of the challenge for DCs, especially in GATT negotiations, is to identify policies that promote growth internationally but that also strengthen domestic political constituencies' support of trade liberalization. Although it is not a surplus nation, the United States bears some responsibility for the low level of global economic activity in the 1980s and early 1990s. U.S. policies in the early 1980s, including tight monetary policy, high interest rates affecting global rates, and no tax collection on foreign capital, dampened the demand for LDC exports and attracted an excessive capital outflow from LDCs to the United States. Moreover, since 1973, increased unemployment rates and trade deficits (exacerbated in the 1980s) increased domestic pressure in the United States for protection.

Keynes's view at Bretton Woods in 1944 was that when international disequilibrium occurs, the IMF should place the burden of monetary and fiscal policy adjustment on surplus nations. The asymmetry of monitoring deficit countries but not surplus countries reduces the growth of the world economy, especially the LDC periphery. The IMF, United States, and European deficit countries should pressure Japan and other surplus countries to expand financial policies through monetary ease and increased government spending, thus reducing the frequency and severity of recessions in low-income countries and requiring less painful disinflation and spending reductions (but also easing the pressure on the monetary and fiscal policies of the United States and other Western deficit countries).

Imperialism

While Chinese indemnities after 1897 (which strengthened the yen) and the military expenses of the 1904–05 Russo–Japanese War strained the international balance of trade, World War I's export demand spurred a large trade surplus. Overall, from 1897 through 1939, Japan's trade balance benefited from imperial ventures. Nakamura contends that "in an international environment where imperialist expansion was the rule, it is not likely that a precocious late-developing country" (1983: 40) could afford *not* to be imperialistic. According to W.B. Beasley (1987: 39, 69, 120), to avoid the West obstructing Japanese trade and investment with neighboring China, Japan felt compelled to acquire commercial privilege and extraterritorial legal concessions in the 1894–95 war with China.

Meiji Japan, similar to many developing countries today with large GNPs relative to neighboring countries, perceived imperialism or economic expansion overseas as a way to safeguard economic security and enhance future economic development. Perhaps an economic imperial venture can be viewed as similar to an investment, where a country acquires an asset today to raise future expected streams of returns. Developing countries today, with substantial GNPs compared with their neighbors—China, India, Indonesia, Brazil, and South Africa—have also attempted to become subimperial powers to reduce their peripheral status in the global politicoeconomic order, but have been less successful than was Meiji, Taisho (1912–26), and early Showa (1926–39) Japan.

We cannot avoid mentioning imperialism with Japan's economic experience, as imperialism was endemic to Japan's development. Both Japan's decades of success as an imperialist and the devastating price it paid for its military and imperial expansion during World War II indicate the relevance of imperialism when discussing the applicability of Japan's development for today's developing countries. It is probably not possible to estimate the net costs or benefits of Japan's imperialism (including those for classes, regions, and communities within Japan). However, the contemporary international economic milieu, with the global involvement of DCs and their MNCs, makes it more difficult for LDCs today to benefit from imperialism toward neighboring countries than it was for Japan during the late decades of the nineteenth century and first four decades or so of the twentieth century.

Summary

From the Meiji Restoration through the 1930s, Japan's foreign-trade policy, unlike in today's LDCs, did not discriminate against exports. Nineteenth-century Meiji Japan, with low tariffs, few protective subsidies, and close to a market-clearing exchange rate, was more open to foreign commerce than are today's LDCs. Japan's liberal trade and exchange-rate policies contributed to rapid export growth.

The late nineteenth-century international economy was more conducive to Meiji's export enhancement than today's international environment is to LDC export growth. The greatest export growth potential is in labor-intensive manufactures, where technology is widely available, yet the competition from other LDCs is more severe than it was for Meiji Japan.

Meiji Japan felt compelled to participate in the scramble for commercial privilege and extraterritorial economic concessions in order to avoid unequal treatment by the West and to acquire gains from trade and investment in Asia. While Meiji Japan's experience indicates that imperialism can help remove a country's peripheralness in the global economy, the extreme cost paid by early to mid-twentieth-century Japan for its imperial expansion provides a warning for today's potential subimperial Asian and African countries.

Notes

1. For an elaboration of the theory of comparative advantage applied to LDCs, see Nafziger (1990a: 390–93). For greater detail on comparative advantage, the Heckscher–Ohlin thesis on factor proportions, and the Leontief paradox contradicting that thesis, see Kenen (1989: 51–68).

2. Most of these arguments are from Black (1959: 124–34).

3. When demand is elastic, the percentage decline in the quantity imported exceeds the percentage increase in price from the tariff, so that import value, price multiplied by quantity, falls. When demand is inelastic, import payments increase, but by less than the government's gain in tariff revenue.

4. Highly populated India had an export commodity concentration ratio of 24 percent, but see the discussion above of the substantial cost of its price distortions and industrial protection.

5. Nurkse (1961) also contributed to these ideas.

Chapter 9

Applying the Japanese Development Model

Since the early 1980s, the development model of the Soviet Union, whose growth was slow since 1970, lost its appeal in LDCs. After the collapse of Soviet and Central European socialism in 1989–91, many Western intellectuals began to celebrate the triumph of economic (and political) liberalism. Indicative of this was Francis Fukuyama's *The End of History and the Last Man* (1992), which contended that liberalism's victory meant there were no major ideological battles left. In their assistance and adjustment programs today, the IMF, World Bank, and Organisation for Economic Cooperation and Development (OECD) prescribe liberalism for LDCs. In this concluding chapter, I examine how this IMF–World Bank–OECD liberal prescription compares with the 1868–1939 Japanese model.

This first two sections of this chapter discuss the similarities and differences between the OECD and 1868–1939 Japanese strategies. After these two sections, we investigate the success of the ASEAN four and the extent to which they have followed the Japanese model. Before concluding, we examine the more specifically political aspects of the Japanese model.

Similarities between the Early Japanese Model and the OECD Model for LDCs

Since 1980, OECD countries, the major shareholders of the International Monetary Fund and World Bank, have set in motion a new development model for LDCs. In contemporary Asian, African, and Latin American countries (as well as Central Europe and the former Soviet Union), the World Bank, OECD or DC governments, and DC commercial banks—whose funding to LDCs and transitional economies depends on the International Monetary Fund "seal of approval"—together with the IMF, form a policy cartel. Because of these interlocking interests, we will henceforth label this OECD/Bank/Fund/DC commercial bank policy model for LDCs the OECD model.

Ostensibly, OECD countries prefer that developing countries be democracies. However, since lenders and aid-givers depend on IMF approval, the OECD and World Bank rarely provide concessional funds to compensate for the additional inflationary and external payments pressures faced by countries making the transition to democracy. In practice, the OECD provides funds to LDCs on the basis of their economic liberalization and other economic criteria, while paying little attention to the achievement of political democracy. Thus, except for its lack of emphasis on indigenous economic decision making, the OECD model closely resembles the development model of pre–World War II Japan—economic liberalism with state action but without political democracy. The Japanese model, like the contemporary OECD approach, emphasizes the acquisition of foreign technology, encouragement and subsidies for local entrepreneurs, the strengthening of indigenous financial institutions, reduction of industrial wages to market rates, increased profits, the achievement of market-clearing exchange rates, the expansion of exports, and the eschewal of import substitution.

Investment in Human and Other Capital

Meiji Japan received a high return from its investment priority on primary, vocational, and scientific education. Basic literacy facilitates technological adaptation and learning. Asia and Africa would benefit from a similar emphasis on investment. While the OECD model for developing countries matches Meiji Japan's emphases, OECD/Bank/Fund policies toward LDC adjustment programs contributed to low investment rates in education and literacy, especially in the highly indebted countries of low-income sub-Saharan Africa.

For sub-Saharan countries, the actual debt service (interest and principal paid) in 1990 was 24 percent of export earnings; the *scheduled* debt-service ratio, which includes default on or rescheduling of debt, was 37 percent. This debt overhang in the sub-Sahara was so large that investment, especially in education and social services, was inefficiently low in the midst of the paucity of new loans or debt writedowns from DC commercial banks, governments, and multilateral agencies. Sub-Saharan expectations of future debt burdens reduce the incentive for investment in people and domestically initiated adjustment, and future growth becomes less attractive as higher proportions have to be transferred abroad. When future repayments are large, these obligations act as a tax on investment because a share of returns goes to creditors. A high-debt country, then, invests at less than the most efficient level and overconsumes or engages in capital flight (Claessens and Diwan 1989: 213–25; Husain and Underwood 1992: 24; World Bank 1990a: vol. 1).

Having endured years of austerity and stagnation, many African countries cannot afford to reduce consumption to effect an external transfer, and thus they shift the burden to investment. The sub-Sahara's gross domestic investment as a percentage of GDP fell from 23 percent in 1979 to 15 percent in 1989; the gross savings rate declined from 20 percent to 13 percent. Indeed, except for Ghana from 1984 to 1990, which had started with a low investment rate base in the 1960s and 1970s, Bank/Fund adjustment programs contributed to reduced investment rates in sub-Saharan Africa, thus wiping out the investment gains of the 1970s (Mkandawire 1991: 81; Mosley, Harrigan, and Toye 1991: vol. 1, pp. 196–98; World Bank 1981: 147, 1991a: 221). Reduced investment had a particularly adverse effect on investment in social services (education and nutrition), contributing to reductions in school enrollment rates (especially in primary schools), literacy, and daily calorie supply per capita in sub-Saharan Africa in the 1980s (World Bank 1989a: 274–76).

Low-income countries would do well, of course, to emulate a major component of the early Japanese approach: high rates of investment in education. However, contemporary developing countries need to be selective in using Japanese schools as models; Japanese schools emphasized rote memory and subservience to authority, legitimized militarism and imperialism, and were antithetical to creativity, democracy, human rights, and female equality.

High Labor Supply Elasticities

High labor supply elasticities resulting from vast reserves from the agricultural and informal industrial sectors, together with low industrial wage premiums, kept Japanese unskilled industrial wage rates relatively low before World War I, increasing business profits and reducing urban unemployment. Before the Bank/Fund adjustment programs of the 1980s, minimum-wage legislation, strong trade union movements, and unadaptive capital-intensive technologies in LDCs contributed to much higher wages than were found in Meiji Japan, reducing the profits and savings of today's LDCs. Most Third World governing elites were afraid of losing political support from revising labor codes, curtailing wages, eliminating capital subsidies, adjusting foreign exchange rates, or making pay scales more flexible. Today, with austere policies essential to obtain loans of last resort from the IMF, World Bank, or OECD member countries, LDC political leaders have frequently resorted to repression to retain power.

The Role of the State

In Japan, government and private businesspeople formed a consensus on the key function of the state in development, avoiding the individualism and cutthroat competition of U.S. capitalism that many leaders of developing countries oppose. Japanese-type guided capitalism involved a major governmental role in infrastructure, educational expansion, directly productive investment, selling factories cheaply to private business, industrial extension, subsidies, revenue growth, and probusiness legislation. These government policies helped create samurai, merchant, and landlord entrepreneurs to spearhead industrialization. Many samurai, mobilizing capital from government-paid pensions and debt instruments and cooperating closely with a samurai-dominated bureaucracy, emerged as leading Meiji entrepreneurs.

Today, despite Bank/Fund/OECD conditions, the state is expected to have a major role in LDCs. Indeed, accords between a Third World government and the Bank/Fund force the state to monitor closely the financial flows essential to reverse external imbalances and reduced living standards. To deal with the Bank/Fund, the state needs to improve its analytical, planning, and data-gathering capabilities, provide technical assistance and training, reform state-owned enterprises, and privatize public enterprises (Callaghy 1989: 116–17). Stein's (1991) study indicates that IMF structural adjustment lending in Tanzania in the late 1980s reinforced the post-Nyerere strategy of state centralization and production, including state monitoring of parastatal enterprises operating on a commercial basis. Moreover, those in control of the state protected those sectors containing their vital interests (and those of their allies) during negotiations with the IMF and subsequent implementation of the adjustment loan. Polyani's (1944: 140–41) words apply to the IMF, World Bank, and their liberal African allies in the 1990s: "Even those who wished most ardently to free the state from all unnecessary duties, and whose whole philosophy demanded the restriction of state activities, could not but entrust the self-same state with the new powers, organs and instruments required for the establishment of *laissez-faire.*" Ironically, for adjustment policies to be successful, the Bank/Fund must strengthen the capacity of the African state (Migdal 1988: 3–41; Sandbrook 1991: 101).

Guided capitalism, however, is limited in its effectiveness in today's LDCs because of inadequate government capability to spur private enterprise and elite and populist opposition to large business subsidies, high industrial concentration, high income inequality between businesspeople and others, and favorable legal and labor policies for business. Moreover, today's Asian and African capitalist class, dependent on support from government and collaboration with foreign capital, is weaker than was Japan's nineteenth-century capitalist class.

Financial Institutions

Japanese economic history also demonstrates the importance of a state role in creating and regulating financial institutions, without tolerating growing concentration of private financial institutions. Like Meiji Japan, however, most contemporary LDCs lack the ability and the will to prevent indigenous concentration.

Differences between the Early Japanese Model and the OECD Model for LDCs

Tradeoffs between Growth and External Balance

Unlike the early Japanese model, which focused on both external and domestic fiscal balance, the IMF and its major shareholders from OECD countries do not focus on economic development but on correcting external-account deficits. The FAO contends: "An important aspect of [IMF] loans and their associated policies is that they do not present a growth package as such, . . . [but] their primary role is to serve as a balance-of-payments support" (1991: 89). Since IMF loans are short-term (one to two years), and supply-side (structural) changes take years, IMF programs almost always require demand restraint, with contractional monetary and fiscal policies (spending reductions and slow growth in the money supply) (Stewart 1990: 3).

The World Bank's microeconomic objectives, on the other hand, enhance resource efficiency by removing price distortions, opening up competition, and deregulation. Since the Bank has been slicing up adjustment loans into smaller and smaller elements, and since the release of each slice (or *tranche*) is dependent on the performance of certain conditions, the Bank's planning horizon in practice is almost as short as the Fund's. Indeed, the Bank increasingly frontloads conditionality, so key conditions are fulfilled in advance of the release of any part of the loan, as in the reform and stabilization before Tanzania's 1988 and 1989 sectoral adjustment loans (SECALs) (Mosley, Harrigan, and Toye 1991: vol. 1, p. 45). And while post-1988 publications of the Bank, which has been increasingly on the defensive in international fora, have recognized growth and income distribution as goals of long-term structural adjustment, the Bank's goals, as expressed in adjustment programs, are similar to those of the Fund.

The Planning Horizon

The OECD model, in contrast to the early Japanese model, has a short-term planning horizon. While the crises in Ghana, Zambia, and Senegal—countries undergoing Bank/Fund adjustment programs in the 1980s—developed over ten to twenty years, stabilization may take at least that long. Zambia, facing rapidly deteriorating terms of trade, had too little time to stabilize, let alone restructure its economy. Liberalizing and privatizing, while probably an appropriate goal, work more effectively if planned over a longer period. Zambia faced major political opposition to the elimination of food subsidies and increased farm prices—tasks that are less daunting if part of a long-range plan. Except for 1988, Zambia's GDP per capita fell every year from 1984, the beginning of Bank SECALs, to 1990.

Evolutionary versus Comprehensive Change

The OECD model stresses immediate comprehensive changes to liberalization for LDCs while the Japanese model emphasized gradual adjustment. Indeed, Japan exemplifies the importance of improving capital and technology step by step, learning by doing within existing small industry and craft firms rather than making substantial leaps to the most advanced technologies available.

In addition, today's low-income countries have far more price, exchange-rate, and other market distortions than Meiji Japan had. The theory of the second best states that if economic policy changes cannot satisfy *all* the conditions necessary for maximizing welfare, then satisfying one or several conditions may not increase welfare. This theory indicates that liberalizing one price while other prices are still repressed may be worse than having all prices distorted. As Alec Nove put it, "To change everything at once is impossible, but partial change creates contradictions and inconsistencies" (1983: 168).

Agricultural and informal industrial sectors especially benefit from an evolutionary strategy that emphasizes extension service, technical training, improvement engineering, management assistance, and credit facilities. Early industrial growth need not eliminate dualism; indeed, expanding electricity spurs dualism, reducing internal economies of scale and improving small-industry productivity. In fact, small industry still thrives in contemporary Japan, despite its technological leadership in numerous sectors.

Ghana's adjustment program from 1984 to 1989 focused on a relatively few policy instruments, concentrated primarily in agriculture. Commercial agriculture, which requires fewer wage and outside price changes, may gain more from liberalization than does industry. Cocoa in Ghana exemplifies this, as does agricultural reform in China since 1979. China decontrolled (and increased) prices for farm commodities, virtually eliminated their compulsory deliveries to the state, reduced multitiered pricing, relaxed restrictions on interregional farm trade, encouraged rural markets, allowed direct sales of farm goods to urban consumers, and decollectivized agriculture, instituting individual household management of farm plots under long-term contracts with collectives and allowing farmers to choose cropping patterns and non-farm activities. From 1979 to 1986, China's 2.2 percent annual growth in food grain output per capita (not even as rapid as gains in oilseed, livestock, and cotton output) was among the fastest in the world, and faster than its 0.3 percent growth from 1954 to 1977 (using a five-year moving average to reduce distortions from weather fluctuations from both series). China's industrial reform, plagued by inconsistencies from partial change, was much less successful (China, State Statistical Bureau, *Statistical Yearbook of China* [Beijing], various annuals; Nafziger 1990a: 141–43, 448–51).

Trade, Exchange-Rate, and Capital Liberalization

Successful trade liberalization and exchange-rate equilibration usually require, as in Meiji Japan, the domestic ability to produce inputs previously bought overseas. Ghana was a fortunate exception in that its increased volume of cocoa exports resulting from cedi depreciation relied largely on inputs already produced internally. In contrast, Zambia exporters suffered from liberalization during the 1980s because domestic industry lacked the capability of producing inputs previously purchased abroad. Moreover, as the preference for them declined during liberalization, indigenous firms in Zambia found it increasingly difficult to compete with well-established foreign firms with oligopolistic power that could benefit from monopoly advantages such as patents, technical knowledge, superior managerial and marketing skills, better access to capital markets, economies of large-scale production, and economies of vertical integration (that is, cost savings from decision coordination at various production stages) (Kindleberger 1974: 267–88).

Although price controls, exchange-rate misalignments, and government budget deficits contributed to Africa's external crisis, the immediate freeing of markets and contraction of spending will not resolve the disequilibrium. Many African and Asian governments feel that the Bank and Fund, in contrast to the Japanese pre–World War II strategy, focus only on demand reduction. After 1981, the IMF emphasized shock treatment for demand restraint in low-income countries, rarely provided financing for external adjustments, and cut programs from three years to one year, applying Reaganomics internationally. One year is not enough time for adjustment. Demand restrictions, inflation deceleration, and currency depreciation do not switch expenditures to exports and import substitutes or expand primary production quickly enough to have the desired effect on prices and trade balances. Studies indicate that, even in DCs (for example, the United States from 1985 to 1992), the current-account improvement from devaluation usually takes two to five years, usually beginning with a worsening trade balance in the first year. The time required for adjustment is due to the lags between changes in relative international prices (from exchange-rate changes) and responses in quantities traded. Lags include time for decision (assessing the change), delivery, replacement (waiting to use up inventories and wear out machines), and production (Grubel 1981: 349–88). Even after 1988, despite increased emphasis on structural adjustment programs on productive capacity and long-term sectoral change, in practice LDCs still face unrealistically short adjustment times, resulting in severe economic disruption and excessive hardship for the poor.

Bank/Fund adjustment programs in LDCs increased agricultural income inequality. Agricultural export expansion, higher farm producer prices, and reduced food subsidies disproportionately benefited landed classes and affluent commercial farmers and had little impact on smallholders producing food for subsistence, whose output expansion was limited by lack of labor, land, credit, or appropriate technology. But adjustment usually reduced the surplus captured by monopsony marketing agencies (often controlled by political leaders and their clients) at the expense of agricultural classes generally (Bates 1989: 222–26; FAO 1991: 97).

Samora Moises's FRELIMO government in Mozambique and Robert Mugabe's ZANU government in Zimbabwe tried to shift the terms of trade from industry (under the previous white supremacist policies) to agriculture. Zimbabwe's 1982 IMF agreement resulted in a wage freeze and real wage decline, substantial food price increases, and reduced health expenditures from 1982 to 1984. The Ministry of Health found that the percentage of underweight children less than six years old in rural areas rose from 18–22 percent in 1982 to 48 percent in 1984. The *Zambia Basic Needs Report* in the early 1980s records how reduced recurrent allocation after adjustment discouraged a rural woman with a sick child from walking fifteen kilometers to the nearest health center, since the woman knew the center was frequently out of drugs (Davies and Saunders 1987: 3–23; Parfitt and Riley, 1989: 33).

Uma Lele's (1990: 1209) study of the World Bank's approach to agricultural development castigated the shift away from integrated rural development with its emphasis on supply intervention such as infrastructure, credit, research, and extension, to private-sector initiatives and adjustment programs. This shift, she argues, is flawed by its inadequate recognition of causal factors underlying growth, the effects of price-based policies on supply, the nonprice actions essential to sustain policy reforms, and harmonization with long-terms goals. Indeed, World Bank economist Kevin M. Cleaver (1985) argues that farm prices have a minor role relative to state agricultural services in affecting agricultural growth.

The IMF has stressed devaluation and foreign-exchange decontrols to improve the balance of trade, increase domestic prices and terms of trade for agriculture, and reduce shortages of foreign inputs, along with market interest rates to improve capital allocation. Reginald Herbold Green (1989: 36) supports African states' complaints that World Bank or IMF adjustment programs fail to consider market imperfections. Government, however, frequently creates market imperfections through policies of financial repression, encouraging interest-rate ceilings, foreign-exchange controls, high reserve requirements, and restrictions on private capital markets to increase the flow of domestic resources to the public sector without higher taxes, inflation, or interest rates. Yet, even though government helped to create these market imperfections, the state cannot immediately decontrol all prices and liberalize foreign exchange and capital markets. Although devaluation raises import prices, the demand for foreign exchange may not be restrained, since relaxing foreign-exchange licenses and import restrictions spurs the use of foreign inputs and probably increases capital flight in the short run. Indeed, substantial devaluation may generate hyperinflation, as the domestic currency experiences a free fall which is made irreversible by expectations (Zambia in 1985–87 and Sierra Leone in 1986–87).

Meiji Japan's markets for labor, capital, inputs, and commodities were responsive to exchange-rate changes. In comparison, the effect of devaluation in LDCs today (say, from C90 = $1 to C222 = $1) on the trade balance depends on demand and supply elasticities, which are considered by critics to be low in African and Asian agriculture, especially over a one- to two-year period. The elasticity of demand for LDC primary products like tea, coffee, sugar, and cocoa is so low that increasing the output of agricultural exports to undertake Bank/Fund-sponsored adjustment might result in reduced revenues from increased output. On the supply side, farmers in developing countries have little short-run (one year or less) but substantial long-run elasticity (0.3–0.9) for cash crops, as farmers respond to allocate labor and land variously to commercial output, subsistence commodities, black-market activity, nonfarm work, or leisure. Supply response would be at least a year or two for cotton and tobacco, and between five and six years for tree crops such as coffee, tea, cashews, and sisal in Tanzania. Cost-induced inflationary pressures due to devaluation (from economic interests fighting to maintain income and consumption shares) should reduce output expansion. Inadequate infrastructure, such as poor transport for Ghanaian cocoa, limits supply increases, slowing export response to higher cedi prices for a given dollar price of cocoa. Indeed, most low-income countries remove balance-of-payments deficits quickly not from exchange-rate changes (and expenditure switching) but from reduced import demand due to a fall in real income (or a depressed economy). Still, most LDCs no longer oppose devaluation but want more control over its size, timing, structure (such as single versus multiple exchange rates), and accompanying policy measures (Campbell and Stein 1992: 20–22; Loxley 1989: 13–36).

When IMF conditions require devaluation and improved trade balance to extend further credit in a year or so, developing countries have little choice in adjustment. While it is sufficient for the sums of the export and import demand elasticities to be at least one for devaluation to improve the trade balance, actual short-run LDC elasticities often appear considerably below necessary and sufficient levels. Most African and Asian finance ministers are elasticity pessimists, doubting that devaluation will improve the trade balance, certainly not in the short run, over which period empirical studies suggest elasticities are perverse even in the industrialized countries. In any event, governments rarely know the "correct" market rate or how exchange-rate changes will affect income and trade variables that feed back to affect the equilibrium price of foreign exchange.

Trade liberalization in the midst of stabilization, even if politically possible, is more likely to perpetuate a government budget crisis in contemporary LDCs than in Meiji Japan, with better-developed factor and input markets. As Mosley, Harrigan, and Toye (1991) argue, given labor and resource immobility, early liberalization of external trade and supply-side stimulation in "one glorious burst" result in rising unemployment, inflation, and capital flight, and subsequently undermine adjustment programs. This trade-reform failure is consistent with second-best theory, which indicates that removing one distortion in a highly distorted economy may reduce overall welfare.

Mosley, Harrigan, and Toye, and FAO (1991) suggest the following trade, exchange, and capital market liberalization sequence: (1) liberalize imports of critical capital and other inputs; (2) devalue domestic currency to a competitive level, while simultaneously restraining monetary and fiscal expansion to curb inflation and convert a nominal devaluation to a real devaluation, (3) promote exports through liberalizing commodity markets, subsidies, and other schemes; (4) allocate foreign exchange for maintaining and repairing infrastructure for production increases; (5) remove controls on internal interest rates to achieve positive real rates, and expand loans agencies to include farmers and small businesspeople; (6) reduce public-sector deficits to eliminate reliance on foreign loans at banking standards without decreasing real development spending, and reform agricultural marketing to spur farmers to sell their surplus; (7) liberalize other imports, rationalizing the tariff structure, and removing price controls and subsidies to the private sector; and (8) abandon external capital-account controls.

The eighth step recognizes the necessity of reforming internal capital markets before liberalizing international capital markets, the sequences in Meiji Japan. However, neither Bank/Fund recommendations nor implementation bore much relationship to this eight-stage sequence. In most cases, the Bank asked that trade be liberalized early without limiting the imports to which it should be applied. For example, the foreign-exchange requirements associated with trade liberalization, the major component of the Bank's first structural adjustment program in Kenya (1980), became unsustainable, so liberalization had to be abandoned. In addition, import liberalization preceded agricultural export expansion based on commodity market liberalization, price decontrol, and export promotional schemes. On the other hand, Ghana, under a Bank SECAL beginning in 1983, allocated foreign exchange through an auction, and the goods eligible for entry to the auction expanded over time in line with the increased supply of foreign currency.

Recipients should implement IMF demand-reducing programs before the Bank's supply-increasing ones. If countries begin with supply reforms, which take a longer time, the lack of demand restraint will contribute to inflation and an unmanageable current-account deficit. Still, adjustment loan recipients also need to avoid excessive initial demand restraint that depresses the economy; simultaneous devaluation, as in stage 2, could avoid its contractionary effect (FAO 1991: 101–3; Mosley, Harrigan, and Toye 1991: vol. 1, 110–16).

Privatization

OECD strategies for LDC privatization provide even fewer safeguards for preventing industrial concentration than did Meiji Japan's policies, which exacerbated zaibatsu domination. The OECD/Bank/Fund emphasis was not just an extension of the domestic economics of U.S. President Ronald Reagan and British Prime Minister Margaret Thatcher to Western-dominated multilateral aid and lending programs; it was also a Third World response to the failure of public enterprises to match expectations. In February 1986, Babacar N'Diaye, president of the African Development Bank, criticized the private sector for performing inefficiently and claimed that it needed a more conducive environment for growth. Yet, as Stewart (1990) argues, the Bank's focus should be on substituting local private ownership for public ownership or reforming parastatals, rather than on wholesale privatization. Even the World Bank's *World Development Report, 1983,* contends, "the key factor determining the efficiency of an enterprise is not whether it is publicly or privately owned, but how it is managed" (1983b: 50). If entry barriers are removed, the report states, there is no presumption that the private sector has better management. Moreover, Bank/Fund analyses in the mid-1980s indicated that public enterprises can perform well with competition, no investment licensing, managerial autonomy and accountability, hard budget constraints, and firm size commensurate with technical and managerial skills (Ayub and Hegstad 1987: 26–29; Kohli and Sood 1987: 34–36; Marsden and Belot 1989: 163–68; Nafziger 1990a: 446–67; Park 1987: 25–27).

The transition from centrally managed state enterprises to a liberal, privatized economy is politically and technically difficult. Prices masked by controls inevitably rise. Forcing inefficient firms to close is likely to be unacceptable where labor is not mobile. Pent-up demand for imports may hurt the balance of payments. Skilled people are usually lacking (Mills 1989: 14–18). Moreover, government may require parastatals to achieve social objectives, such as setting quality standards, investing in infrastructure, producing social goods for low-income earners, controlling sectors vital for national security, wresting control from foreign owners or minority ethnic communities, rescuing bankrupt firms in key sectors, avoiding private oligopolistic concentration, raising capital essential for overcoming indivisibilities, producing vital inputs cheaply for the domestic market, capturing gains from technological learning, and creating other external economies that would be overlooked by private firms. To illustrate, Nigeria's abolition in 1987 of the government Cocoa Marketing Board and licenses for marketing cocoa resulted in poor quality control and fraudulent trading practices, which adversely affected the reputation of Nigerian cocoa. The government subsequently incurred substantial costs reintroducing inspection procedures and marketing licenses (Hackett 1990: 776).

Moreover, the effectiveness of creating market incentives and deregulating state controls presupposes a class able and willing to respond by innovating, bearing risk, and mobilizing capital, as the samurai did in Meiji Japan. While significant groups of indigenous entrepreneurs have emerged in India, Kenya, Nigeria, and Côte d'Ivoire, the private sector in Bangladesh, Sri Lanka, Tanzania, Ghana, and Zambia, for example, is much more limited. In addition, some regimes have restricted the commercial and industrial enterprises of such visible minorities as the Chinese in Southeast Asia, the Asians in East Africa, and the Lebanese in West Africa.

Even where privatization is desirable, government may want to proceed slowly to avoid a highly concentrated business elite being created from newly privatized firms falling into a few hands, as was true during Meiji Japan during the late nineteenth century and of much of Africa during its indigenization since the early 1970s. It would be ironic if two goals of privatization—improvements of efficiency and competition—were sabotaged because of the creation of new oligopolies from a limited number of buyers. Moreover, the fact that the private sector may lack the business skills and experience means that an emphasis on providing private competition to the private sector and a gradual reduction of the relative size of the public sector may be preferable to abrupt privatization. To quote a publication of the World Bank/IMF: "The rationale for privatization is most straightforward and least controversial where a public enterprise is engaged in a purely commercial activity and is already subject to competition" (World Bank and IMF 1990: 83).

While Ghana's reform of state-owned enterprises (SOEs) in the mid-1980s was to enhance their competitiveness and management responsibility, restructuring failed to modify management or corporate boards, criteria for management promotion and pay, or rules for allocating capital between SOEs. Indeed, existing managers, many of whom should have been discharged, oversaw enterprise divestiture, viewing work-force retrenchment and restructuring as unrelated activities, disproportionately laying off production workers and retaining administrative and clerical staff, and sometimes in the absence' of guidelines for work-force requirements, reporting no redundant staff (Davis 1991: 987–1005).

Sectoral Transfer of Surplus

Like Meiji Japan, many of today's low-income countries aspire to transfer agricultural savings to industry for investment. Unlike Meiji Japan, however, few agrarian classes in contemporary African and Asian countries have the potential to start ventures in manufacturing and finance. Except for landowners, few LDC farmers have the funds to invest in industry. Yet African and Asian landlords rarely undertake industrial activity, as they usually place a high value on consumption and real-estate expenditures, and lack experience in managing a production process with specialized work tasks and machinery and in overseeing secondary labor relations. Feudal and postfeudal Japan's landed interests had a high preference for industrial investment because of the lack of financial security in land, conditions that were quite different from those in LDCs today. Moreover, the lower rural incomes and nutritional levels and higher agrarian political consciousness of low-income Africa and Asia than were found in Meiji Japan mean that taxes and other forced savings in agriculture in excess of today's substantial resource transfers might spur additional agrarian discontent. To increase agricultural–industrial capital transfers, LDCs need to accelerate their agricultural technical progress and growth, and increase their industrial lending, training, and extension programs.

Factor Intensity in Industry

Meiji Japan, benefiting from its labor surplus and low wage rates, had a more labor-intensive industrial growth than contemporary LDCs. This growth, together with Meiji's lower fertility rates and slower population and labor-force growth rates, contributed to much lower Meiji rates of unemployment than is true in today's developing countries. Asia and Africa can apply lessons from the Japanese experience, eschewing specialization in high-technology, capital-intensive products, while emphasizing improved engineering in existing labor-intensive small industry and (where values are less conducive to fertility control than in Meiji Japan) investing in family-planning education and programs.

Export Expansion

Although today's international economic conditions are less favorable to developing countries than the late nineteenth century was to Japan, LDCs could still benefit from the Japanese approach of using international competition and market-clearing exchange rates to spur rapid export expansion. Still, restoring external equilibrium should be a long-term goal. Indeed, attaining a long-run foreign-exchange equilibrium might exacerbate the immediate trade deficit, since the elasticities for primary-product exports are low in the short run. In addition, Third World countries should resist Bank/Fund pressures to restore the trade balance in one to two years by reducing government spending. The African and Asian LDCs may need temporary restrictions to avoid the adverse short-run impact of foreign-exchange decontrol on inflation and the balance of payments.

Moreover, like nineteenth-century Japan, LDCs can gain from the product cycle, in which Japan's, Germany's, and the United States' comparative advantage in unstandardized goods embodying research, innovation, and advanced technology becomes a comparative disadvantage as markets grow, techniques become common knowledge, and the good becomes standardized, so less-sophisticated countries can mass-produce the item with less skilled labor (as in the Japanese-led borderless economy which includes Thailand, Malaysia, Indonesia, and the Philippines, discussed in chapter 2). Developing countries are at a disadvantage, however, compared with nineteenth-century Japan, as LDC firms today do not face atomistic competition or competition among the many, but rather, they face competition in an integrated global economy against oligopolistic multinational corporations that enjoy monopoly advantages in management, marketing, technology, and access to capital. Furthermore, the potential primary and light manufacturing export expansion industries overlap substantially among low-income countries. DCs must resist increasing trade barriers in response to the export expansion of newly industrialized developing countries, a response similar to the West vis-à-vis developing Japan in the 1930s. Indeed, the comparative-advantage theorem, which most neoclassical and heterodox economists support as valid for DCs, indicates that DC expanding trade restrictions is analogous to "cutting off your nose to spite your face."

Self-Directed Development

The Japanese (and earlier OECD) experience indicates the advantages of self-directed development to transform a country away from its peripheral position in the global economy. The OECD model for LDCs, however, neglects self-direction, emphasizing a close IMF and World Bank monitoring of lending and policy. To be sure, many small countries are limited in their options to reduce dependence on DC trade and capital movements. But the Japanese development model underlines the importance of Asian and African governments controlling DC capital flows and the employment of DC personnel introducing technology into the country. This is especially important since the technological distance between contemporary LDCs and DCs, emphasizing labor-saving technology, is large, making it less likely that foreign experts will adapt technology to indigenous conditions unless developing countries insist that foreigners stress appropriate technology.

Malaysia and Thailand, however, have enjoyed limited prosperity while sacrificing their economic autonomy to less-sophisticated, labor-intensive, low-value-added production in a Japanese-organized division of knowledge (see chapter 2 on the Asian borderless economy). However, Aoki Takeshi (1992) and Tessa Morris-Suzuki (1991) contend that the short-run prosperity from integration within the Japanese-led trading system came at the expense of the technological learning and skill acquisition that will be essential for rapid growth in the late 1990s and early twenty-first century. Takeshi mentions the inadequate spending on R&D, the lack of indigenous mastery of industrial technology, the few Malay entrepreneurs, the sparse linkages within the industrial economy, and the substantial shortage of skilled workers, technicians, and engineers as major obstacles to Malaysia's future growth. For Morris-Suzuki, some major barriers to Thailand's prospective development are the concentration of technological transfer within multinational enterprises rather than local firms, the lack of innovation and adaptation by indigenous personnel, the falling R&D capability, the poor communications facilities, and the low secondary-school enrollment rates. Indeed, Malaysia and Thailand have emphasized peripheral intermediation in technologically complex industrial production rather than indigenous innovation and technology generation in less complex industry that provides more scope for gains from learning (Morris-Suzuki 1992: 135–52; Takeshi 1992: 73–110). Ironically, for Malaysia and Thailand to follow the early Japanese model means less dependence on technology, capital, and imports from Japanese multinational corporations.

As chapter 8 contends, the struggle of Meiji and pre–World War II Japan to escape a peripheral position in the world order and to attain economic and political autonomy was inextricably linked to Japan's scramble for imperial power in Asia. The economic success of Japan, South Korea, Taiwan, Singapore, and Hong Kong after World War II, however, demonstrates that economic growth and security in the contemporary global system do not require imperialist expansion. Indeed, Steven Schlossstein, who observed that, in the early 1990s, Japan was the leading foreign investor in the NICs, as well as in Malaysia, Thailand, and Indonesia, asks whether contemporary Japan has "creatively gained the benefits of colonization without its administrative burden—in other words, a kinder, gentler co-prosperity sphere" (1991: 22).

The Early Japanese Model and the ASEAN Four

As indicated in the first chapter, my purpose is not to apply the early Japanese model to South Korea, Taiwan, Hong Kong, and Singapore—successful NICs that are advanced enough to learn lessons from the post–World War II Japanese approach. Rather, my focus is on low- and lower-middle-income countries. Among these countries, economists stress the success of the ASEAN four (Malaysia, Indonesia, the Philippines, and Thailand). According to the World Bank, however, the Philippines' annual real growth in GNP per capita from 1980 to 1991 was −1.2 percent. Thus, the World Bank's *East Asian Miracle* study does not include the Philippines among the eight high-performing Asian economies; I also exclude the Philippines from this analysis and I eliminate Indonesia, although *Miracle* includes it among these high-performing economies. In its *World Development Report, 1993,* the World Bank still ranked Indonesia among low-income countries. Moreover, Indonesia's growth rate from 1980 to 1991 was only the average among these low-income countries (World Bank 1993a: 1, 1993b: 238–39; Indonesia's growth rate falls by two to three percentage points when Repetto [1989] measures natural asset depletion).

We focus here on Malaysia and Thailand, arguably the two most successful among the ASEAN four. Thailand's 5.9 percent growth rate (1980–91) is the highest among all lower-middle-income countries (except tiny Mauritius). In the case of Malaysia, its 1991 GNP per capita of $2,520 is the highest of all lower-middle-income countries (World Bank 1993b: 238–39).

To what extent have Malaysia and Thailand's successes been the result of "looking East" to follow the Japanese model? Malaysia's and Thailand's positions in an international division of labor (as a part of Japan's borderless economy since the mid-1980s) seem to be based, as in Meiji Japan, on near-market exchange rates that expedite labor-intensive exports.

The Malaysian ringgit has been convertible since 1968, and the Thai baht since 1990, although as of 1993, Thailand still retained formal restrictions on capital outflows by domestic residents. Previously, in the 1970s and 1980s, both Thailand and Malaysia, like Meiji Japan, avoided appreciating the real value of their currencies vis-à-vis the dollar, keeping exports competitive. Both countries, like the late nineteenth-century Meiji regime, offset import restrictions and currency controls with export incentives and subsidies that maintained relative prices close to international prices. For Malaysia, for example, the stimulus to exports came from export-processing zones, free trade zones, licensed manufacturing warehouses, and income tax breaks, credit guarantees, and duty-free raw-material imports for exporters (World Bank 1993a: 22, 114–15, 135, 236).

Economic growth in post-1970 Malaysia and Thailand, as in Meiji Japan, was not limited by the balance of payments. Although Malaysia undertook structural adjustment and liberalization in 1986–90 on its own to prevent its external debt and deficit from becoming chronic, neither ASEAN country was compelled as a last resort to borrow funds from the IMF or World Bank. This freedom from external crises enabled both countries to enjoy a longer planning horizon.

Like Meiji Japan, modern Malaysia and Thailand emphasized building financial institutions to improve the capital and foreign-exchange markets. Since independence in 1963 and separation from Singapore in 1965, the government of Malaysia, a predominantly Muslim country, established and facilitated conventional financial intermediaries (commercial, development, and postal banks; stock and bond markets; and pension, provident, and insurance funds) along with Islamic banks. These banks, which treat depositors as if they were shareholders, receive returns through markup pricing or profit-sharing, interest-free deposits. In Thailand, banks are predominantly privately owned. In both countries, the banks have exercised independent authority over lending. Malaysia and Thailand experienced few major financial crises since the 1960s, although both countries lost resources from endemic corruption.

Malaysia and Thailand, like Meiji and contemporary Japan, had extended periods of mild financial repression, in which interest rates were held below market rates and credit was allocated to activities with high social returns. Even the World Bank's *Miracle* concedes that modest capital market distortion did not inhibit (and may even have enhanced) growth (World Bank 1993a: 17–19).

Malaysia and Thailand financed their rapid economic growth through high domestically generated savings (30 percent of GDP in Malaysia and 32 percent of GDP in Thailand in 1991), augmented by capital imports (6 percent of GDP in Malaysia and 7 percent in Thailand in the same year) (World Bank 1993b: 254–55). The ratio of these countries' foreign capital to income was in excess of Japan's peak at the turn of the twentieth century.

There are drawbacks to the position of Malaysia and Thailand in Japan's borderless economy. The other side of the coin concerning Schlossstein's remarks about Japan's gentler coprosperity sphere is the growing dependence of contemporary Malaysia and Thailand on Japan. As pointed out, in contrast to Malaysia and Thailand, Meiji Japan, which received no foreign aid and virtually no foreign direct investment, controlled capital flows and technology transfer. The industrial export growth of early Japan was based on self-directed technological learning and innovation, rather than peripheral growth within a trading system dominated by foreign corporations.

Despite the reliance of Malaysia and Thailand on labor-intensive exports, their industrial wages since the 1970s have been high relative to other contemporary low-income countries and, unlike Meiji Japan, much in excess of subsistence wages. Both Malaysia and Thailand, with higher agricultural productivity and faster farm-income growth than Southeast Asia generally, lacked cheap labor reserves. For example, the primary sector in Malaysia included rubber, petroleum, palm oil, tin, timber, and cocoa, much of which was commercialized. Yet, the governments of Malaysia and Thailand, like that of Meiji Japan, repressed labor organization and radicalism.

Contemporary Thailand has a low income concentration and Malaysia a high income inequality compared with LDCs generally. Both ASEAN countries, however, have a much lower inequality than Meiji Japan had and a faster reduction in poverty rates (World Bank 1993a: 29–33, 294–95).

In 1991, the primary and secondary enrollment rates as percentages of the relevant age groups for upper-middle-income Malaysia were between the rates for low-income and middle-income countries. In the same year, Thailand's enrollment rates were not much in excess of those of low-income countries generally. The primary enrollment rate as a percentage of the age group was 93 percent in Malaysia and 85 percent in Thailand, below the virtually 100 percent rate achieved by Meiji Japan in 1911. Neither Malaysia nor Thailand placed the priority on investment in science and education that Japan did throughout its modern history.

Japan's population growth in the late nineteenth century was about 1 percent yearly, a rate less than those for contemporary ASEAN countries. Thailand's population growth rate in 1988–89 was 1.5 percent yearly; Malaysia's growth for the same period was 2.5 percent annually. Thus, the dependency burden of primary-school-age children, the number of these children as a percentage of the total population, was less in late nineteenth-century Japan than it is for Thailand, Malaysia, or the other ASEAN four members. In a similar sense, however, Thailand and Malaysia had more favorable dependency ratios than other LDCs such as Pakistan, with a 3.0 annual growth rate, and Kenya, with a 3.8 percent annual rate (Population Reference Bureau 1990; see table 6.1). The World Bank (1993a: 194–96) estimates that in 1988–89 Malaysia and Thailand each saved 1–2 percent of GNP due to growth rates of the school-age population that were lower than Kenya.

The Malaysian and Thai states, like Meiji Japan, have tried to play a major role in facilitating private business, especially from overseas. A focus on large-scale foreign firms has reduced the success of programs to support domestic business in both countries. The government of Thailand, plagued by political instability from 1932 to 1994, has lacked effectiveness in supporting an indigenous business class, which is primarily ethnic Chinese. The Malaysian government, on the other hand, since enacting the New Economic Policy in 1969, has provided preferences for business ownership and assistance, loans, licenses, and employment to *bumiputras* (Malays and tribes of Sarawak and Sabah, sons of the soil) relative to Chinese, Indians, and other non-Malay ethnic communities. Since most large domestic businesspeople are Chinese and the bureaucracy is virtually all Malay, Malaysia's consultation between government and business has been contentious, failing to achieve the effectiveness that Japan enjoyed during its modern history (Schlossstein 1991: 21, 136; World Bank 1993a: 178–87).

Both ASEAN countries, lacking the Japanese tradition of a well-paid, merit-based government service, were hurt by widespread inefficiency and corruption. In Malaysia, in the 1980s, the government lost billions of dollars in fraudulent loans and investments involving politicians, public managers, civil servants, and intermediaries. These losses resulted from the channeling of the Employee Pension Fund into a public corporation and speculative stocks to boost the stock exchange, the collapse of the Cooperative Central Bank from politicians' unpaid debts, the fraudulent use of a commercial bank for local small industry for speculative loans to three Hong Kong real estate firms, and other schemes where hundreds of millions of dollars "disappeared" (Schlossstein 1991: 261–65).

Thailand and Malaysia, like early Japan, have had near-market exchange rates, labor-intensive export promotion, mild financial repression, and high savings rates. However, the two ASEAN countries lack not only the low wages and high income concentration but also the bureaucratic excellence, stress on investment in education, the slow population growth, the well-designed assistance programs for domestic entrepreneurs, and the self-directed technological learning of Japan in the late nineteenth and early twentieth centuries.

The economic approaches of Thailand, Malaysia, Indonesia, and the Philippines deviate in major ways from the early Japanese models. Yet the ASEAN four are similar to Meiji Japan in their lack of political liberalism and democracy. The *Human Development Report, 1991,* independently written by a United Nations Development Programme team (1991: 18–21), ranks the ASEAN four relatively low in their Human Freedom Index (HFI). This index is based on civil and legal rights, freedom from torture and censorship, electoral and religious freedom, ethnic and gender egalitarianism, independent media, courts, and trade union, and related indicators. Among 88 countries, Thailand's rank, in the medium category, is 41, after Mexico, South Korea, and Colombia. The other three ASEAN four are ranked low in freedom, with the Philippines ranked 53, Malaysia 55, and Indonesia 77.

The OECD and Early Japanese Models:
Liberalism without Democracy

While the OECD model stresses liberalism, its implementation accentuates only economic liberalism, while deemphasizing political democracy. This OECD/IMF/World Bank emphasis is consistent with the Japanese model of economic transformation through economic liberalism from 1868 to 1939, which was commingled with political authoritarianism during the same period, and is discussed in the two concluding sections to this chapter.

On July 8, 1991, IMF Managing Director Michel Camdessus deplored statements "that countries that have recently introduced democracy lack the maturity to manage rigorously [and] that we must facilitate their task by closing our eyes to the abandonment or temporary suspension of the adjustment process" (Camdessus 1991: 227). While World Bank economists Stanley Fischer and Ishrat Husain (1990: 27) think that LDCs not undertaking Bank/Fund reform and adjustment should carry their debt burden until they attain the political will, African and Asian finance ministers complain that the Bank/Fund neglects political constraints faced by LDCs in undertaking adjustment. How does the Bank or Fund expect to persuade Third World officials to implement adjustment programs that tarnish their prestige as political leaders (Martens 1988: 15–21; Mills 1989: 21–23)?

Deepak Lal, an economic liberal, contends "that a courageous, ruthless and perhaps undemocratic government is required to ride roughshod over . . . newly-created special interest groups" (1983: 33). Lal views democratic governments as the source of irrational economic policies to placate interest groups. As a World Bank study points out, transitional democratic systems have been remarkably unsuccessful in implementing IMF adjustment programs. Indeed, authoritarian systems appear to be especially successful, the study contends, in controlling rapid inflation in polarized environments (World Bank 1991b: 50, 132–34).

Since the empirical research on the compatibility between Bank/Fund economic adjustment and reform and Asian and African democratic government is sparse, we will use evidence from LDCs generally. Louellen Stedman and Peter Hakim (1989: 166–74) report that in 1982–87, under existing civilian rule, the opposition candidate won seven of eight Latin American presidential elections, primarily because of external debt crises and Bank/Fund adjustment programs. Although the winning candidates called for higher wages, greater social spending, price controls, domestic protection, and sometimes debt suspension or default, no winner ameliorated the economic crisis. Indeed, the Acapulco Summit Meeting of Latin American Presidents (1987) stated: "The economic crisis undermines democracy in the region because it neutralizes the legitimate efforts of our people to improve their living standards."

Stephen Haggard and Robert R. Kaufman, examining twenty-five African, Asian, and Latin American countries from 1978 to 1986, find no difference between the macroeconomic policies of established democratic and authoritarian governments, but countries undergoing transitions to democracy pursued more expansionary central-bank credit and expenditures policies than before and after the transition and compared with established regimes. Established governments gave more discretion to national monetary authorities and economic ministries than do countries changing regime types (Haggard and Kaufman 1989: 57–77).

Albert O. Hirschman agrees:

> [W]hen a civilian, democratic government first comes into power after a long period of repressive military rule, it is normal for various, newly active groups of the reborn civil society—particularly the long-repressed trade unions—to stake substantial claims for higher incomes.... New inflationary and balance-of-payments pressures are of course likely to result from the granting of such demands ... [I]nflation can nevertheless be a useful mechanism in this situation: it permits newly emerging or re-emerging social groups to flex their muscles, with inflation acting as a providential safety valve for accumulated social pressure. [1986: 17]

In Nigeria, the repression and control of partisan and ethnic-regional politics under military rule between 1966 and 1979 gave way to demands for increased patronage, income shares, and social spending during the Second Republic, from 1979 to 1983. Indeed, in 1979–80, the ports lacked the capacity for imports such as cement going to government agencies controlled by politicians distributing benefits to contractors and other clients. South Korea, though, attained high growth, current-account surpluses, and financial stability before democratic transition, increasing policy flexibility after 1988. As in Korea, coalitional strategies that limit mass appeal and dampen expectations contributed to greater domestic financial and external economic stability (Mosley, Harrigan, and Toye 1991: vol. 1, p. 146; Whitehead 1989: 85–86).

In Africa and Asia, many heads of state feared that economic mistakes might hasten their removal through irregular power transfer such as coups, assassinations, and military takeovers. The strongest opposition comes from vested interests (mainly upper and middle classes) threatened by privatization, currency devaluation, farm-price decontrol, and other reforms. Measures helping the poorest third rarely contribute to ruling-class sustainability, except where the poor's interests overlap with those of the middle deciles. Indeed, Joan M. Nelson's study of seven Muslim majority countries—five Middle Eastern states plus Pakistan and Turkey—showed the most populous group, the peasantry, not to be a part of any politically dominant coalition, and organized labor to be a part of only three of the seven (Nelson 1989: 100–105; Waterbury 1989: 40–46).

In designing adjustment programs, the IMF neglects the domestic political pressures that economies face when undergoing declining terms of trade and export purchasing power, as in Nigeria (1984–90) and Zambia (1983–91). In 1987, President Kenneth Kaunda, who lost the IMF "seal of approval" by restricting debt servicing to 10 percent of export earnings in the face of Zambia's 70 percent obligation, asked the Bank and Fund, "Which is a better partner for you in the long run, a nation which devotes all of its resources to paying the debt and, therefore, grinds to an economic and political halt, or a stable nation capable of sustaining the repaying of its entire debt?" (Seshamani 1990: 120).

Economic Liberalism, Authoritarianism, and Fascism

Ronald P. Dore (1959: 115–25) argues that agrarian poverty and distress from land taxes and tenancy contributed to the rise of Japanese totalitarian and military expansion abroad in the following ways: (1) tenant distress and farm population pressures provided a powerful motive for securing emigration opportunities through expansion; (2) rural poverty and the interrelated low industrial wages limited domestic market size, spurring Japan to use force to acquire external markets for its industry; (3) ruling elites used overseas expansion to divert attention from agrarian distress and foster national unity; and (4) landlord paternalism and agrarian pressures for social conformity facilitated susceptibility to authoritarianism.

Many components of the Japanese model associated with industrial growth also engendered emperor-system authoritarianism. The nationalism and militarism that provided a motive force for rapid technological change and substantial government investment also contributed to imperial expansion and fascism. The universal primary educational system of the late nineteenth century that improved Japanese productivity also proclaimed the virtues of the emperor and state worship.

In the economic crisis of 1929–31, Japan became more militaristic, its state became more coercive, dissent was suppressed, and the populace became disillusioned with even a limited parliamentarianism. By the end of the 1930s, Japan had acquired an "emperor-system fascist" authoritarian regime. The emperor and imperial household at the apex of national identity and authority were the basis for state absolutism and industrial concentration (Bix 1982: 2–19).

Japan's government of the 1930s used foreign aggression and war as tools for forging macroeconomic expansion and domestic integration. After the Great Depression, low tariffs—a legacy of the late nineteenth century—gave way to increased protection, cartelization, and military expansion, policies to expand spending and employment. During the 1930s, however, the state intervened to freeze workers' pay and dissolve unions, reducing the low real wages even further. This policy, consistent with mass repression and rising inequality, contributed to high profits and savings. Indeed, the military and bureaucracy's alliance with the zaibatsu enabled their share of industry and banking and their monopoly profits to skyrocket during the total mobilization of war (Bix 1982).

In general, discontented tenants, landless laborers, and urban workers, who mobilized to change Japan's economic and political system, were diverted to channeling their dissatisfaction into pressing for a stronger national state that was committed to improving Japan's economic and military power within the global system. State action by Japan helped the country become a regional imperial power to acquire privileged access to trade and investment in Taiwan, Korea, China, and other countries in Asia. Building state power also enabled Japan to transform itself from a peripheral to a semiperipheral position within the world economy. Given the oligopolistic concentration of DC-based corporations in today's world economy, Asian and African countries will find it more difficult to undertake an international transformation similar to that of Japan from the mid-nineteenth century to the early twentieth century.

Conclusion: Selecting Components of the Japanese Model

While a contemporary LDC can learn useful lessons from the Japanese development model, these lessons are limited because of Meiji Japan's historically specific conditions, and because some aspects of the Japanese approach also contributed to pathologies of growth, such as zaibatsu concentration, income inequality, labor union repression, militarism, and imperialism. In the seven decades before World War II, the parental indenturing of young workers, the increased tenancy rates and greater tenure insecurity, the slums in major cities, the serious environmental noise and pollution problems, the cost of soldiers and civilians killed, crippled, and disabled under imperialism, the torture and imprisonment of opponents to the regime, the suffering of colonial peoples in Taiwan and Korea, the distress of adversaries (especially in Asia) during World War II, the independence of the military command from cabinet control, the rampant militarism in the 1930s, and authoritarianism were endemic to an economic strategy emphasizing economic autonomy, low wages, samurai subsidies, zaibatsu facilitation, capital transfers from agriculture, meager spending on so-

cial welfare, and the neglect of human rights. These pathologies were not reduced until after the revolutionary momentum in 1945–47, with massive unemployment from large-scale factory closings, hyperinflation, the rapid growth of
union membership, workers seizing control of factories and mines, a wave of
strikes, a Tokyo rally demanding popular control over food distribution, a mili-
tant raid on the emperor's kitchens, a call for a general strike to bring down the
occupation-backed Yoshida government, and the occupational government's fear
of a communist takeover. The supreme commander of the allied powers in Japan,
General Douglas MacArthur, quelled the strike through his threat of arrest and
military intervention. As Selden points out, the democratization reforms, promulgated under a U.S. occupation government in response to the events of 1945–47,
were an attempt to preserve the elite structure of the Japanese state and society,
including the emperor system, its ultimate embodiment, while changing many
ground rules under which the Japanese polity functioned (Halliday 1975; Norman 1975; Selden 1983: 100–106; Yoshihara 1986: 167–81).

These occupational reforms laid the groundwork for improved income equality, accelerated economic growth, and democratization of the political economy
for the subsequent half-century, but they took place during a period too unique to
serve as a blueprint for developing countries. Today's Asian and African countries cannot wholly adopt the Japanese model but must select components piece-
meal, such as self-directed development planning, technological adaptation,
scientific and practical education, state role in infrastructure and human capital
investment, labor-intensive industrial export expansion, and learning by doing.

References

Abelson, Philip H., ed. 1975. *Food, Politics, Economics, Nutrition, and Research.* Washington, DC: American Association for the Advancement of Science.

Abramovitz, Moses. 1956. "Resources and Output Trends in the United States since 1870." *American Economic Review 44* (May): 5–23.

Acapulco Summit Meeting of Latin American Presidents. 1987. "Final Communique." November 30.

Ake, Claude. 1981. "The Political Context of Indigenization." In Adebayo Adedeji (ed.), *Indigenization of African Economies.* London: Hutchinson University Library for Africa, pp. 32–41.

Alavi, Hamza, and Khusro, Amir. 1970. "Pakistan: The Burden of U.S. Aid." In Robert I. Rhodes (ed.), *Imperialism and Underdevelopment: A Reader.* New York: Monthly Review Press.

Ali, Tariq. 1970. *Pakistan: Military Rule or People's Power.* New York: William Morrow.

Allan, Pyarali G. 1969. "Tax and Fiscal Policy and its Impact on Private Enterprise." In Agha M. Ghouse (ed.), *Pakistan in the Development Decade: Problems and Performance.* Lahore: Economic Development Seminar, pp. 211–25.

Allen, G. C. 1964. *A Short Economic History of Modern Japan.* London: Macmillan.

——. 1982. *The Japanese Economy.* New York: Simon and Schuster.

Amin, Samir. 1973. *Neo-Colonialism in West Africa.* Trans. Francis McDonagh. New York: Monthly Review Press.

Anyang' Nyong'o, Peter. 1987. "The Development of Agrarian Capitalist Classes in the Ivory Coast, 1945–1975." In Paul M. Lubeck (ed.), *The African Bourgeoisie: Capitalist Development in Nigeria, Kenya, and the Ivory Coast.* Boulder, CO: Lynne Rienner, pp. 185–86.

Appleyard, Dennis R., and Field, Alfred J., Jr. 1992. *International Economics.* Homewood, IL: Irwin.

Arrow, Kenneth. 1962. "The Economic Implications of Learning by Doing." *Review of Economic Studies 29* (June): 154–94.

Aukrust, O., and Bjerke, J. 1959. "Real Capital and Economic Growth in Norway, 1900–1956." In International Association for Research in Income and Wealth, *The Measurement of National Wealth.* Income and Wealth series VIII. London: Bowes and Bowes.

Avramovic, Dragoslav. 1991. "Africa's Debts and Economic Recovery." North–South Roundtable. Abidjan, Côte d'Ivoire, July 8–9.

Ayoob, Mohammed. 1971. "Pakistan's Political Development, 1947 to 1970: Bird's Eye View." *Economic and Political Weekly 6,* 3–5 (January): 199–204.

Ayub, Mahmood A., and Hegstad, Sven O. 1987. "Determinants of Public Enterprise Performance." *Finance and Development 24* (December): 26–29.

Balakrishna, R. 1961. *Review of Economic Growth in India.* Bangalore: Bangalore Press.

Balogh, Thomas, and Streeten, Paul P. 1963. "The Coefficient of Ignorance." *Bulletin of the Oxford Institute of Statistics 25* (May): 99–107.

Bank of Japan. Statistics Department. 1966. *Hundred-Year Statistics of the Japanese Economy.* Tokyo.

Baran, Paul A. 1957. *The Political Economy of Growth.* New York: Modern Reader.

Bates, Robert H. 1981. *Markets and States in Tropical Africa: The Political Basis of Agricultural Policies.* Berkeley: University of California Press.

———. 1989. "The Reality of Structural Adjustment." In Simon Commander (ed.), *Structural Adjustment and Agriculture: Theory and Practice in Africa and Latin America.* London: Overseas Development Institute, pp. 222–26.

Beasley, W.B. 1987. *Japan Imperialism, 1894–1945.* Oxford: Clarendon Press.

———. 1990. *The Rise of Modern Japan.* London: Weidenfeld and Nicolson.

Bennett, M.B. 1951. "International Disparities in Consumption Levels." *American Economic Review 61* (September): 632–49.

Bettelheim, Charles. 1978. *Class Struggles in the USSR.* Vol. 1. New York: Monthly Review Press.

Bhagwati, Jagdish N., and Desai, Padma. 1970. *India: Planning for Industrialization—Industrialization and Trade Policies since 1951.* London: Oxford University Press.

Biersteker, Thomas J. 1987. "Indigenization and the Nigerian Bourgeoisie: Dependent Development in an African Context." In Paul M. Lubeck (ed.), *The African Bourgeoisie: Capitalist Development in Nigeria, Kenya, and the Ivory Coast.* Boulder, CO: Lynne Rienner, pp. 249–79.

Birdsall, Nancy; Ross, David; and Sabot, Richard. 1994. "Inequality and Growth Reconsidered." Paper presented to the American Economic Association meetings, Boston.

Bix, Herbert P. 1982. "Rethinking 'Emperor-System Fascism': Ruptures and Continuities in Modern Japanese History." *Bulletin of Concerned Asian Scholars 14* (April–June): 2–19.

Black, John. 1959. "Arguments for Tariffs." *Economic Journal 69* (June): 191–208.

Bose, Swadesh R. 1972. "East–West Contrast in Pakistan's Agricultural Development." In Keith Griffin and Azizur Rahman Khan (eds.), *Growth and Inequality in Pakistan.* London: Macmillan, pp. 69–93.

Brandner, James A., and Spencer, Barbara J. 1981. "Tariffs and the Extraction of Foreign Monopoly Rents under Potential Entry. *Canadian Journal of Economics 3* (August): 371–89.

Brimmer, Andrew F. 1955. "The Setting of Entrepreneurship in India." *Quarterly Journal of Economics 29* (November): 554–61.

Bruno, M. 1962. *Interdependence, Resource Use, and Structural Change in Israel.* Jerusalem: Bank of Israel Research Department.

Bruton, Henry J. 1967. "Productivity Growth in Latin America." *American Economic Review 57* (December): 1099–1116.

Cairncross, Alex K. 1955. "The Place of Capital in Economic Progress." In Leon H. Dupriez (ed.), *Economic Progress: Papers and Proceedings of a Round Table Held by the International Economic Association.* Louvain, France: Institut de Recherches Economiques et Sociales, pp. 235–48.

————. "Essays in Bibliography and Criticism. XLV: The Stages of Economic Growth." *Economic History Review 14* (April): 451–56.

Callaghy, Thomas M. 1989. "Toward State Capability and Embedded Liberalism in the Third World: Lessons for Adjustment." In Joan Nelson (ed.), *Fragile Coalitions: The Politics of Economic Adjustment.* New Brunswick, NJ: Transaction Books, pp. 115–38.

Camdessus, Michel. 1991. "Managing Director's Address: A Viable Economic System Is a Priority for Emerging Democracies." *IMF Survey* (July 29, 1991): 227.

Campbell, Horace, and Stein, Howard, eds. 1992. *Tanzania and the IMF: The Dynamics of Liberalization.* Boulder, CO: Westview.

Cesaire, Aimé. 1970. "On the Nature of Colonialism." In Irving Leonard Markovitz (ed.), *African Politics and Society: Basic Issues and Problems of Government and Development.* New York: Free Press.

Claessens, Stijn, and Diwan, Ishac. 1989. "Liquidity, Debt Relief, and Conditionality." In Ishrat Husain and Ishac Diwan (eds.), *Dealing with the Debt Crisis.* Washington, DC: World Bank, pp. 213–28.

Cleaver, Harry M., Jr. 1972. "The Contradictions of the Green Revolution." *American Economic Review 52* (May): 177–86.

Cleaver, Kevin. 1985. "The Impact of Price of Exchange Rates Policies on Agriculture in Sub-Saharan Africa." World Bank Staff Working Paper No. 728. Washington, DC.

Cole, William E., and Sanders, Richard D. 1985. "Internal Migration and Urban Employment in the Third World." *American Economic Review 75* (June): 481–94.

Committee for Academic Freedom in Africa (CAFA). 1991. "The World Bank and Education in Africa." *CAFA Newsletter*, no. 2 (Fall): 2–12.

Cornia, Giovanni Andrea; Jolly, Richard; and Stewart, Frances, eds. 1987. *Adjustment with a Human Face: Protecting the Vulnerable and Promoting Growth.* 2 vols. Oxford: Clarendon Press.

Curtin, Philip; Feierman, Steven; Thompson, Leonard; and Vansina, Jan. 1978. *African History.* Boston: Little, Brown.

Davey, Brian. 1975. *The Economic Development of India: A Marxist Analysis.* Nottingham, UK: Spokesman.

Davies, Rob, and Saunders, David. 1987. "Stabilisation Policies and the Effect of Child Health in Zimbabwe," *Review of African Political Economy*, no. 38 (April): 3–23.

Davis, J. Tait. 1991. "Institutional Impediments to Workforce Retrenchment and Restructuring in Ghana's State Enterprises." *World Development 19* (August): 987–1005.

Datt, Ruddar, and Sundharam, K.P.M. 1968. *Indian Economy.* New Delhi: Niraj Prakashan.

Denison, Edward F. 1967. *Why Growth Rates Differ: Postwar Experience in Nine Western Countries.* Washington, DC: Brookings Institution.

DeRosa, Dean. 1991. "Protection in Sub-Saharan Africa Hinders Exports." *Finance and Development 28* (September): 42–45.

Dore, Ronald P. 1959. *Land Reform in Japan.* London: Oxford University Press.

————. 1965a. *Education in Tokugawa Japan.* Berkeley: University of California Press.

————. 1965b. "Land Reform and Japan's Economic Development." *Developing Economies 3*, 4 (December): 487–96.

Drummond, Ian. 1961. Review of Rostow's *"The Stages of Economic Growth."* *Canadian Journal of Economics and Political Science 13* (February): 111–13.

Duus, Peter; Myers, Ramon H.; and Peattie, Mark R., eds. 1989. *The Japanese Informal Empire in China, 1895–1937.* Princeton, NJ: Princeton University Press.

Economic Commission for Africa. 1983a. *Commodity Market Structures, Pricing, Policies and Their Impact on African Trade.* E/ECA/TRADE/3. Addis Ababa.

————. 1983b. *ECA and Africa's Development, 1983–2000: A Preliminary Perspective Study*. Addis Ababa.

Economist Intelligence Unit. 1985. *Country Profile: Kenya*. London.

Eicher, Carl K., and Baker, Doyle C. 1982. *Research on Agricultural Development in Sub-Saharan Africa: A Critical Survey*. East Lansing: Michigan State University International Development Paper No. 1.

El Samhouri, Mohammed. 1989. "Flexible Exchange Rates and Export Instability: The Impact of the Post-1973 International Monetary System on the Developing Countries." Ph.D. diss., Kansas State University.

Fajana, O. 1981. "Aspects of Income Distribution in the Nigerian Urban Sector." In Henry Bienen and Victor P. Diejomaoh (eds.), *The Political Economy of Income Distribution in Nigeria*. New York: Holmes and Meier, pp. 193–236.

Fei, John C.H., and Ranis, Gustav. 1964. *Development of the Labor Surplus Economy*. Homewood, IL: Irwin.

Fischer, Stanley, and Husain, Ishrat. 1990. "Managing the Debt Crisis in the 1990s." *Finance and Development 27* (June): 24–27.

Food and Agriculture Organization of the United Nations. 1991. *The State of Food and Agriculture, 1990*. Rome.

Forrest, Tom. 1987. "State Capital, Capitalist Development, and Class Formation in Nigeria." In Paul M. Lubeck (ed.), *The African Bourgeoisie: Capitalist Development in Nigeria, Kenya, and the Ivory Coast*. Boulder, CO: Lynne Rienner, pp. 307–42.

Francks, Penelope. 1992. *Japanese Economic Development: Theory and Practice*. London: Routledge.

Frank, Andre Gunder. 1969. *Latin America: Underdevelopment or Revolution?* New York: Monthly Review Press.

Frankel, Francine R. 1978. *India's Political Economy, 1947–1977*. Princeton, NJ: Princeton University Press.

Franko, Lawrence G. 1983. *The Threat of Japanese Multinationals—How the West Can Respond*. Chichester, UK: John Wiley.

Fransman, Martin. 1986. *Technology and Economic Development*. Boulder, CO: Westview.

Fujino, Shozaburo; Fujino, Shiro; and Ono, Akira. 1979. *Sen-i Kogyo*. In Kazushi Ohkawa, Miyohei Shinohara, and Mataji Umemura (eds.), *Choki Keizai Tokei; Suikei to Bunseki* [Estimates of Long-term Economic Statistics since 1868]. Vol. 11. Tokyo: Toyokeizai Shinposha.

Fukuyama, Francis. 1992. *The End of History and the Last Man*. New York: Free Press.

Furtado, Celso. 1968. *The Economic Growth of Brazil: A Survey from Colonial to Modern Times*. Trans. Ricardo W. de Aguiar and Eric Charles Drysdale. Berkeley: University of California Press.

————. 1970. *Economic Development of Latin America: A Survey from Colonial Times to the Cuban Revolution*. Cambridge: Cambridge University Press.

————. 1973. "The Concept of External Dependence in the Study of Underdevelopment." In Charles K. Wilber (ed.), *The Political Economy of Development and Underdevelopment*. New York: Random House, pp. 118–23.

Gaathon, A.L. 1961. *Capital Stock, Employment, and Output in Israel, 1950–59*. Jerusalem: Bank of Israel Research Department.

Gadgil, Dhananjaya Ramchandra. 1959. *Origins of the Modern Indian Business Class—An Interim Report*. New York: Institute of Pacific Relations.

Gallagher, John, and Robinson, Ronald. 1953. "The Imperialism of Free Trade." *Economic History Review* (second series) *6*: 1–15.

Galtung, Johan. 1971. "A Structural Theory of Imperialism." *Journal of Peace Research* 8, 2: 81–118.

Gavan, James D., and Dixon, John A. 1975. "India: A Perspective on the Food Situation." In Philip H. Abelson (ed.), *Food, Politics, Economics, Nutrition, and Research*. Washington, DC: American Association for the Advancement of Science.

Gerschenkron, Alexander. 1962. *Economic Backwardness in Historical Perspective*. Cambridge, MA: Harvard University Press.

Ghai, Dharan, ed. 1991. *The IMF and the South: The Social Impact of Crisis and Adjustment*. London: Zed Books.

Ghai, Dharan, and Radwan, Samir, eds. 1983. *Agrarian Policies and Rural Poverty in Africa*. Geneva: International Labour Office.

Ghouse, Agha M., ed. 1969. *Pakistan in the Development Decade: Problems and Performance*. Lahore: Economic Development Seminar.

Gillis, Malcolm; Perkins, Dwight H.; Roemer, Michael; and Snodgrass, Donald R. 1987. *Economics of Development*. New York: Norton.

Goldsmith, Raymond W. 1983. *The Financial Development of India, Japan, and the United States: A Trilateral Institutional, Statistical, and Analytical Comparison*. New Haven, CT: Yale University Press.

Goode, Richard. 1962. "Personal Income Tax in Latin America." In Joint Tax Program, Organization of American States/Inter-American Development Bank/Economic Commission for Latin America, *Fiscal Policy for Economic Growth in Latin America*. Baltimore: Johns Hopkins University Press, pp. 157–71.

Gordon, Andrew. 1985. *The Evolution of Labor Relations in Japan: Heavy Industry, 1853–1955*. Cambridge, MA: Harvard University Press.

Grant, James P. 1989. *The State of the World's Children, 1989*. New York: Oxford University Press.

Green, Reginald Herbold. 1989. "Articulating Stabilisation Programmes and Structural Adjustment: Sub-Saharan Africa." In Simon Commander (ed.), *Structural Adjustment and Agriculture: Theory and Practice in Africa and Latin America*. London: Overseas Development Institute, pp. 34–39.

Gregory, Paul R., and Stuart, Robert C. 1986. *Soviet Economic Structure and Performance*. New York: Harper and Row.

Griffin, Keith, and Khan, Azizur Rahman, eds. 1972. *Growth and Inequality in Pakistan*. London: Macmillan.

Grubel, Herbert G. 1981. *International Economics*. Homewood, IL: Irwin.

Hackett, Paul. 1990. "Economy." In *Africa South of the Sahara, 1990*. London: Europa Publications.

Hagen, Everett E. 1975, 1980. *The Economics of Development*. Homewood, IL: Irwin.

Haggard, Stephan, and Kaufman, Robert R. 1989. "Economic Adjustment in New Democracies." In Joan Nelson (ed.), *Fragile Coalitions: The Politics of Economic Adjustment*. New Brunswick, NJ: Transaction Books, pp. 57–77.

Halliday, Jon. 1975. *A Political History of Japanese Capitalism*. New York: Pantheon.

Hamid, Naved. 1970. "A Critical Appraisal of Foreign Aid Strategy." *Punjab University Economist 8* (December): 132–46.

Hane, Mikiso. 1982. *Peasants, Rebels, and Outcastes: The Underside of Modern Japan*. New York: Pantheon Books.

———. 1992. *Modern Japan: A Historical Survey*. Boulder, CO: Westview.

Harris, John R., and Todaro, Michael P. 1970. "Migration, Unemployment and Development: A Two-sector Analysis." *American Economic Review 60* (March): 126–42.

Harrod, Roy F. 1939. "An Essay in Dynamic Theory." *Economic Journal 49* (March): 14–33.

Hayami, Yujiro. 1975. *A Century of Agricultural Growth in Japan: Its Relevance to Asian Development.* Tokyo: University of Tokyo Press.

Hayami, Yujiro, and Ruttan, Vernon W. 1971. *Agricultural Development: An International Perspective.* Baltimore: Johns Hopkins University Press.

Hayami, Yujiro, and Yamada, S. 1969. "Agricultural Productivity at the Beginning of Industrialization." In Kazushi Ohkawa, Bruce Johnston, and H. Kaneda (eds.), *Agriculture and Economic Growth: Japan's Experience.* Tokyo: Tokyo University Press.

Heckscher, Eli F. 1950. "The Effect of Foreign Trade on the Distribution of Income." In H.S. Ellis and L.M. Metzler (eds.), *Readings in the Theory of International Trade.* Homewood, IL: Irwin, pp. 272–300.

Heston, Alan, and Summers, Robert. 1980. "Comparative Indian Economic Growth: 1870–1970." *American Economic Review 70* (May): 96–101.

Hicks, John R. 1965. *Capital and Growth.* New York: Oxford University Press.

Higgins, Benjamin. 1968. *Economic Development: Problems, Principles, and Policies.* New York: W.W. Norton.

Hirschman, Albert O. 1986. "The Political Economy of Latin American Development: Seven Exercises in Retrospect." Paper for the 13th International Congress of the Latin American Studies Association. Boston. October.

Hirschmeier, Johannes. 1964. *The Origins of Entrepreneurship in Meiji Japan.* Cambridge, MA: Harvard University Press.

Hirschmeier, Johannes, and Yui, Tsunehiko. 1975. *The Development of Japanese Business, 1600–1973.* London: George Allen and Unwin.

Hogan, Warren T. 1958. "Technical Progress and Production Functions." *Review of Economics and Statistics 40* (November): 407–11.

Humphrey, Clare E. 1990. *Privatization in Bangladesh: Economic Transition in a Poor Country.* Boulder, CO: Westview Press.

Huntington, Samuel P. 1968. *Political Order in Changing Societies.* New Haven, CT: Yale University Press.

Husain, Ishrat, and Underwood, John. 1992. "The Problem of Sub-Saharan Africa's Debt—and the Solutions." Unpublished paper. Washington, DC: World Bank.

Hymer, Stephen. 1970. "The Efficiency (Contradictions) of Multinational Corporations." *American Economic Review 60* (May): 441–53.

India Planning Commission. 1969. *Fourth Five-Year Plan, 1969–74.* Delhi.

International Development Center of Japan. 1977a. "Japan's Historical Development Experience and the Contemporary Developing Countries: Issues for Comparative Analysis." Prepared for the Economic Planning Agency, Tokyo, March.

———. 1977b. "The Nigerian Economy in Transition: An Analytical Framework for a Comparative Study." Prepared for the Economic Planning Agency, Tokyo, March.

———. Kazushi Ohkawa, team leader. 1980. "Japan's Development Experience and the Development Strategy for the Contemporary Developing Countries." Tokyo, March.

———. 1982a. "Japan's Historical Development Experience and the Contemporary Developing Countries: Issues for Comparative Analysis." Tokyo, January.

———. 1982b. "Japan's Historical Development Experience and the Contemporary Developing Countries: Issues for Comparative Analysis." Phase 2. Tokyo, February.

International Monetary Fund. 1984. *Government Finance Statistics Yearbook.* Washington, DC.

———. 1986. *World Economic Outlook.* Washington, DC. October.

———. 1987. *World Economic Outlook.* Washington, DC. October.

———. 1989. *World Economic Outlook.* Washington, DC. October.

———. 1990. *World Economic Outlook.* Washington, DC. October.

———. 1991. *World Economic Outlook.* Washington, DC. October.

Inukai, Ichirou. 1979. "The Kogyo Iken: Japan's Ten Year Plan, 1884." *Kyoto Sangyo University Economic and Business Review* (May): 1–100.

──────. 1981. "Experience in Transfer of Technology from the West: Lessons from False Starts." In Haruo Nagamine (ed.), *Nation-Building and Regional Development: The Japanese Experience*. U.N. Centre for Regional Development, vol. 10. Hong Kong: Maruzen Asia, pp. 77–98.

Ishikawa, Shigeru. 1981. *Essays on Technology, Employment, and Institutions in Economic Development: Comparative Asian Experience*. Tokyo: Kinokuniya.

──────. 1982. "Relevance of the Experiences of Japan to Contemporary Economic Development." *The Philippine Review of Economics and Business 19*: 255–79.

Jagannathan, N. Vijay. 1987. *Informal Markets in Developing Countries*. New York: Oxford University Press.

Jain, Shail. 1975. *Size Distribution of Income: A Compilation of Data*. Washington, DC: World Bank.

Jansen, Marius B. 1975. *Japan and China: from War to Peace, 1894–1972*. Chicago: Rand McNally.

Jamal, Vali, and Weeks, John. 1988. "The Vanishing Rural-Urban Gap in Sub-Saharan Africa." *International Labour Review 127, 3*: 271–92.

Jiliani, M.S. 1969. "Social Welfare and Economic Development." In Agha M. Ghouse (ed.), *Pakistan in the Development Decade: Problems and Performance*. Lahore: Economic Development Seminar, pp. 346–69.

Johnson, B.L.C. 1983. *Development in South Asia*. Harmondsworth, UK: Penguin.

Johnston, Bruce F., and Mellor, John W. 1961. "The Role of Agriculture in Economic Development." *American Economic Review 51* (September): 571–81.

Kenen, Peter B. 1989. *The International Economy*. Englewood Cliffs, NJ: Prentice-Hall.

Keynes, John Maynard. 1936. *The General Theory of Employment, Interest and Money*. Cambridge: Cambridge University Press.

Khan, Mohsin S. 1991. "Comments." In Vinod Thomas, Ajay Chhibber, Manssor Dailami, and Jaime de Melo (eds.), *Restructuring Economies in Distress: Policy Reform and the World Bank*. Oxford: Oxford University Press, pp. 435–39.

Khan, Taufiq M., and Bergan, Asbjorn. 1966. "Measurement of Structural Change in the Pakistan Economy: A Review of the National Income Estimates, 1949/50 to 1963/64." *Pakistan Development Review 6* (Summer): 173–91.

Kilby, Peter, ed. 1971. *Entrepreneurship and Economic Development*. New York: Free Press.

Kindleberger, Charles P. 1956. *The Terms of Trade: A European Case Study*. New York: Wiley.

──────. "The Theory of Direct Investment." In Robert E. Baldwin and J. David Richardson (eds.), *International Trade and Finance*. Boston: Little, Brown, pp. 267–85.

Kitching, Gavin. 1987. "The Role of a National Bourgeoisie in the Current Phase of Capitalist Development: Some Reflections." In Paul M. Lubeck (ed.), *The African Bourgeoisie: Capitalist Development in Nigeria, Kenya, and the Ivory Coast*. Boulder, CO: Lynne Rienner, pp. 27–55.

Kling, Blair B. 1966. "The Origins of the Managing Agency System in India." *Journal of Asian Studies 26* (November): 37–47.

Kohli, Harinder S., and Sood, Anil. 1987. "Fostering Enterprise Development." *Finance and Development 24* (March): 34–36.

Krause, Lawrence B. 1971. *Brookings Papers on Economic Activity*. Washington, DC: Brookings Institution.

Krueger, Anne O. 1978. *Foreign Trade Regimes and Economic Development: Liberalization Attempts and Consequences*. Cambridge: Ballinger.

———. 1983. *Trade and Employment in Developing Countries: Synthesis and Conclusions.* Chicago: University of Chicago Press.

Krueger, Anne O.; Lary, Hal B.; Monson, Terry; and Akrasenee, Narongchai, eds. 1981. *Trade and Employment in Developing Countries,* vol. I, *Individual Studies.* Chicago: University of Chicago Press.

Krugman, Paul R. 1984. "Import Protection as Export Promotion: International Competition in the Presence of Oligopoly and Economies of Scale." In Henryk Kierzkowski (ed.), *Monopolistic Competition in International Trade.* Oxford: Oxford University Press, pp. 180–93.

Kuznets, Simon. 1956. "Quantitative Aspects of the Economic Growth of Nations: I. Levels and Variability of Rates of Growth," *Economic Development and Cultural Change 5* (October): 5–94.

———. 1966. *Modern Economic Growth: Rate, Structure, and Spread.* New Haven, CT: Yale University Press.

———. 1971. *Economic Growth of Nations—Total Output and Production Structure.* Cambridge, MA: Harvard University Press, 1971.

Lal, Deepak. 1983. *The Poverty of "Development Economics."* London: Institute of Economic Affairs.

Lall, Sanjaya. 1985. *Multinationals, Technology and Exports: Selected Papers.* New York: St. Martin's Press.

Lamb, Helen B. 1955. "The Rise of Indian Business Communities." *Pacific Affairs 23* (June): 101–16.

Langdon, Steven. 1987. "Industry and Capitalism in Kenya: Contributions to a Debate." In Paul M. Lubeck (ed.), *The African Bourgeoisie: Capitalist Development in Nigeria, Kenya, and the Ivory Coast.* Boulder, CO: Lynne Rienner, pp. 343–81.

Larrain, Jorge. 1989. *Theories of Development: Capitalism, Colonialism and Dependency.* Cambridge: Polity Press.

Lecaillon, Jacques; Paukert, Felix; Morrisson, Christian; and Germidis, Dimitri. 1984. *Income Distribution and Economic Development: An Analytical Survey.* Geneva: International Labour Office.

Lee, Teng-hui. 1971. *Intersectoral Capital Flows in the Economic Development of Taiwan, 1895–1960.* Ithaca, NY: Cornell University Press.

Leibenstein, Harvey. 1966. "Allocative Efficiency vs. 'X-Efficiency.' " *American Economic Review 56* (June): 392–415.

Lele, Uma. 1990. "Structural Adjustment, Agricultural Development and the Poor: Some Lessons from the Malawian Experience." *World Development 18* (September): 1207–19.

Levine, Herbert S. 1960. "A Small Problem in the Analysis of Growth." *Review of Economics and Statistics 42* (May): 225–28.

Levy, Marion, Jr. 1955. "Contributing Factors in the Modernization of China and Japan." In Simon Kuznets, W.E. Moore, and J.J. Spengler (eds.), *Economic Growth: Brazil, India, Japan.* Durham, NC: Duke University Press, pp. 496–536.

Lewis, W. Arthur. 1954. "Economic Development with Unlimited Supplies of Labor." *Manchester School 22* (May): 139–91.

Lipton, Michael. 1977. *Why Poor People Stay Poor: A Study of Urban Bias in World Development.* London: Maurice Temple Smith.

Lockwood, William W. 1954. *The Economic Development of Japan: Growth and Structural Change, 1868–1938.* Princeton, NJ: Princeton University Press.

Loxley, John. 1989. "The Devaluation Debate in Tanzania." In Bonnie K. Campbell and John Loxley (eds.), *Structural Adjustment in Africa.* New York: St. Martin's Press.

Lubeck, Paul M., ed. 1987. *The African Bourgeoisie: Capitalist Development in Nigeria, Kenya, and the Ivory Coast.* Boulder, CO: Lynne Rienner.

MacEwan, Arthur. 1971. "Contradictions in Capitalist Development: The Case of Pakistan." *Review of Radical Political Economics 3* (Spring): 40–57.

Maddison, Angus. 1969. *Economic Growth in Japan and the USSR.* New York: Norton.

———. 1970. *Economic Progress and Policy in Developing Countries.* London: Allen and Unwin.

———. 1971. *Class Structure and Economic Growth: India and Pakistan since the Moghuls.* New York: Norton.

Mahajan, V.S. 1976. *Development Planning: Lessons from the Japanese Model.* Calcutta: Minerva Associates.

Malthus, Thomas Robert. 1963. *Essay on the Principles of Population.* Homewood, IL: Irwin.

Maniruzzaman, Talukder. 1966. "Group Interests in Pakistani Politics, 1947–1958." *Pacific Affairs 39,* 1 & 2 (Spring/Summer): 83–98.

Markovitz, Irving Leonard. 1977. *Power and Class in Africa: An Introduction to Change and Conflict in African Politics.* Englewood Cliffs, NJ: Prentice-Hall.

Markovitz, Irving Leonard, ed. 1970. *African Politics and Society: Basic Issues and Problems of Government and Development.* New York: Free Press.

Marsden, Keith, and Belot, Therese. 1989. "Impact of Regulations and Taxation on Private Industry." In Gerald M. Meier and William F. Steel (eds.), *Industrial Adjustment in Sub-Saharan Africa.* New York: Oxford University Press, pp. 163–68.

Martens, Andre. 1988. "Structural Adjustment in the Sahel: Beyond the Point of No Return?" In North–South Institute, *Structural Adjustment in Africa: External Financing for Development.* Ottawa, Canada, February 25–26.

Massell, Benton F. 1960. "Capital Formation and Technological Change in United States Manufacturing." *Review of Economics and Statistics 42* (May): 182–88.

———. 1962. "Another Small Problem in the Analysis of Growth." *Review of Economics and Statistics 44* (August): 330–35.

McCleary, William A. 1991. "Pakistan: Structural Adjustment and Economic Growth." In Vinod Thomas, Ajay Chhibber, Manssor Dailami, and Jaime de Melo (eds.), *Restructuring Economies in Distress: Policy Reform and the World Bank.* Oxford: Oxford University Press, pp. 414–34.

McClelland, David C. 1961. *The Achieving Society.* Princeton, NJ: D. Van Nostrand.

McClelland, David C., and Winter, David G., 1971. *Motivating Economic Achievement— Accelerating Economic Development through Psychological Training.* New York: Free Press.

McCord, William. 1973. "The Japanese Model." In Charles K. Wilber (ed.), *The Political Economy of Development and Underdevelopment.* New York: Random House, pp. 278–83.

McHale, Magda, and McHale, John. 1979. "World of Children." *Population Bulletin 33,* 6 (January): 14.

Medhora, Phiroze B. 1965. "Entrepreneurship in India." *Political Science Quarterly 80* (September): 558–78.

Migdal, Joel S. 1988. *Strong Societies and Weak States: State-Society Relations and State Capabilities in the Third World.* Princeton, NJ: Princeton University Press.

Mills, Cadman Atta. 1989. "Structural Adjustment in Sub-Saharan Africa." Economic Development Institute Policy Seminar Report No. 18. Washington, DC: World Bank.

Millward, Robert. 1988. "Measured Sources of Inefficiency in the Performance of Private and Public Enterprises in LDCs." In Paul Cook and Colin Kirkpatrick (eds.), *Privatisation in Less-Developed Countries.* Sussex, UK: Wheatsheaf, pp. 143–61.

Minami, Ryoshin. 1973. *The Turning Point in Economic Development: Japan's Experience.* Tokyo: Kinokuniya.

————. 1976. "The Introduction of Electric Power and its Impact on the Manufacturing Industries: With Special Reference to Smaller Scale Plants." In Hugh T. Patrick (ed.), *Japanese Industrialization and Its Social Consequences.* Berkeley: University of California Press, pp. 299–325.

————. 1986. *The Economic Development of Japan: A Quantitative Study.* Trans. Ralph Thompson and Ryoshin Minami. Houndmills, UK: Macmillan.

Mitsuru, Hashimoto. 1982. "The Social Background of Peasant Uprisings in Tokugawa Japan." In Tetsuo Najita and J. Victor Koschmann (eds.), *Conflict in Modern Japanese History: The Neglected Tradition.* Princeton: Princeton University Press, pp. 145–63.

Mkandawire, Thandika. 1991. "Crisis and Adjustment in Sub-Saharan Africa." In Dharan Ghai (ed.), *The IMF and the South: The Social Impact of Crisis and Adjustment.* London: Zed Books, pp. 80–94.

Mody, Ashoka; Mundle, Sudipto; and Raj, K.N. 1982. "Resource Flows from Agriculture and Industrialization: A Comparative Analysis of Japanese and Indian Experiences." In International Development Center of Japan, "Japan's Historical Development Experience and the Contemporary Developing Countries: Issues for Comparative Analysis," Phase 2. Tokyo, February.

————. 1985. "Resource Flows from Agriculture: Japan and India." In Kazushi Ohkawa and Gustav Ranis (eds.), *Japan and the Developing Countries: A Comparative Analysis.* Oxford: Basil Blackwell.

Morawetz, David. 1974. "Employment Implications of Industrialization in Developing Countries." *Economic Journal 84* (September): 492–523.

————. 1977. *Twenty-five Years of Economic Development, 1950 to 1975.* Baltimore: Johns Hopkins University Press.

Morris-Suzuki, Tessa. 1992. "Japanese Technology and the New International Division of Knowledge in Asia." In Tokunaga Shojiro (ed.), *Japan's Foreign Investment and Asian Economic Interdependence.* Tokyo: University of Tokyo Press, pp. 135–52.

Morss, Elliot R. 1984. "Institutional Destruction Resulting from Donor and Project Proliferation in Sub-Saharan Countries." *World Development 12* (April): 465–70.

Mosley, Paul; Harrigan, Jane; and Toye, John. 1991. *Aid and Power: The World Bank and Policy-based Lending.* 2 vols. London: Routledge.

Moulder, Frances V. 1977. *Japan, China, and the Modern World Economy: Toward a Reinterpretation of East Asian Development ca. 1600 to ca. 1918.* Cambridge: Cambridge University Press.

Mukherjee, M. 1969. *National Income of India.* Calcutta: Statistical Publishing Society.

Müller, Ronald. 1979. "The Multinational Corporation and the Underdevelopment of the Third World." In Charles K. Wilber (ed.), *The Political Economy of Development and Underdevelopment.* New York: Random House, pp. 151–78.

Munakata, Seiya. 1965. "The Course and Problems of National Education." *Developing Economies 3* (December): 540–59.

Mundle, Sudipto. 1981. *Surplus Flows and Growth Imbalances.* New Delhi: Allied Publishers.

Myint, Hla. 1958. "The 'Classical Theory' of International Trade and the Underdeveloped Countries." *Quarterly Journal of Economics 68* (June): 190–207.

Myrdal, Gunnar. 1968. *Asian Drama: An Inquiry into the Poverty of Nations.* 3 vols. Middlesex, UK: Penguin Books.

Nafziger, E. Wayne. 1976. "A Critique of Development Economics in the U.S." *Journal of Development Studies 13* (October): 18–34.

————. 1977. *African Capitalism: A Case Study in Nigerian Entrepreneurship.* Stanford, CA: Hoover.

————. 1978. *Class, Caste, and Entrepreneurship: A Study of Indian Industrialists.* Honolulu: University Press of Hawaii.

————. 1983. *The Economics of Political Instability.* Boulder, CO: Westview.

————. 1986. *Entrepreneurship, Equity, and Economic Development.* Greenwich, CT: JAI Press.

————. 1988a. *Inequality in Africa: Political Elites, Proletariat, Peasants, and the Poor.* Cambridge: Cambridge University Press.

————. 1988b. "Society and the Entrepreneur." *Journal of Development Planning,* no. 18: 127–52.

————. 1990a. *The Economics of Developing Countries.* Englewood Cliffs, NJ: Prentice-Hall.

————. 1990b. *Indian National Development Strategy and National Power.* Beijing: International Technology and Economic Institute, Development Research Center of the State Council.

————. 1993. *The Debt Crisis in Africa.* Baltimore: Johns Hopkins University Press.

Nagamine, Haruo, ed. 1981. *Nation-building and Regional Development: The Japanese Experience.* U.N. Centre for Regional Development. Vol. 10. Hong Kong: Maruzen Asia.

Nakamura, James. 1966. *Agricultural Production and the Economic Development of Japan, 1873–1922.* Princeton, NJ: Princeton University Press.

Nakamura, Takafusa. 1983. *Economic Growth in Prewar Japan.* Trans. Robert A. Feldman. New Haven, CT: Yale University Press.

Nelson, Joan M. 1989. "The Politics of Pro-Poor Adjustment." In Joan Nelson (ed.), *Fragile Coalitions: The Politics of Economic Adjustment.* New Brunswick, NJ: Transaction Books, pp. 95–113.

Nelson, Joan M., ed. 1989. *Fragile Coalitions: The Politics of Economic Adjustment.* New Brunswick, NJ: Transaction Books.

Nicolson, I.F. 1969. *The Administration of Nigeria, 1900–1960; Men, Methods, and Myths.* Oxford: Clarendon Press.

Niitamo, Olavi. 1958. "The Development of Productivity in Finnish Industry, 1925–52." *Productivity Measurement Review 33* (November): 30–41.

Norman, E. Herbert. 1975. *Origins of the Modern Japanese State: Selected Writings of E.H. Norman.* Ed. by John W. Dower. New York: Pantheon.

Nove, Alec. 1983. *The Economics of Feasible Socialism.* London: George Unwin.

Nurkse, Ragnar. 1961. *Patterns of Trade and Development.* New York: Oxford University Press.

Ofer, Gur. 1987. "Soviet Economic Growth: 1928–1985." *Journal of Economic Literature 25* (December): 1769–82.

Ogbuagu, Chibuzo S.A. 1983. "The Nigerian Indigenization Policy: Nationalism or Pragmatism?" *African Affairs 82* (April): 241–66.

Ohkawa, Kazushi. 1983. "Japan's Development: A Model for Less-Developed Countries?" *Asian Development Review 1,* 2: 45–57.

Ohkawa, Kazushi, and Hayami, Yujiro, eds. 1976. *Papers and Proceedings of the Conference on Japan's Historical Development Experience and the Contemporary Developing Countries.* Tokyo: International Development Center of Japan.

Ohkawa, Kazushi, and Ranis, Gustav, eds. 1985. *Japan and the Developing Countries: A Comparative Analysis.* Oxford: Basil Blackwell.

Ohkawa, Kazushi, and Rosovsky, Henry. 1973. *Japanese Economic Growth: Trend Acceleration in the Twentieth Century.* Stanford, CA: Stanford University Press.

Ohkawa, Kazushi; Shimizu, Yutaka; and Takamatsu, Nobukiyo. 1982. " 'Agricultural Surplus' in Japan's Case: Implication for Various Possible Patterns in the Initial Phase of Development," International Development Center of Japan Working Paper No. 19, March.

Ohkawa, Kazushi, and Shinohara, Miyohei, eds. 1979. *Patterns of Japanese Economic Development: A Quantitative Appraisal.* New Haven, CT: Yale University Press.

Ohkawa, Kazushi; Shinohara, Miyohei; Umemura, M.; Ito, M.; and Noda, T. 1957. *The Growth Rate of the Japanese Economy since 1878.* Tokyo: Kinokuniya.

Ohlin, Bertil. 1933. *Interregional and International Trade.* Cambridge, MA: Harvard University Press.

Okita, Saburo. 1980. *The Developing Economies and Japan: Lessons in Growth.* Tokyo: University of Tokyo Press.

———. 1981. "Development Strategy: A Japanese Perspective." In Haruo Nagamine (ed.), *Nation-Building and Regional Development: The Japanese Experience.* U.N. Centre for Regional Development, vol. 10. Hong Kong: Maruzen Asia, pp. 1–12.

Ono, Keinosuke, and Odaka, Konosuke. 1979. "Ancillary Firm Development in the Japanese Automobile Industry—Selected Case Studies (I)." Hitotsubashi University Institute of Economic Research Discussion Paper Series No. 24. December.

Organisation for Economic Cooperation and Development. 1988. *Historical Statistics, 1960–1986.* Paris.

Oshima, Harry T. 1965. "Meiji Fiscal Policy and Agricultural Progress." In William W. Lockwood (ed.), *The State and Economic Enterprise in Japan: Essays in the Political Economy of Growth.* Princeton, NJ: Princeton University Press, pp. 353–89.

Osterhammel, Jürgen. 1986. "Semi-colonialism and Informal Empire in Twentieth-century China: Towards a Framework of Analysis." In Wolfgang J. Mommsen and Jürgen Osterhammel (eds.), *Imperialism and After: Continuities and Discontinuities.* London: Allen and Unwin.

Pakistan. Ministry of Finance. 1971. *Pakistan Economic Survey (1970–71).* Islamabad.

———. 1972. *Pakistan Economic Survey (1971–72).* Islamabad.

Papanek, Gustav F. 1962. "The Development of Entrepreneurship." *American Economic Review 52* (May): 46–58.

Parfitt, Trevor W., and Riley, Stephen P. 1989. *The African Debt Crisis.* London: Routledge.

Park, Young C. 1987. "Evaluating the Performance of Korea's Government-Invested Enterprise." *Finance and Development 24* (June): 25–27.

Patrick, Hugh T. 1967. "Japan, 1868–1914." In Rondo Cameron (ed.), *Banking in the Early Stages of Industrialization: A Study in Comparative Economic History.* New York: Oxford University Press, pp. 239–89.

Patrick, Hugh T., ed. 1976. *Japanese Industrialization and Its Social Consequences.* Berkeley: University of California Press.

Perry, David B. 1980. "International Tax Comparisons." *Canadian Tax Journal 28* (January–February): 89–93.

Polyani, Karl. 1944. *The Great Transformation: The Politics and Economics of Our Time.* Boston: Beacon Press.

Population Reference Bureau. 1988. *1988 World Population Data Sheet.* Washington, DC.

———. 1990. *1990 World Population Data Sheet.* Washington, DC.

———. 1991. *1991 World Population Data Sheet.* Washington, DC.

———. 1993. *1993 World Population Data Sheet.* Washington, DC.

Power, John H. 1979. "Trade Trends in Asia." *Asia Pacific Community* (Fall): 44–55.

Prebisch, Raul. 1962. "The Economic Development of Latin America and its Principal Problems." *Economic Bulletin for Latin America 7* (February): 1–22. [First published in Spanish in 1950.]

Ranis, Gustav. 1955. "The Community-centered Entrepreneur in Japanese Development." *Explorations in Entrepreneurial History 8,* 2: 80–98.

Ray, Edward John. 1989. *U.S. Protectionism and the World Debt Crisis.* New York: Quorum Books.

Raychaudhuri, Tapan. 1968. "A Re-interpretation of Nineteenth Century Economic History." *Indian Economic and Social History Review 5*: 77–100.

Reddaway, W.B., and Smith, A.D. 1960. "Progress in British Manufacturing Industries in the Period, 1948–1954." *Economic Journal 70* (March): 6–37.

Redlich, Fritz. 1963. "Economic Development, Entrepreneurship, and Psychologism." *Explorations in Entrepreneurial History/Second Series 1* (Fall): 10–35.

Reich, Robert B. 1991. *The Work of Nations: Preparing Ourselves for 21st-Century Capitalism.* New York: Alfred A. Knopf.

Reischauer, Edwin O., and Fairbank, John K. 1958. *East Asia: The Great Tradition.* Boston: Houghton Mifflin.

Repetto, Robert. 1989. *Wasting Assets: Natural Resources in the National Income Accounts.* Washington, DC: World Resources Institute.

Rimmer, Douglas. 1984. *The Economies of West Africa.* London: Weidenfeld and Nicolson.

Robinson, Sherman. 1971. "Sources of Growth in Less Developed Countries: A Cross Section Study." *Quarterly Journal of Economics 85* (August): 391–408.

Rosenstein-Rodan, Paul N. 1943. "Problems of Industrialization of Eastern and Southeastern Europe." *Economic Journal 53* (June–September): 202–11.

Rostow, Walter W. 1961. *The Stages of Economic Growth: A Non-communist Manifesto.* Cambridge: Cambridge University Press.

Rostow, Walter W., ed. 1963. *The Economics of Take-off into Sustained Growth.* London: Macmillan.

Rungta, Radhe Shyam. 1970. *The Rise of Business Corporations in India, 1851–1900.* Cambridge: Cambridge University Press.

Ruttan, Vernon. 1972. "Induced Technical and Institutional Change and the Future of Agriculture." In the Fifteenth International Conference of Agricultural Economists. *Papers and Reports.* Sao Paulo.

Sablo, Yves. 1975. "Employment and Unemployment, 1969–90." *International Labour Review 112* (December): 408–17.

Sachs, Jeffrey. 1993. *Poland's Jump to the Market Economy.* Cambridge, MA: MIT Press.

Sandbrook, Richard. 1991. "Economic Crisis, Structural Adjustment and the State in Sub-Saharan Africa." In Dharan Ghai (ed.), *The IMF and the South: The Social Impact of Crisis and Adjustment.* London: Zed Books, pp. 95–114.

Saxonhouse, Gary R. 1976. "Country Girls and Communication among Competitors in the Japanese Cotton-spinning Industry." In Hugh T. Patrick (ed.), *Japanese Industrialization and Its Social Consequences.* Berkeley: University of California Press, pp. 97–125.

Saxonhouse, Gary, and Kiyokawa, Yukihiko. 1985. "Supply and Demand for Quality Workers in Cotton Spinning in Japan and India." In Kazushi Ohkawa and Gustav Ranis (eds.), *Japan and the Developing Countries: A Comparative Analysis.* Oxford: Basil Blackwell, pp. 177–211.

Schatz, Sayre P. 1965. "n Achievement and Economic Growth: A Critical Appraisal." *Quarterly Journal of Economics 79* (May): 234–41.

Schlossstein, Steven. 1991. *Asia's New Little Dragons: The Dynamic Emergence of Indonesia, Thailand, and Malaysia.* Chicago: Contemporary Books.

Schultze, Charles L. 1983. "Industrial Policy: A Dissent." *Brookings Review 2* (Fall): 3–12.

Schumpeter, Joseph A. 1939. *Business Cycles.* 2 vols. New York: McGraw-Hill.

———. 1942. *Capitalism, Socialism, and Democracy.* New York: Harper and Row.

———. 1961. *The Theory of Economic Development.* Cambridge, MA: Harvard University Press. [First German ed., 1911.]

Seers, Dudley; Nafziger, E. Wayne; Cruise O'Brien, Donal; and Bernstein, Henry. 1979. *Development Theory: Four Critical Studies*. London: Frank Cass.

Selden, Mark. 1983. "The Proletariat, Revolutionary Change, and the State in China and Japan, 1850–1950." In Immanuel Wallerstein (ed.), *Labor in the World Social Structure*. Beverly Hills, CA: Sage Publications.

———. 1988. *The Political Economy of Chinese Socialism*. Armonk, NY: M.E. Sharpe.

Sender, John, and Smith, Sheila. 1986. *The Development of Capitalism in Africa*. London: Methuen.

Seshamani, Venkatash. 1990. "Zambia." In Adebayo Adedeji, Sadig Rasheed, and Melody Morrison (eds.), *The Human Dimensions of Africa's Persistent Economic Crisis*. London: Hans Zell, pp. 104–23.

Sethuraman, S. V. 1981. *The Urban Informal Sector in Developing Countries*. Geneva: International Labour Office.

Sewell, John W.; Tucker, Stuart K.; et al. 1988. *Growth, Exports, and Jobs in a Changing World Economy: Agenda 1988*. New Brunswick, NJ: Transaction Books.

Shinohara, Miyohei. 1962. *Growth and Cycles in the Japanese Economy*. Tokyo: Kinokuniya.

———. 1970. *Structural Changes in Japan's Economic Development*. Tokyo: Kinokuniya.

———. 1982. *Industrial Growth, Trade, and Dynamic Patterns in the Japanese Economy*. Tokyo: University of Tokyo Press.

Shishido, Toshio. 1983. "Japanese Industrial Development and Policies for Science and Technology." *Science 219* (January 21): 259–64.

Shojiro, Tokunaga. 1992a. "Japan's FDI-Promoting Systems and Intra-Asia Networks: New Investment and Trade Systems Created by the Borderless Economy." In Tokunaga Shojiro (ed.), *Japan's Foreign Investment and Asian Economic Interdependence*. Tokyo: University of Tokyo Press, pp. 5–48.

Shojiro, Tokunaga, ed. 1992b. *Japan's Foreign Investment and Asian Economic Interdependence*. Tokyo: University of Tokyo Press.

———. 1992c. "Moneyless Direct Investment and Development of Asian Financial Markets: Financial Linkages Between Local Markets and Offshore Centers." In Tokunaga Shojiro (ed.), *Japan's Foreign Investment and Asian Economic Interdependence*. Tokyo: University of Tokyo Press, pp. 153–90.

Short, R.P. 1983. "The Role of Public Enterprises: An International Statistical Comparison." International Monetary Fund Working Paper, Fiscal Affairs Department. Washington, DC, May 17.

Singer, Hans. 1950. "The Distribution of Gains between Investing and Borrowing Countries." *American Economic Review 40* (May): 473–85.

———. 1990. "The Role of Food Aid." In James Pickett and Hans Singer (eds.), *Toward Economic Recovery in Sub-Saharan Africa: Essays in Honour of Robert Gardiner*. London: Routledge, pp. 178–93.

Singh, Pritam. 1963. "Essays Concerning Some Types of Entrepreneurship in India." Ph.D. diss., University of Michigan.

Sklar, Richard L. 1979. "The Nature of Class Domination in Africa." *Journal of Modern African Studies 17* (December): 531–52.

Sobhan, Rehman. 1983. "Bangladesh and the World Economic System: The Crisis of External Dependence." *Asian Affairs 5* (1983): 379–89.

Solow, Robert. 1957. "Technical Change and the Aggregate Production Function." *Review of Economics and Statistics 39* (August): 312–20.

Spear, Percival. 1965. *A History of India*. 2 vols. Baltimore: Penguin.

Spraos, John. 1985. *Inequalising Trade? A Study of Traditional North/South Specialisation in the Context of Terms of Trade Concepts.* Oxford: Clarendon Press.

Squire, Lyn. 1981. *Employment Policy in Developing Countries: A Survey of Issues and Evidence.* New York: Oxford University Press.

Stedman, Louellen, and Hakim, Peter. 1989. "Political Change and Economic Policy in Latin America and the Caribbean in 1988." In John F. Weeks (ed.), *Debt Disaster? Banks, Governments, and Multilaterals Confront the Crisis.* New York: New York University Press, pp. 165–74.

Stein, Howard. 1991. "Deindustrialization, Adjustment, and the IMF in Africa." *World Development 19* (December).

Stewart, Frances. 1990. "Are Adjustment Policies in Africa Consistent with Long-run Development Needs?" Paper presented to the American Economic Association. Washington, DC, December 30.

Sugiyama, Shinya. 1988. *Japan's Industrialization in the World Economy, 1859–1899.* London: Athlone Press.

Sumiya, Mikio, and Taira, Koji, eds. 1979. *An Outline of Japanese Economic History, 1603–1940: Major Works and Research Findings.* Tokyo: University of Tokyo Press.

Swainson, Nicola. 1987. "Indigenous Capitalism in Postcolonial Kenya." In Paul M. Lubeck (ed.), *The African Bourgeoisie: Capitalist Development in Nigeria, Kenya, and the Ivory Coast.* Boulder, CO: Lynne Rienner, pp. 137–63.

Tachi, Minoru, and Okazaki, Yoichi. 1965. "Economic Development and Population Growth—with Special Reference to Southeast Asia," *Developing Economies 3* (December): 497–515.

Takeda, Takao. 1965. "The Financial Policy of the Meiji Government." *Developing Economies 3* (December): 427–49.

Takeshi, Aoki. 1992. "Japanese FDI and the Forming of Networks in the Asia-Pacific Region: Experience in Malaysia and Its Implications." In Tokunaga Shojiro (ed.), *Japan's Foreign Investment and Asian Economic Interdependence.* Tokyo: University of Tokyo Press, pp. 73–110.

Tanzi, Vito. 1987. "Quantitative Characteristics of the Tax Systems of Developing Countries." In David Newbery and Nicholas Stern (eds.), *The Theory of Taxation for Developing Countries.* New York: Oxford University Press, pp. 205–41.

Taylor, Lance. 1979. *Macro Models for Developing Countries.* New York: McGraw-Hill.

Teranishi, Juro. 1976. "The Pattern and Role of Flow of Funds between Agriculture and Non-agriculture in Japanese Economic Development." In Kazushi Ohkawa and Yujiro Hayami (eds.), *Papers and Proceedings of the Conference on Japan's Historical Development Experience and the Contemporary Developing Countries.* Tokyo: International Development Center of Japan.

Thomas, Vinod; Chhibber, Ajay; Dailami, Mansoor; and de Melo, Jaime, eds. 1991. *Restructuring Economies in Distress: Policy Reform and the World Bank.* Oxford: Oxford University Press.

Toyama, Shigeki. 1966. "Politics, Economics, and the International Environment in the Meiji and Taisho Periods." *Developing Economies 4,* 4: 419–46.

Tripp, Ali. 1989. "Women and the Changing Urban Household in Tanzania." *Journal of Modern African Studies 27* (December): 601–23.

Tsurumi, E. Patricia. 1990. *Factory Girls: Women in the Thread Mills of Meiji Japan.* Princeton, NJ: Princeton University Press.

Turner, Terisa. 1978. "Commercial Capitalism and the 1975 Coup." In Keith Panter-Brick (ed.), *Soldiers and Oil: The Political Transformation of Nigeria.* London: Frank Cass, pp. 166–97.

United Nations. 1973–85. *Yearbook of International Trade Statistics.* New York.

————. 1987. *National Accounts Statistics: Main Aggregates and Detailed Tables, 1985.* New York.

United Nations Children's Fund (UNICEF). 1992. *The State of the World's Children, 1992.* New York: Oxford University Press.

United Nations Conference on Trade and Development (UNCTAD). 1978. *Intra-firm Transactions and Their Impact on Trade and Development.* Report Series no. 2, UN-CTAD/OSG/74, May.

————. 1991. *Trade and Development Report, 1991.* New York.

United Nations Department of Economic Affairs. 1949. *Relative Prices of Exports and Imports of Underdeveloped Countries.* New York.

United Nations Development Programme. 1991. *Human Development Report, 1991.* New York: Oxford University Press.

————. 1993. *Human Development Report, 1993.* New York: Oxford University Press.

United Nations Development Programme and World Bank. 1989. *African Economic and Financial Data.* Washington, DC.

United States Congress. Joint Economic Committee. 1988. "Gorbachev's Economic Program: Problems Emerge." A Report by the Central Intelligence Agency and the Defense Intelligence Agency presented to the Subcommittee on National Security Economics. Washington, DC., April 13.

United States Department of Agriculture. 1986a. *World Indices of Agricultural and Food Production, 1950–85.* Washington, DC.

————. 1986b. *World Indices of Agricultural and Food Production, 1976–85.* Washington, DC.

————. 1988. *World Indices of Agricultural and Food Production, 1977–86.* Washington, DC.

United States Department of State. 1945. *National Income of Japan.* Washington, DC.

Uppal, Jogindar S. 1977. *Economic Development in South Asia.* New York: St. Martin's Press.

Van der Hoeven, Ralph. 1989. "External Shocks, Adjustment, and Income Distribution." In John F. Weeks (ed.), *Debt Disaster? Banks, Governments, and Multilaterals Confront the Crisis.* New York: New York University Press, pp. 21–40.

Vernon, Raymond. 1966. "International Investment and International Trade in the Product Cycle." *Quarterly Journal of Economics 2* (May): 190–207.

Wade, Nicholas. 1975. "International Agricultural Research." In Philip H. Abelson (ed.), *Food, Politics, Economics, Nutrition, and Research.* Washington, DC: American Association for the Advancement of Science, pp. 91–95.

Wallerstein, Immanuel. 1974. *The Modern World-System I: Capitalist Agriculture and the Origins of the European World-Economy in the Sixteenth Century.* New York: Academic Press.

————. 1975. "The Present State of the Debate on World Inequality." In Immanuel Wallerstein (ed.), *World Inequality.* Montreal: Black Rose Books, pp. 19–37.

————. 1980a. "The Future of the World-economy." In Terence K. Hopkins and Immanuel Wallerstein (eds.), *Processes of the World System.* Vol. 3. *Political Economy of the World-System Annuals.* Beverly Hills, Calif.: Sage Publications, pp. 167–223.

————. 1980b. *The Modern World-System II: Mercantilism and the Consolidation of the European World-economy, 1600–1750.* New York: Academic Press.

————. 1983. "Capitalism and the World Working Class: Some Premises and Some Issues for Research and Analysis." In Immanuel Wallerstein (ed.), *Labor in the World Social Structure.* Beverly Hills, CA: Sage Publications, pp. 17–21.

————. 1989. *The Modern World-System III: The Second Era of Great Expansion of the Capitalist World-economy, 1730–1840s.* New York: Academic Press.

Waterbury, John. 1989. "The Political Managements of Economic Adjustment and Reform." In Joan Nelson (ed.), *Fragile Coalitions: The Politics of Economic Adjustment.* New Brunswick, NJ: Transaction Books, pp. 39–56.

Waterston, Albert. 1963. *Planning in Pakistan: Organization and Implementation.* Baltimore: Johns Hopkins Press.

Weeks, John F., ed. 1989. *Debt Disaster? Banks, Governments, and Multilaterals Confront the Crisis.* New York: New York University Press.

Weisskopf, Thomas E. 1973. "Dependence and Imperialism in India." *Review of Radical Political Economics 5* (Spring): 53–96.

Westney, Eleanor. 1987. *Imitation and Innovation: The Transfer of Western Organizational Patterns to Meiji Japan.* Cambridge, MA: Harvard University Press.

Wheeler, David. 1984. "Sources of Stagnation in Sub-Saharan Africa." *World Development 12* (January): 1–23.

Whitehead, Laurence. 1989. "Democratization and Disinflation: A Comparative Approach." In Joan Nelson (ed.), *Fragile Coalitions: The Politics of Economic Adjustment.* New Brunswick, NJ: Transaction Books, pp. 79–93.

Wilber, Charles K., ed. 1973. *The Political Economy of Development and Underdevelopment.* New York: Random House.

World Bank. 1975. *Kenya: Into the Second Decade.* Washington, DC.

———. 1978. *World Development Report, 1978.* New York: Oxford University Press.

———. 1979. *World Development Report, 1979.* Washington, DC.

———. 1980a. *World Development Report, 1980.* Washington, DC.

———. 1980b. *World Tables, 1980.* Baltimore: Johns Hopkins University Press.

———. 1981. *Accelerated Development in Sub-Saharan Africa: An Agenda for Action.* Washington, DC.

———. 1982. *World Development Report, 1982.* New York: Oxford University Press.

———. 1983a. *China: Socialist Economic Development.* 3 vols. Washington, DC.

———. 1983b. *World Development Report, 1983.* New York: Oxford University Press.

———. 1984. *World Development Report, 1984.* New York: Oxford University Press.

———. 1986a. *Financing Adjustment with Growth in Sub-Saharan Africa, 1986–90.* Washington, DC.

———. 1986b. *World Development Report, 1986.* New York: Oxford University Press.

———. 1987a. *World Bank Atlas, 1987.* Washington, DC.

———. 1987b. *World Development Report, 1987.* New York: Oxford University Press.

———. 1988. *World Development Report, 1988.* New York: Oxford University Press.

———. 1989a. *Sub-Saharan Africa: From Crisis to Sustainable Growth: A Long-term Perspective Study.* Washington, DC.

———. 1989b. *World Development Report, 1989.* New York: Oxford University Press.

———. 1990a. *World Debt Tables, 1989–90: External Debt of Developing Countries.* Washington, DC.

———. 1990b. *World Development Report, 1990.* New York: Oxford University Press.

———. 1991a. *World Debt Tables, 1991–92: External Debt of Developing Countries.* 2 vols. Washington, DC.

———. 1991b. *World Development Report, 1991.* New York: Oxford University Press.

———. 1992a. *Global Economic Prospects and the Developing Countries.* Washington, DC, April.

———. 1992b. *World Development Report, 1992.* New York: Oxford University Press.

———. 1993a. *The East Asian Miracle: Economic Growth and Public Policy.* New York: Oxford University Press.

———. 1993b. *World Development Report, 1993.* New York: Oxford University Press.

World Bank and International Monetary Fund. Joint Ministerial Committee of the Boards of Governors. 1990. *Problems and Issues in Structural Adjustment.* Washington, DC.

World Bank and U.N. Development Programme. 1989. *Africa's Adjustment and Growth in the 1980s.* Washington, DC.

Wright, Theodore P. 1973. "Indian Muslim Muhajirin in the Politics of Pakistan." Paper presented to the Annual Meeting of the American Political Science Association, New Orleans.

Yamada, Yuzo. 1951. *Nihon Kokumin Shotoku Suikei Shiryo.* Tokyo: Kinokuniya.

Yamamura, Kozo. 1968. "A Re-examination of Entrepreneurship in Meiji Japan (1868–1912)." *Economic History Review 21* (February): 148–58.

Yamazawa, Ippei, and Yamamoto, Yuzo. 1979. "Trade and Balance of Payments." In Kazushi Ohkawa and Miyohei Shinohara (eds.), *Patters of Japanese Economic Development: A Quantitative Appraisal.* New Haven, CT: Yale University Press, pp. 126–42.

Yasuba, Yasukichi. 1976. "The Evolution of Dualistic Wage Structure." In Hugh T. Patrick (ed.), *Japanese Industrialization and Its Social Consequences.* Berkeley: University of California Press, pp. 249–98.

Yasuba, Yasukichi, and Dhiravegin, Likhit. 1982. "Initial Conditions, Institutional Changes, Policy and their Consequences: An Essay in the Comparative Economic History of Siam and Japan, 1850–1914." In International Development Center of Japan, "Japan's Historical Development Experience and the Contemporary Developing Countries: Issues for Comparative Analysis," Phase 2. Tokyo, February.

Yasuba, Yasukichi, and Dhiravegin, Likhit. 1985. "Initial Conditions, Institutional Changes, Policy and their Consequences: Siam and Japan, 1850–1914." In Kazushi Ohkawa and Gustav Ranis (eds.), *Japan and the Developing Countries: A Comparative Analysis.* Oxford: Basil Blackwell.

Yasuzo, Horie. 1965. "The Transformation of the National Economy." *Developing Economies 3* (December): 404–26.

Yonekawa, Shin'ichi and Yoshihara, Hideki, eds. 1987. *Business History of General Trading Companies.* Tokyo: University of Tokyo Press.

Yoshihara, Kunio. 1986. *Japanese Economic Development.* Tokyo: Oxford University Press.

Yotopoulos, Pan A., and Nugent, Jeffrey B. 1976. *Economics of Development: Empirical Investigations.* New York: Harper and Row.

Zuvekas, Clarence, Jr. 1979. *Economic Development: An Introduction.* New York: St. Martin's.

Glossary

Commodity terms of trade The price index of exports divided by the price index of imports. For example, if export prices increase 10 percent and import prices 22 percent, the commodity terms of trade drops 10 percent, that is, $1.10/1.22 = 0.90$.

Conditionality Conditions for lending set by the International Monetary Fund or the World Bank.

Current account balance An international balance comprising exports minus imports of goods and services, plus net grants, remittances, and unilateral transfers received.

Debt External debt stock owed to nonresidents and repayable in foreign currency, goods, or services.

Economic growth The rate of growth of GNP per capita.

Formal sector Government sector and firms with ten or more employees in the private sector.

Gini index of inequality A measure of concentration that indicates how far a distribution is from perfect equality. It ranges from a value of 0 representing perfect equality to 1 representing maximum inequality (e.g., where the richest individual has all the income).

Gross domestic product (GDP) A measure of the total output of goods and services in terms of income earned within a country's boundaries. GDP includes income earned by foreign residents and companies, even if it is transferred abroad, and excludes income earned abroad by a country's residents and companies.

Gross National Product (GNP) A measure of the total output of goods and services in terms of income earned by a country's residents. GNP includes income by the country's residents abroad and excludes income earned domestically by foreign residents.

GNP per capita GNP divided by the population.

Group of Seven (G7) Major industrialized countries (United States, Canada, Japan, Germany, United Kingdom, France, and Italy).

Import substitution Domestic production replacing imports.

Income terms of trade The commodity terms of trade times export volume. For example, if the commodity terms of trade drop 10 percent but export volume increases by 22 percent, the income terms of trade increase by 10 percent, that is, $0.90 \times x\ 1.22 = 1.10$.

International balance of (merchandise) trade Exports minus imports of goods.

Least developed countries Forty-six of the poorest countries designated by the United Nations on the basis of low per-capita income, low share of manufacturing in gross product, and low literacy rates.

Monopsony A market in which there is only one buyer of a product.

Oligopoly A market with few sellers making interdependent pricing decisions.

Parastatal enterprises Public corporations and statutory boards owned by the state, but responsible for day-to-day management to boards of directors, at least partially appointed by the state.

Price elasticity of demand The absolute value of the percentage change in quantity demanded divided by the percentage change in price. Values of more than one are elastic; of less than one, inelastic.

Primary products Food, raw materials, and organic oils and fats.

Real economic growth Inflation adjusted growth in GNP per capita (usually expressed per annum).

Samurai   Japanese feudal warrior class.

Surplus   Output minus wages, depreciation, and purchases from other firms.

Technology   The practical arts, ranging from hunting, fishing, and agriculture through manufacturing, communication, and medicine. Technologies are skills, knowledge, procedures, and activities for transforming inputs into outputs, and an increase in technology reduces inputs per output.

Total economic growth   The rate of GNP growth.

Zaibatsu   Hierarchical groups of companies, legally separate but linked by close personal, financial, and trading relationships. The zaibatsu dominated industry and banking from the late nineteenth century through World War II.

Index

Acapulco Summit Meeting of Latin
American Presidents (1987), 172
Adjustment: design of, 173; financing of,
159; by LDC debtors, 32, 33; by
Malaysia, 168; and malnutrition, infant
mortality, and illiteracy, 60; loans for,
81; loans for, in Tanzania, 157; policies
for, 57; political opposition to, 172; and
the poor, 107; process of, 171;
programs of, 59, 84, 123, 155, 158, 162;
programs of, initiated by the IMF and
World Bank, 64, 96, 116, 160, 161;
programs of, OECD/Bank/Fund
policies toward, 154; requirement of
export expansion for, 150; structural,
programs of, 148, 156; time for,
159. *See also* Structural
Administrators: in Africa, 69, 83; in India,
70; shortages of, 58
Africa: acquiring knowledge in, 40;
admonishment by World Bank to, 146;
adoption of Japanese model by, 175;
application of lessons from Japan to,
165; benefits to, from investment in
education, 154; calorie intake in, 16;
capitalist class in, 156; capitalists in,
share of benefits, 118; colonial state in,
66–69; commercial triangle in, 126;
competition by, 48; concentration of
business elites in, 164; cost of
inward-looking policies to, 147; DC
tariff structure in, 150; declining prices
in, 143; death rate in, 115; deficits by
SOEs in, 125; in the demographic
transition, 108; difficulty of, in

Africa *(continued)*
emulating early Japan strategies, 174;
discrimination against exports by, 138;
disruption of, by colonialism, 8;
economic mistakes in, 172; effect of
reduction of tariffs in, 148; end of
growth in, 83; export expansion in, 45,
140; external crisis of, 158; finance
ministers of, 161, 171; food crisis in,
99–100; food output (production) per
capita in, 98, 111; governments of,
control of capital and employment by,
166; informal sector in, 123; labor force
growth in, 112; lack of control in
economic affairs in, 51; as lagging in
agricultural research, 97; landlords in,
in industrial activity, 164; life
expectancy in, 15; high worker-land
ratios in, 41; as peripheral region, 49;
policy cartel for, 153–54; policy
conditionality faced by, 74; policy
toward agriculture in, 95; ratio of urban
to rural income, 121; regime survival in,
54; secondary enrollment rate in, 36;
sources of growth in, 33; taxes as a
percentage of GNP in, 59; trade by
MNCs in, 48. *See also* Sub-Saharan
African Development Bank, 33, 163
Agrarian: classes, in manufacturing, 164;
political consciousness, 165; poverty
and distress, 173
Agricultural: development, the approach of
the World Bank to, 160; experiment
stations, 38; export expansion, 148,
159; goods, export of, 146; labor shares

E. Wayne Nafziger is professor of economics at Kansas State University, Manhattan. He has been visiting scholar at the International University of Japan, Cambridge University, the East-West Center, and in Nigeria and India, and has lectured in Moscow, Beijing, Prague, and Mexico City. His many publications include *Poverty and Wealth; The Debt Crisis in Africa; The Economics of Developing Countries; Inequality in Africa; The Economics of Political Instability; Class, Caste, and Entrepreneurship*; and *African Capitalism*, and articles in the *American Economic Review* and *Economic Development and Cultural Change.*